Biblical Refigurations

Jesus and the Chaos of History

BIBLICAL REFIGURATIONS

General Editors: James G. Crossley and Francesca Stavrakopoulou

This innovative series offers new perspectives on the textual, cultural, and interpretative contexts of particular biblical characters, inviting readers to take a fresh look at the methodologies of Biblical Studies. Individual volumes employ different critical methods including social-scientific criticism, critical theory, historical criticism, reception history, postcolonialism, and gender studies, while subjects include both prominent and lesser-known figures from the Hebrew Bible and the New Testament.

Published Titles Include:

Jeremy Schipper	*Disability and Isaiah's Suffering Servant*
Keith Bodner	*Jeroboam's Royal Drama*
Mark Leuchter	*Samuel and the Shaping of Tradition*
Louise J. Lawrence	*Sense and Stigma in the Gospels: Depictions of Sensory-Disabled Characters*
William John Lyons	*Joseph of Arimathea: A Study in Reception History*

JESUS AND THE CHAOS OF HISTORY

Redirecting the Life of the Historical Jesus

JAMES G. CROSSLEY

UNIVERSITY PRESS

OXFORD
UNIVERSITY PRESS

Great Clarendon Street, Oxford, OX2 6DP,
United Kingdom

Oxford University Press is a department of the University of Oxford. It furthers the University's objective of excellence in research, scholarship, and education by publishing worldwide. Oxford is a registered trade mark of Oxford University Press in the UK and in certain other countries

First Edition published in 2015

Impression: 2

Published in the United States of America by Oxford University Press
198 Madison Avenue, New York, NY 10016, United States of America

British Library Cataloguing in Publication Data
Data available

Library of Congress Control Number: 2014946128

ISBN 978–0–19–957057–7 (hbk.)
ISBN 978–0–19–957058–4 (pbk.)

Printed and bound by
CPI Group (UK) Ltd, Croydon, CR0 4YY

In memory of Maurice Casey (1942–2014)

Contents

Introduction

This book is not a comprehensive 'life of Jesus' and nor is it intended to be a mini-biography. Rather, it is better understood as a proposal to rethink some of the ways we approach the historical Jesus, or, as I prefer, the earliest Palestinian tradition.[1] The main thrust of the argument here is that rather than seeing Jesus as a Great Man who, implicitly, changed history by himself, we should investigate what happened when the social upheavals in Galilee and Judea intersected with a range of different ideas and interests and if, or how, this contributed to the generation of historical change. In particular, this book looks at the accidental, purposeful, discontinuous, and implicit meanings in the developments of ideas as they appear across times and places, often justifying things that are seemingly contradictory. Another thread running through this book is less chaotic in that it looks at how seemingly egalitarian and countercultural ideas can lead to, or coexist with, ideas of dominance and power and how human reactions to socio-economic inequalities can end up replicating dominant and imperial power. In this sense, the book is an extended presentation (albeit tweaked) of the popular argument that the revolution and the revolutionary can lay the ideological foundations for the totalitarian state; or, in the case of this book, how a Galilean protest movement could lay the foundations for its own brand of imperial rule. In this sense, the book as a whole functions as an implicit critique of the idea of a subversive, revolutionary, and anti-empire Jesus movement in that it also takes into account the reactionary, counter-revolutionary, and imperial aspects of the Jesus movement. To bring us back to more traditional historical Jesus territory, this book will give three detailed case studies focusing on: the kingdom of God and 'Christology'; 'sinners' and purity; and gender. Prior to that, the first two chapters are broadly akin to 'a survey of the field of historical Jesus studies' and 'methodology in historical reconstruction'.

The level of secondary literature in historical Jesus studies alone is extraordinarily high and this is a relatively short book. With some exceptions, the book is not an extensive engagement with scholarly positions, though such engagement is referenced in the endnotes. Sometimes I have referenced more recent literature. This is not because it is necessarily better than that which came before it or that it is necessarily saying anything dramatically new. More recent literature does, however, typically give more updated discussions than its predecessors. Fortunately for a sub-field within biblical studies with such an extended bibliography, a lot of the literature is repetitive,[2] often building on and strengthening previous ideas, so at least it is easier to engage with a range of perspectives.[3] Yet, on a number of occasions I do turn to older scholarship and engage less with more recent scholarship when it proves helpful and, as we will see, one of the main inspirations behind this book is a prediction by a nineteenth-century radical. But to return to the original point: this is not a 'life of Jesus' as such; it is more a proposal or extended essay arguing for a modest redirection of the ways we do historical Jesus studies. My proposal may or may not be along the right lines but I would settle for historical Jesus studies looking more closely at the intersection of ideas and material conditions involved in historical change.

For abbreviations of primary and secondary sources, see the *SBL Handbook of Style*.[4]

1

Does Jesus Plus Paul Equal Marx Plus Lenin?

Redirecting the Historical Jesus

Are all Jesuses created liberal?

One of the major things I want to do in this book is to critique the following kinds of claims paralleling Jesus and Paul with Marx and Lenin:

> I am not the first to risk the comparison that makes of him [Paul] a Lenin for whom Christ will have been the equivocal Marx.[1]

> Paul goes on to his true Leninist business, that of organizing the new party called the Christian community. Paul as a Leninist: was not Paul, like Lenin, the great 'institutionalizer,' and, as such, reviled by the partisans of 'original' Marxism–Christianity? Does not the Pauline temporality 'already, but not yet' also designate Lenin's situation in between two revolutions, between February and October 1917? Revolution is already behind us, the old regime is out, freedom is here—*but* the hard work still lies ahead.[2]

These are not the kinds of claims usually found in books on the historical Jesus. They are, however, claims made in some very prominent treatments of Paul by two of the most famous contemporary thinkers: Alain Badiou and Slavoj Žižek. These readings of Christian origins are in no small part designed to challenge dominant postmodern or liberal understandings of Jesus and Paul. The focus here will, of course, be on Jesus but, like Badiou and Žižek, I will consistently be working with a bigger materialist picture.

As anachronistic as the statements by Badiou and Žižek may seem (and they would admit and embrace this), we should hesitate should we wish to condemn them too quickly. Over the past forty years, arguably the most dominant rhetorical generalization about the historical Jesus has become something of a cliché: Jesus the Jew. This dominant scholarly construction has in fact been partly a product of postmodern and liberal forms of identity and dominant political trends. For those unaware of the extensive work carried out in recent scholarship on the ideological functions of contemporary Jesus studies, this alternative approach to the discredited 'three quests' model for understanding the quest for the historical Jesus may need spelling out and summarizing in further detail.[3] If we leave aside fascist and Nazi scholarship, no contemporary scholar denies Jesus was Jewish. However, prior to the 1970s, mainstream scholarship—as well as more broadly popular views—typically argued that Jesus rejected much of what was believed to be central to Judaism. Put crudely, Jesus was said to have abolished (say) Sabbath laws and purity laws. Moreover, these Sabbath and purity laws deemed so central to Judaism were also deemed to be cold, harsh, inadequate, and so on, until Jesus came along and changed everything.

But something changed in the 1970s. Geza Vermes published his famous book, *Jesus the Jew*, in 1973 and in it constructed Jesus as a figure firmly within Judaism, and Judaism itself was presented positively, as other, less influential Jewish scholars had also done before him. Yet, ever since Vermes' book, and particularly with the accompanying influence of E. P. Sanders' work on Jesus, Paul, and early Judaism,[4] most historical Jesus scholars will now go out of their way to tell us how Jewish their Jesus is, with book titles regularly emphasizing Jesus' Jewishness common enough—and all the while no one denying he was Jewish. However, as has been argued in different ways in recent ideological critiques of historical Jesus scholarship, scholars will regularly construct or assume a construction of what constituted Jewish identity in the first century, before having their Jesus transcend this Jewish identity in some way, or at least present Jesus as doing something new and unparalleled either generally or on some specific (and often crucial) issue, and typically involving the Torah and/or Temple. Subtly or otherwise, this pattern is found from the more obscure Jesus scholarship through to the major works on the historical Jesus, such as those by Sanders, Wright, Dunn, Meier, Theissen and Merz, Allison, Hengel and Schwemer, to name a few.[5] This, it should be added, is subtly different from Vermes' construction of Jesus the Jew because Vermes' Jesus was to do things that were effectively all paralleled in early Judaism. And so Vermes' challenge has been absorbed and domesticated, and with any problematic Otherness of this Jesus removed. Or as N. T. Wright put it about his Jesus: 'a very Jewish Jesus who was nevertheless opposed to some high-profile features of first-century Judaism'.[6]

There are historical reasons for this dominant emphasis on a 'Jewish... but not *that* Jewish' Jesus (as well as a 'Jewish... but not *that* Jewish' Paul[7]). The 1967 Six Day War brought about major shifts in Anglo-American understandings of Israel and Judaism in popular, political, religious, and intellectual culture, from indifference to a dominant discourse of staunch support, support which nevertheless has included attitudes of cultural and religious superiority in relation to Jews, Judaism, and Israel. A crucial post-1967 cultural shift included a new widespread interest in the Holocaust, at least in America (e.g. Holocaust memorials, museums, changes in Jewish assimilation, and identity politics), an important point to stress given the strange suggestion sometimes made that scholarly positivity towards Judaism emerged as a direct reaction to the Holocaust; strange because this means it would have taken over twenty-five years to register a widespread concern.

Thinking about the quest for the historical Jesus in such politicized and historicized ways shows how interconnected with major geopolitical trends scholarship is. It further provides us with ways of understanding how the startling readings of Christian origins by Badiou and Žižek challenge the dominant postmodern Jesuses. We can go further still. As I have argued elsewhere, contemporary constructions of Jesus are intimately tied in with a dominant manifestation of capitalism we call neoliberalism which emphasizes, for instance, the power of the individual, image, free trade, the private sector, and freedom, the very economic model which has been facing such a crisis these past few years.[8] As Fredric Jameson and David Harvey in particular have shown, the general connections between late capitalism/neoliberalism and the cultural 'condition' of postmodernity—with its emphasis on eclecticism, multiple identities, indeterminacy, depthlessness, scepticism towards grand narratives, and so on—are clear enough.[9] In this context, especially when we recall the 'liberal' in 'neoliberal', we might begin by thinking of the marketplace of multiple, sometimes competing, Jesuses (eschatological prophet, sage, Cynic-like social critic, wisdom teacher, Mediterranean Jewish peasant apocalyptic eschatological wisdom teacher, etc.).

One key corollary of these intersecting trends in contemporary capitalism has been multiculturalism, which helps us understand the latest chapter in the long history of racializing Jesus.[10] One dominant liberal form of thinking about multiculturalism (which is hardly incompatible with the more right-wing attacks on multiculturalism) that has emerged over the past forty years embraces others but has to ensure that anything problematic is removed; or, as Žižek defined this discourse of contemporary multiculturalism, the Other is welcomed but without the Otherness in this liberal democratic embrace.[11] Popular statements on 'religion', or specific religious practices, highlight this point neatly. For instance, we regularly hear of liberal phrases like 'true Islam', which is deemed to be spiritual and not violent. In this tradition, 'true Christianity' is also a religion of peace, with the Crusades some kind of perversion, or understanding Jesus as a peace-loving figure crucified for his message of love rather than the man who called Gentiles 'dogs' (Mark 7.27–8; Matt. 15.24–7). It is, of course, increasingly recognized that 'religion', or religions such as Islam and Christianity, cannot be boiled down to a pure 'spiritual', non-violent, or indeed violent,[12] core but it is equally clear that common discourses on, for instance, 'true Islam' or 'true Christianity' (or 'false Islam' or 'false Christianity') are of ideological significance. To state the obvious, violent and non-violent beliefs can be, and are, associated with what some people would believe to be 'true Islam' or 'true Christianity' but it is the rhetorical move to decide which is the 'true' manifestation that attempts to make sure such people are, or are not, part of liberal discourses on 'religion'.[13] This multicultural acceptance of the Other deprived of Otherness is precisely what we see with dominant views on Jesus the Jew: scholarship regularly embraces this 'very Jewish' Jesus but the stranger bits of, say, Law observance are now 'redundant', to use another phrase from Wright.[14]

This is one reason why I am tempted to label almost all mainstream historical Jesuses as 'liberal', if by liberal we mean certain central ideas broadly conforming to some of the general tendencies and trends in contemporary discourses of liberal democracy.[15] Of course, some of the new supersessionism comes from Christian tradition (Wright perhaps being the most obvious high-profile example) but it ultimately has the same political function as the work of many mainstream scholars, if by political function we read scholarship in terms of broad consensual trends as outlined here. But what do we make of the numerous anti-imperial (and even anti-capitalist) Jesuses that have been common over the past forty years (and, of course, before)? Surely they would buck such trends! I am not entirely convinced that they do, even if we should not throw the baby out with the bathwater (see below). For a start, the awkward relationship with the construction of Judaism remains present.[16] But the neoliberal context of the past forty years also absorbs such seemingly radical critique in that anti-capitalist rhetoric is simultaneously widespread.[17] As Žižek put it:

> Today, when everyone is 'anticapitalist,' up to the Hollywood 'socio-critical' conspiracy movies (from *The Enemy of the State* to *The Insider*) in which the enemy are the big corporations with their ruthless pursuit of profit, the signifier 'anticapitalism' has lost its subversive sting. What one should problematize is rather the self-evident opposite of this 'anticapitalism': the trust in the democratic substance of the honest Americans to break up the conspiracy.[18]

One example of this in practice can be found in Žižek's review of the film *Avatar* for the *New Statesman*. Žižek pointed out that at the same time as *Avatar* was generating one billion dollars in under three weeks, there was in fact something resembling its plot happening in the Indian state of Orissa. Here land was sold to mining companies, which provoked an armed rebellion. Consequently, there were propaganda and military attacks from the Indian state and a vicious conflict ensued. Žižek added:

> So where is Cameron's film here? Nowhere: in Orissa, there are no noble princesses waiting for white heroes to seduce them and help their people, just the Maoists organising the starving farmers. The film enables us to practise a typical ideological division: sympathising with the idealised aborigines while rejecting their actual struggle. The same people who enjoy the film and admire its aboriginal rebels would in all probability turn away in horror from the Naxalites, dismissing them as murderous terrorists. The true avatar is thus *Avatar* itself—the film substituting for reality.[19]

Putting the motivations, beliefs, and practices of individual scholars to one side, it is difficult to see how contemporary historical Jesus scholarship as a field of study (or the sub-field of radical historical Jesuses) is having any significant oppositional political impact. That sounds blindingly obvious and it is—we never really expect it to! Crossan and Borg may have Jesuses who are radical political figures but arguably their most significant ideological function is to sell books to liberal audiences on a large scale and Borg's mystical, Buddhist-esque Jesus effectively ends up looking internally, like the ultimate capitalist subject.[20]

Strands of liberation theology provide an important point of comparison because here we have influential church organizations dedicated to socio-economic liberation in contexts which have faced serious peasant exploitation and the brutal effects of imperialism of the sort that might form the backdrop for a historical Jesus book. And liberation theology *has* had an impact, hence the reason various figures came under lethal attack.[21] This is not something we might expect to happen to Borg-inspired liberal American church groups; while violence and death threats certainly do happen, they are more typically located in the context of 'culture wars' rather than a direct and overt challenge to state, corporate, or multinational power. Or, we might think about how Wright views the importance of his bodily resurrected Jesus: 'in the real world ... the tyrants and bullies (including intellectual and cultural tyrants and bullies) try to rule by force, only to discover that in order to do so they have to quash all rumours of resurrection, rumours that would imply that their greatest weapons, death and deconstruction, are not after all omnipotent.'[22] Aside from the obvious non-impact of Wright's books in the face of tyrants,[23] it might be wondered how the former Bishop of Durham's market would react if people who really believed in resurrection went and confronted death like Razis in 2 Macc. 14.43–6. And all the while radical historical Jesus books sell to mass audiences; to paraphrase Mark Fisher's analysis of *Wall-E*, radical historical Jesuses perform our anti-capitalism and radicalism for us, allowing us to consume books about him with impunity.[24]

And to this we might add: why do we need the historical Jesus to critique contemporary manifestations of power? What if Jesus suggested things we might find unpleasantly racist? Would we really agree with him if he thought that a theocracy would be imposed on the world imminently with the wrong kind of people being punished terribly? It is hardly as if such thinking is absent from the Gospel tradition (see Chapter 3) and so we need to find alternative ways of understanding the historical process and the structures of power in human societies, incorporating any problematic Otherness this might entail and without so easily displacing our anti-capitalist fantasies into the long, distant past.

There have been attempts to retrieve Jesus' Otherness by locating him in the context of the strange 'Mediterranean' but these too seem to me to be by-products of dominant politicized discourses,[25] even though some contributions of the Context Group-influenced scholarship on the structures of power remain important (e.g. Moxnes, Oakman, Hanson, Herzog).[26] For example, the Bruce Malina-inspired social scientific approaches have dominated contemporary approaches to social sciences and the New Testament, particularly over the past thirty years, and have brought a number of now well-known issues to the fore (e.g. honour and shame, limited good, dyadic personality). Following a virtual absence of social scientific approaches in New Testament studies between (approximately) the 1930s and the 1970s (partly because of the not wholly unjustified association of social sciences with atheistic Marxism and, by implication, Soviet Communism), they came back powerfully. As is widely recognized, this was due to the prominence and influence of 1960s protest movements, the increasing influence of sociology in the universities, declining church numbers, the perception of 'secularism', and the impact of decolonization. I have added several other reasons, including the development of an explicitly non-Marxist (and therefore more palatable) social scientific/anthropological approach (e.g. Keith Thomas on magic), translations of Weber into English, and overt shifts in West German historiography away from the Nazi cult of the individual towards trends and themes.[27] A significant reason was also the heavy (re-) emphasis in Anglo-American culture from the 1970s onwards on the 'Arab world', 'the Arab mind', 'the Middle East', and a number of Orientalist and ideologically convenient stereotypes which fed into the world of the influential Malina, as well as his key colleagues such as Richard Rohrbaugh and John Pilch, and their use of the static construction of 'the Mediterranean' (even to the extent of 'the Mediterranean' and 'the Arab world' being, at times, synonymous).[28]

The use of 'the Mediterranean'/'the Middle East' is of further significance. It is not only the case that it is intellectually colonized by scholarship but it can produce a certain kind of Jesus. Even scholars not known for their use of social sciences (e.g. Wright, Meier) simply refer to the work of (say) Malina and Neyrey as a given.[29] But note also one function of this backdrop, at least in its reception: to make Jesus better than his strange background. Wright, for instance, claims that social anthropology must be part of 'the equipment of the historian' and helps avoid anachronisms 'by recognizing that different societies operate with different worldviews and social norms'. Wright gives a brief application of this to the story of Mary and Martha (Luke 10.38–42) with the hardly surprising conclusion that 'a subversive note is struck'.[30] Portraits may differ wildly but the logic of superiority remains in important historical Jesus scholarship. Indeed, there are scholars who have systematically applied the backdrop of the Mediterranean to an understanding of the historical Jesus and none more so than John Dominic Crossan. But, despite making some significant advances (to which we will return), Crossan's Mediterranean Jewish peasant becomes arguably the most famous liberalized (in a widely recognized popular sense) Jesus of recent times. For all the anti-imperial rhetoric of Crossan it is noticeable that Crossan's Jesus stands over against the alien Mediterranean world. The world of honour and shame which supposedly characterizes 'the Mediterranean' is, so the argument goes, profoundly challenged. And against this fixed Mediterranean world is a Jesus with common table fellowship and a brokerless kingdom, subverting the system, playing around with gender categories, and so on.[31] Crossan's Jesus is, in many ways, and almost certainly unintentionally, representative of liberal America, or perhaps the liberal West, overcoming the brutal backwards East.

Of course, it still remains that we have Jesuses, or studies of the early traditions, as well as significant elements of Crossan's work and work on Palestine in the first century, which really do point to ways in which to understand the chaos and upheaval of Jesus' time, not to mention the socio-economic structures which have contributed to injustices in human history.[32] This may provide a means to think about historical development without so obviously resorting to Jesus merely as an avatar for anti-capitalist fantasies. On one level, we might reinforce the argument that the critique these Jesuses bring displaces critique safely to the past. But this is where the point about not throwing out the baby with the bathwater becomes significant. What such scholarship potentially shows is that Jesus, or the earliest Palestinian tradition, should also be seen as a product of historical change and development. What I want to do is to shift the focus to using Jesus as a means of understanding historical change and the ways in which power functions in human society, irrespective of whether his teaching is nice, terrible, weird, useful, or seemingly irrelevant. This requires further explanation.

The sigh of an oppressed people?

There is that famous saying of Karl Marx: religion is 'the opium of the people'. This is often taken as an attack on religion. However, there is increasing popular awareness that to argue this is to rip the saying out of context; as Marx fully said: 'The wretchedness of religion is at once an expression of and protest against real wretchedness. Religion is the sigh of the oppressed creature, the heart of a heartless world, and the soul of soulless conditions. It is the *opium* of the people.'[33] There are problems if we take this to assume 'religion' in essentialist terms. In what follows, I am not working with the assumption that there is a natural 'religion' or a religious 'something', whether that something is apparently innate in human beings or some supernatural or 'spiritual' category which we should somehow embrace in our scholarly work. Instead, I will work with the assumption that those discourses we typically understand to be 'religious' are part of a competing network of discourses used by human beings to understand and negotiate the world.[34] With that said, we can acknowledge that the world of what we typically understand as 'religion' is not always as romantic as a more literal reading of the Marx passage might suggest but still accept that there is something in it in the sense that discourses we might find unusual or strange (or usual and familiar) can, of course, tell us something about material and historical change and structure. And it is an important counter to the overtly liberal New Atheism of Richard Dawkins, Sam Harris, Martin Amis, A. C. Grayling, and others that we have been experiencing in recent years. For Dawkins and others it is precisely the problematic 'religion' that is at the heart of so many of the great ills in the world today. Not only does analysis of Dawkins show what is so problematic about assuming the mysterious 'religion' as a cause of violence, including what happened on September 11, but a counter reading shows how a (qualified) understanding of Marx is along the right lines for understanding historical change.[35] For instance, some of the standard reasons given for the rise of revolutionary Islam or 'fundamentalism' are a complex range of issues, including: the decline of secular nationalism in North Africa and the Middle East; the specific context of the key American ally, Saudi Arabia, the homeland of the majority of the September 11 killers; the destructive sanctions on Iraq; Palestine; the petro-crash; the rise of slums and population growth; and US support for various dictators.[36] None of these factors are properly discussed among prominent New Atheists, an alarming oversight given their own emphasis on reason, scholarship, and logic, but the ideological function of blaming 'religion' almost solely masks numerous uncomfortable material and ideological reasons for historical change.

We might also point out the general (and no more) similarities with Christian 'fundamentalism' in America and the emergence of neoliberalism and neoconservatism, in particular the politicization of Christian 'fundamentalism' in recent decades.[37] The mobilization of 'fundamentalist' Christian voters away from their economic interests to 'religious' issues such as gay rights, abortion, and evolution in schools, for instance, has been most beneficial for those wanting to eliminate traditional working-class opposition. Wages have stagnated or declined for the majority over a lengthy period (over twenty years), with working hours increasing and indebtedness rising rapidly while social benefits decreased. By mobilizing Christian 'fundamentalism' into a political force, the discourse and focus was shifted towards those 'fundamentalist' issues. We may or may not like this brand of Christianity, but we can acknowledge that those discourses we label as 'religion' do bring deeply uncomfortable baggage for the more liberal sensibilities, and we can likewise understand these issues as products of the very thing Christian 'fundamentalism' regularly supports. What these sorts of reactions tell us again is that there are deep-rooted and potentially uncomfortable issues that are being masked over when we blame 'religion' or see it as a primary causal factor.

What I want to argue then is that, with all cultural differences duly accepted, what we might understand to be 'religion' in the case of

Christian origins, or indeed any other human discourses we might label entirely differently, can be as much a reaction to the heartless world as some of those more contemporary examples. In fact, in the case of a first-century figure or the associated early tradition we should probably accept one scholarly cliché: 'religion' (however understood) cannot really be separated from the rest of society. As I will hopefully show by the end of this book, it is possible to reconstruct early Palestinian tradition and provide a way of thinking about this Jesus tradition as a useful means of understanding human society and historical change, rather than simply producing yet another Jesus portrait for the marketplace (though that will inevitably also be the case).

Biographies of a Great Man

This approach to history means we also need to critique the dominant approach to biography in historical Jesus studies, which has much in common with a Jesus dissimilar to some degree from the Jewish environment constructed by scholarship: the emphasis on the individual, or Jesus the Great Man.[38] Critiques of the cult of the individual as prime historical mover have not fully permeated the mainstream of historical Jesus studies. Related reflections on historiography typically discuss different ways, including the impact of postmodern challenges to traditional historiography and the nature of 'facts' and 'original meanings', of approaching and understanding the original figure of Jesus rather than anything broader.[39] There are several reasons for this. Two obvious ones would involve biography and faith. In terms of biography, lives of Jesus are, obviously, about one man and therefore it is understandable that emphasis is on the words and deeds of this man. In terms of faith, Jesus is the central figure in the Christian faith and in theology, and the history of New Testament scholarship is overwhelmingly theologically driven. Therefore it is understandable that the words and deeds of the individual Jesus are analysed so heavily.[40]

Consequently, there are countless portraits of Jesus that have become famous: the Cynic-like figure, the revolutionary, the charismatic, the eschatological prophet, the sage, the rabbi, the social critic, and so on. Underlying all these is a serious scholarly fact-finding mission to find the individual. One of the most famous things for which E. P. Sanders' influential books on Jesus are remembered is the establishment of basic *facts* about Jesus (born *c.*4 BCE, grew up in Nazareth, baptized by John the Baptist, preached kingdom of God, executed under Pilate, etc.).[41] In this sense, one of Sanders' key aims is explicitly to shift away from theological concerns and interpret as a conventional historian, the sort of historian that might be found (say) in a history or ancient history department or faculty. But he explicitly locates himself in the tradition of modern historical biography in order to analyse what the subjects *thought*.[42] In many ways poles apart from Sanders are the members of the North American Jesus Seminar. Yet their concerns are still with the facts about Jesus and what Jesus *thought* or *believed*, as can be seen not only in the subtitle to their flagship book (*The Search for the Authentic Words of Jesus*) but also their famous colour coding used to describe to what extent Jesus did or did not say something.[43] Harking back to the nineteenth-century historical narratives, and with echoes of Renan, Bruce Chilton's *Rabbi Jesus* reads more like a conventional biography than any other recent scholarly work on Jesus (and note the subtitle: *An Intimate Biography*). Here we even get exclusive snapshots of Jesus as a *kabbalah*-loving Galilean celebrity, a once adolescent geek whose weight fluctuated when he grew up and whose hair was ever diminishing.[44] The concern with establishing facts gets taken to another kind of extreme in the massive multi-volume work on the historical Jesus by John Meier. If the celebrity biographer (see 'Biography and history') is interested in all things gossipy, then it may be fair to say that Meier is interested in the more sober hard facts ('the detection of reliable data... keep interpretation to a minimum... ascertaining reliable data... the particular data needed for historical reconstruction of individual persons and events').[45]

These examples highlight the obvious: the study of the historical Jesus is overwhelmingly concerned with fact finding,[46] description, and descriptive interpretation in its various forms, with little concern for materialistic questions relating to *why* the Jesus movement emerged when and where it did and *why* it led to a new movement. In terms of historical explanation such detail must at least imply that the individual Jesus of Nazareth (along with Paul) is thought to be the most significant figure (and factor?) in the emergence of Christianity.

Indeed, several historical Jesus scholars are keen to show the connections between Jesus and the emerging Christian movement. Sanders and Wright, for instance, virtually make this a methodological necessity. Indeed, Wright has been heavily critical of those like the members of the Jesus Seminar for reconstructing a Jesus which cannot account for the emergence of Christianity. In contrast, Sanders famously saw the connection between Jesus and the early church on the issue of eschatology. The very first followers had problems with the 'troublesome fact' that the kingdom had not yet come and so, Sanders argues not unreasonably, it is 'almost impossible to explain these historical facts on the assumption that Jesus himself did not expect the imminent end or transformation of the present world order'.[47]

For all Wright's analysis of Jesus' theology, the connections he makes with Christianity are slightly different. With reference to Jesus' storytelling, Wright claims that it is both similar and dissimilar to the Jewish context and the early Christian world. If we recognize this *double dissimilarity*, he argues, 'when something can be seen as credible... within first century Judaism, and credible as the implied starting-point... of something in later Christianity, there is the strong possibility of our being in touch with the genuine history of Jesus'.[48] But here again we remain in the realm of *description*, without any serious discussion of social, economic, and any problematic ideological trends that are invariably present in historical change and developments and that may have aided and abetted the shift from Jesus to early Christianity. When Wright does look beyond the surface level of events and stories he bypasses the route of social and historical causes by taking a historically bizarre turn, claiming that the 'proposal that Jesus was bodily raised from the dead possessed unrivalled power to explain the historical data at the heart of early Christianity'.[49]

On one level it should be obvious that there would be little if any useful socio-economic analysis if there were not a significant amount of factual data and reconstruction of ideas and beliefs, an issue we will turn to in the next chapter. While this book is still one about ideas (but always grounded in social change), one of my problems is that the sheer amount of emphasis given in scholarship to detail and description over against socio-economic causal explanations runs the risk of giving the impression that there is little more to historical change than a large enough number of people being convinced by an argument based on the benefits of the god of Jesus over against others (or a tacit assumption that Christianity *really was* the work of the Holy Spirit). E. H. Carr's scathing critique of such history still holds true:

> ... the Bad King John view of history—the view that what matters in history is the character and behaviour of individuals ... In this country, in particular, we all learned this theory, so to speak, at our mother's knee; and today we should probably recognize that there is something childish, or at any rate childlike, about it.[50]

In terms of broader historical trends, an obvious but useful analogy might be the argument that the Second World War happened not simply because of what Hitler did but because of a whole host of social and economic factors, most obviously including the conditions in Germany after Versailles. Thematically closer to home, no radical comment is being made in suggesting that the Jewish War happened due to deep-rooted socio-economic problems and not *simply* because of a few hot-headed radicals. So, presumably, can we not apply the old idea to Christian origins, that broader historical change frequently happens because something is going on beneath the surface?

It might be thought that the increasing use of social sciences could provide an alternative approach.[51] Such approaches do indeed point to some significant ways forward (see below) but much use of the social sciences in historical Jesus and New Testament studies has been either descriptive or feeds into the idea of individual influence.[52] The idea of Jesus as charismatic leader—the social scientific model of the individual *par excellence*—shows no signs of losing its popularity and, probably more than any other social scientific model, it highlights Jesus as notably different from his social context, not to mention its descriptive importance by portraying Jesus as a 'type'.[53] There have of course been historical Jesus studies grounded in social and economic histories that have potential for wide-ranging explanations for the emergence of the Jesus movement and the Christian movement but ultimately, whether intended or not, the reception of such works tends to involve discussions of theology and description of the individual historical figure's beliefs. For all Horsley's application of Marxist-influenced social sciences it is the resulting Jesus that becomes the object of scrutiny. Wright's problems with Horsley, for instance, involve Jesus' *attitudes* towards violent revolution and social outcasts.[54] In a similar way Dale

Allison's problem with the work of Herzog and others is that it is a 'secular reading', in that such interpretations 'shove our attention away from traditional theological, christological, and eschatological concerns... [but] Jesus himself was a deeply religious personality, who interpreted everything in terms of an unseen world'.[55]

Perhaps more than anyone it is Crossan who has sought to systematize the social sciences in the study of the historical Jesus. For all of Crossan's creative arguments concerning socio-economic change, and his attempts at explaining the shift from Jesus to the birth of Christianity, his portrayals of Jesus and subsequent Christianity still, at least in the reception of Crossan's work, ultimately remain a theological and descriptive enterprise (compare Crossan's own stress on Jesus as social revolutionary, the split between the 'life' and 'death' traditions, etc.) and not without one eye, as his critics frequently point out, on contemporary relevance.[56] It is, therefore, no surprise that in the reception of Crossan's work we get emphases on the individual, descriptive, exegetical, and/or theological. Crossan's work ultimately made Jesus scholars chatter because he portrayed Jesus as a Cynic-like peasant preacher and used all sorts of texts to make his case.[57]

The idea of who Jesus 'really was', and what the texts 'really mean', feeds into the reception of Crossan's use of social sciences. For example, on one level Wright appreciates Crossan's use of social sciences. This is because he thinks, as we saw, that social anthropology helps us avoid anachronisms, and recognizes that different societies have different norms and, predictably, that Jesus' teachings can be described as 'subversive'. This seems a clear indication that social sciences have a descriptive and exegetical function, not to mention an apologetic function, in the hands of Wright. But is this really the best social sciences can offer? Donald Denton's detailed analysis of Crossan's work has a more nuanced take and he accepts that 'important gains' are reflected in his historiographical method which ought to be emulated.[58] I would agree but it is again significant that Denton sees the potential benefits of Crossan's use of social sciences in terms of how Jesus is *portrayed*, how Jesus-the-individual acts and how he can be rescued for intentionality ('Within pan-Mediterranean sociological constructs, Jesus remains a first-century religious figure with genuine religious sensibilities and a historical agent whose actions are intentional, and not reducible to a confluence of environmental factors').[59]

To some extent these reactions to Crossan's work are inevitable: Crossan largely (but not exclusively) deals with how social conditions influence the *teaching* of the historical Jesus and subsequent Christianity, with masses of exegesis and discussion of tradition history.[60] To do this in a field (and I would unambiguously include myself in this critique) dominated by, and obsessed with, exegesis and the historical-critical method makes the response predictable. Of course, I am *not* saying such approaches are necessarily wrong but they do, once again, illustrate that explaining historical change is not high on the agenda.[61]

This dominance of individualism, with heavy doses of description of who Jesus really was, is like the (limited) multicultural 'Jewish... but not *that* Jewish' narrative: another dominant and indeed liberal narrative at work in the field. Jesus in both senses has to be importantly *different from* the world.[62] As Dieter Georgi has shown, there is a long history of Jesus being seen as the great human historical actor in western bourgeois thought and one that cuts across denominational divides.[63] This form of individualism has manifested itself in different ways. Halvor Moxnes shows how this great historical actor has been tied in with European discourses on nationalism and integral to the quest for the historical Jesus.[64] He shows how Schleiermacher's interest in the historical Jesus involved writing a biography, a popular form in nineteenth-century bourgeois German circles. Such biography involved the description of ideal figures who incorporated the ideal values of society, values that were distinct from the more traditional power structures. In other words, what we are dealing with are the biographies of Great Men. In particular, Schleiermacher saw the individual in relation to people, land, and nation, and, in terms of the study of the historical Jesus, to write the life of Jesus as a biography meant using categories within an 'imagined' (German) land, people, and nation. Jesus represented an especially great type of person who had influence over 'all peoples and all ages', and so his relation to people, land, and nation served as an ideal.

In many ways, the links between Great Men and nationalism remain in the field, albeit modified for our times, not least in the case of Jesus as still being constructed in distinction from Judaism. Sanders, one of the most influential historical Jesus scholars, insisted that he would 'propose explanations just as does any historian when writing about history' and suggested that 'Jesus' own theology and the theologies of his first followers' were to be explored, tellingly,

> in the same way as one studies what Jefferson thought about liberty, what Churchill thought about the labour movement and the strikes of 1910 and 1911, what Alexander the Great thought about the union of Greek and Persian in one empire, and what their contemporaries thought about these great men while they still lived... The historian who studies a great human being...[65]

As I have argued in detail elsewhere, one of the additional factors (as well as theological influences, of course) in the perpetuation of the kinds of individualism we find in historical Jesus scholarship has been the dominant ideological trend of neoliberalism.[66] Neoliberalism has typically continued the emphasis on great leaders affecting world history and the myth that individuals have the power to succeed or fail at will, with scant regard for the complexities of socio-economic structure and change. Of course, context and ideological bias do not mean any of the narratives are incorrect in the sense of their portraits of Jesus. As we have seen, while these narratives might help us with descriptions of Jesus the individual, they almost by definition fail to provide a more well-rounded explanation of the role of Jesus in historical change. An alternative narrative might help us to do this.

Biography and history

Biography does not have to be the way of the typical historical Jesus book either. Some historians have not been impressed with a basic descriptive-biographical approach to history. E. H. Carr was particularly scathing of the view stretching from the ancient world to the present that individuals are the decisive factor in history. For Carr, history was all about seeing the role of the human in society. So while he was happy to see biographies concerned with individual behaviour and eccentricities as a different genre to 'history', Carr could also recognize those biographies which located the individual in broader social trends as 'serious contributions to history', citing Isaac Deutscher's biographies of Stalin and Trotsky.[67] Eric Hobsbawm too was not wholly hostile to writing about individual figures and did in fact do so (e.g. Harold Laski, Roy Cohn, Salvatore Giuliano, Karl Korsch).[68]

But Hobsbawm consistently tried to see how the individual illuminates broader historical trends, how successfully the individual reacted to historical conditions in the broader sweep of historical change, and how ideas are intermingled with socio-economic context. We have now more or less arrived at Marx's famous (and widely accepted) saying which can be (and has been) received with a more socio-economic twist: 'Men make their own history, but they do not make it just as they please; they do not make it under circumstances chosen by themselves, but under circumstances directly encountered, given and transmitted from the past.'[69]

For those more biographically inclined, there were similar possibilities raised in a defence of the biographical form as 'serious history' by Ben Pimlott.[70] Pimlott was anything but a member of the sex-obsessed gossipy school of biographical writing (best represented, perhaps, by Andrew Morton's *Diana: Her True Story*) and he would not even entirely side with the all-too-common lengthy and meticulously researched descriptions of Someone-or-Other's life. In fact, he remained upbeat about those factors that Hobsbawm and others think should play a primary role in historical research. As Pimlott put it:

> far from underplaying social factors, the good biographer highlights them, to give *added precision* to the story. Good biography is flexible, *making unexpected connections across periods of time and including unexpected essays on topics which, for the involvement of the subject, might never get written about at all.'* [my italics][71]

As such a statement implies, we are moving beyond the use of social sciences for mere description. Indeed, though writing in a context critical of certain outdated forms of social historical explanation, Pimlott even referred to the 'stress on the role of the individuals' as 'old-fashioned'.[72] From the perspective of at least one prominent figure in biographical writing, then, it follows that there should be nothing contradictory about writing on specific historical figures with a concern for explaining social and historical change.[73] As we will see, socio-economic changes in early first-century Galilee and Judea provide some important reasons for the emphases of the earliest Jesus tradition and why the Jesus movement emerged when and where it did.

We are, of course, into the heart of a major well-worn debate among historians: the role of the individual in historical change. This is a massive area but a brief overview should give some indication of just how one-sided and odd looking the study of the historical Jesus and Christian origins has actually been. On the one hand the humanities have had well-known historians stressing the role of the great individual in history, epitomized (misleadingly it would seem) by Thomas Carlyle's famous sentence: 'The History of the world ... is but the Biography of great men.'[74] On the other hand, the humanities have had a major twentieth-century alternative in various social historians, Marxist historians, and Annalistes like Fernand Braudel. Braudel would even claim that the human was a prisoner of environment and mind and that human events were superficial, like the froth of the ocean tossed around by deeper, slower moving currents, that is social, geographical, and economic trends discernible only over long periods of time.[75] There is no way we can attempt to measure just how much historical change is down to what. The main point here is just how unusual historical Jesus study is, not to mention its relationship to Christian origins: if there are few followers of Braudel, there must be countless followers of (a possibly misinterpreted) Carlyle.

Contextualizing a life of Jesus

As it turns out there is plenty of material in the scholarly histories of Christian origins to provide broader explanations for the rise of the Jesus movement and what followed and which do not require us having to resort as much as is conventional to the history of ideas, events, and heroic individuals. Given the conventional constraints of space, I will have to limit my examples but these should suffice to illustrate the point. The interesting thing about these examples is that they are more or less 'there' waiting to be further exploited in those works which contextualize Jesus in his socio-economic world, as well as the broader work on the socio-economic world of first-century Palestine, not to mention some long-forgotten, provocative, if somewhat flawed, work from the Marxist tradition.[76] As already implied, not too far away has also been a long interdisciplinary tradition of scholars engaging with broader-ranging, socio-economic explanations of historical change.[77] If done properly, this could lead to a very different way of explaining Christian origins and could bring historical

Jesus and Christian origins research more in line with one aspect of conventional historical methodology.

But to leave it at explaining the emergence of the Jesus movement in Galilee is more or less to hover close to the level of description or as another dimension of exegesis and the tradition-historical method. It remains only one step away from describing Jesus' theology (which just so happens to be a result of x, y, and z). If a socio-economically informed explanation wants to look more to the longer term, then it might be helpful to look at what happens next. After all, a major historic movement would eventually emerge through the Jesus movement, to lesser or greater extent. Beyond explanations of those like Sanders and Wright that use the beliefs of the early church to explain the origins of the historical Jesus' teaching, there are, of course, plenty of explanations for the link between Jesus and Paul and the link between Jesus and Christian origins. James Dunn, for example, saw certain legal practices as forming a 'bridge' between Jesus and the Pauline mission.[78] But, typical of works on Christian origins, this is in many ways simply to describe and/or compare, and at best the explanatory force is too often akin to the surface level of events and historically inexplicable (as Braudel or Marx at least would have it) without the deeper movements of social, geographical, economic (etc.) history. Again, there are, no doubt, numerous socio-economic reasons that could be posited but I will have to restrict myself to some brief suggestions as to what this kind of history might involve.

Let us take the blunt fact that 'Christianity' would go on to include a noticeably high number of non-Jews. Irrespective of whether the historical Jesus advocated some inclusion of non-Jews, *how* and *why* did such a significant number of Gentiles become involved in the earliest Christian movement? Some kind of Gentile inclusion in Jewish eschatological thought does not explain this. An eschatological view of the inclusion of non-Jews is certainly one justification ready and waiting to be employed by the first Christians but, as it was 'there' in Judaism, why is it the movement associated with Jesus that gets all the non-Jews? In many ways this is a question of why a major missionary tendency could take off when and where it did. Whatever the reasons, ideas and theology alone simply cannot explain this 'why' question (I deliberately leave aside discussion of supernatural causes).

While this book will be focused on ideas as much as any Jesus book, I want these ideas to be understood as part of socio-economic changes, the most significant of which I will now summarize because, as mentioned above, they have been discussed widely and extensively, including in my own work.[79] The Jesus tradition did not just emerge spontaneously. In fact, we only need to cover some of the key points from the socio-historical work on first-century Galilee to begin to understand why the movement emerged when and where it did. By the time the Jesus tradition was developing, Galilee had witnessed the building and rebuilding of the key urban centres, Tiberias and Sepphoris, with significant socio-economic consequences. Further south in Judea, the Jerusalem Temple had become an extensive building project. Such urbanization can extract surplus from the countryside and is a key feature of the kinds of commercializing activity that John Kautsky believes underlay peasant unrest and the emergence of millenarian or utopian groups in aristocratic or agrarian empires, with calls for change ranging from the reactionary to the revolutionary.[80] It is also linked in with a general argument concerning socio-historical change: significant economic change (perceived or otherwise) and the dislocation of peasant land is a major factor in peasant unrest and reaction, with help often (but not exclusively) coming from outside the peasantry.[81] The labour and materials had to come from somewhere and so people would have faced the possibility of dislocation (cf. Josephus, *Ant.* 18.36–8). It is of some significance that there was a full-scale revolt against Rome in 66–70 CE, accompanied by reports of great hatred levelled at Sepphoris and Tiberias (*Life* 30, 39, 66–8, 99, 374–84), as well as a period that gave us prophetic and millenarian figures such as Theudas and John the Baptist. It is in this context of social upheaval that we can contextualize the emergence of the Jesus movement and the earliest Palestinian traditions.[82] In fear of being misunderstood, the silence of Sepphoris in the Gospel tradition is another issue; what we are dealing with here is the impact of such urbanization projects in Galilee or Judea, irrespective of whether historical actors attributed their changing circumstances to them, or even knew much about what was happening in the major towns.

There are plenty more material and textual details we could discuss were there space but a crucial qualification is especially helpful for understanding social change in Galilee: *perception*. I strongly stress *perception* because Morten Horning Jensen's detailed work on Galilean archaeology has criticized conflict-based approaches to Jesus' Galilean context, suggesting that there is more evidence for a prosperous Herodian economy.[83] Though Jensen may have a point in his criticisms of the use of conflict models in historical Jesus studies, unrest and social upheaval do not simply have to be reaction to or the result of an unambiguous decline in the general standard of living or a reaction to people being explicitly exploited—indeed, the situation would no doubt have been a more complex mix (cf. *Ant.* 18.36–8). The way in which we should alternatively use a conflict-based model is to focus on localized change where at least some among the populace do not *perceive* that this is for the better. As Hobsbawm—an influential figure behind this debate—carefully worded it when discussing peasant land occupations, peasant reaction is due to alienation 'in a manner which they do not regard as valid'.[84] In terms of the context of the earliest Palestinian tradition, the rebuilding of Sepphoris and the building of Tiberias, or, further south, the major extension of the Jerusalem Temple, we can at least suggest that the socio-economic situation would have been significantly changed and not everyone would have *perceived* social and cultural changes in traditional lifestyle for the better, as the Gospel tradition and its intense interest in issues of rich and poor (see chapters 3 and 4) may well attest. I will not add to the already extensive work carried out on the inevitable socio-economic changes brought about by major building projects as Jesus was growing up, but this will form the basis for the historical reconstruction in this book. What I attempt to show is how specified topics (especially kingdom of God, 'Christology', and gender) are partly a negotiation with the socio-economic changes in Galilee and Judea.

But this discussion will also involve some mention of longer-term changes. The emergence of millenarian or utopian groups in aristocratic or agrarian empires is crucial for making those unexpected connections across periods of time. A striking, albeit anachronistic, example is the English civil wars of the mid-seventeenth century. The most obvious reading here would be Christopher Hill's account of the civil wars as a bourgeois revolution paving the way for longer-term capitalist development. As part of this 'revolution', Hill famously gave much attention to radical developments 'from below' involving figures such as Gerrard Winstanley and groups such as the Levellers,

Quakers, and Diggers, all of which would have to be dealt with, tamed, and/or domesticated.[85] This 'world turned upside down' provided a context for unheard of radical claims concerning democracy, sexuality, theology, God, education, millenarianism, and so on and taken together this might provide a general perspective important for understanding Jesus and Christian origins.[86] Hill's work may have long gone out of fashion, his particular Marxist reading seriously challenged, and it is not entirely clear that he read some of his source material accurately.[87] However, the general point that this 'world turned upside down' fed into longer-term changes, suppression, and/or developments in science, theology, literature, politics, democracy, philosophy, and so on, all to be taken up vigorously in the Enlightenment, remains an important one. This is a key point of the more recent major study of the English civil wars by Michael Braddick. The following is worth an extensive quotation:

> Out of a chaos of opinion and anxiety, and of the catastrophe and trauma of civil war, had come ideas about freedom and citizenship, religious toleration and exclusion of secular powers from matters of conscience. These arguments had deeper roots in the English past but were newly public, and newly in power. These English discussions about the origins and limits of political power were of profound significance for Enlightenment Europe—indeed, to the more celebrated revolutions in eighteenth-century America and France. But they were not, as far as we know, representative of average opinions: others sought resolutions to the crisis in astrology, the prosecutions of witches, or the restoration of older forms of religious and political authority... There is much more to say, and to remember, about England's decade of civil war and revolution. Political and religious questions of fundamental importance were thrashed out before broad political audiences as activists and opportunists sought to mobilize support for their proposals... by exposing... presumptions to sustained critical examination, this public discussion changed them. This was a decade of intense debate and spectacular intellectual creativity—not just in politics and religion, but in understandings of the natural world and how political opinion was mobilized. The implications of this English experience reverberated around the world of the Enlightenment and English politics were permanently changed by the experience of popular mobilization...[88]

We might think of analogous contexts of chaotic social upheaval contributing to shifts in, and explosions of, ideas and thinking (whether revolutionary, reactionary, creative, culturally bizarre, peaceful, violent, or accidental) which may have huge long-term impacts, be clamped down almost immediately, or have potential unrealized, from the French Revolution to the Spanish Civil War, from the Peasants' Revolt to the Iranian Revolution. But, with historical and cultural differences duly acknowledged, there is something potentially significant about the logic concerning the emergence of (culturally) radical groups and ideas when we think of more ancient agrarian societies. And, of course, not only did early first-century Galilee witness some significant socio-economic changes but also Palestine of the first-century witnessed some monumental changes, culminating in the two major revolts against Rome. From this, to at least some degree, emerge Christianity and the consolidation of Judaism among the rabbis. These developments should not simply be restricted to the revolts themselves but were part of the thinking that emerged from a series of significant socio-political changes intersecting with specific cultural traditions already present in first-century Palestine. Moreover, we also know that Christianity (and Judaism) would stretch beyond Palestine and across the empire and, in the case of Christianity, would *become* the empire. Within the constraints of space, this means we can also look at some (and only some) of the ways in which broader and long-term trends in the ancient world intersected with the tradition emerging from Palestine. This does not mean, of course, that this book is a grand explanation of Christian origins. It is clearly not. Instead, it remains broadly within the genre of the historical Jesus book and is designed to provide an example of how we might approach this genre differently in future by making creative historical connections.

There are, of course, important methodological echoes of Foucault's genealogies here (not forgetting that Foucault had well-known interests in the ways ideas were generating in the Iranian Revolution).[89] In this sense, historical analysis looks for the somewhat chaotic development of ideas without recourse to implied metaphysical origins. This Foucauldian qualification is especially important because the critique of the quest for origins obviously lies at the heart of the quest for the historical Jesus and could be mistaken for lying at the heart of an approach which looks at social upheaval and the redirection of ideas. However, this present book, while hardly disavowing totalizing history, is not the search for the pure, essential origins of Christianity, as if at the heart of which lies the scholarly construct of the influential historical figure of Jesus. Instead, we are tracing and unravelling the details of the uneasy, accidental, purposeful, discontinuous, and implicit meanings in the developments of ideas as they appeared in particular times and places.

Was Jesus important?

Roland Deines has argued that my insistence on explaining historical development in terms of a mixture of individual influence and social context is 'extreme' (which in New Testament studies it may well be). He then critiques me as follows: 'Adopting his line about Hitler ("...something like what happened in Germany in the 1930s and 1940s would have happened even if Hitler had not been born") in relation to Jesus, one can say (and the title of his book implies it) that Christianity would have happened even without Jesus.'[90] I am not sure how the title of a previous book of mine—*Why Christianity Happened: A Sociohistorical Explanation of Christian Origins*—implies that Christianity would have happened even without Jesus so I leave that to one side until a better explanation is forthcoming. Deines' use of the ellipsis is unfortunate. Here is the sentence I wrote in full: 'Whether correct or not, it would hardly be too revolutionary to say that something like what happened in Germany in the 1930s and 1940s would have happened even if Hitler had not been born.'[91] The qualification is important because the point, as is clear from the paragraph Deines cites, was to challenge the dominance of Jesus as *the* great historical mover and to suggest that we cannot assume from the outset that he was a major influence on the emergence of Christianity and that a range of social, economic, and historical factors might be far more, or at least equally, important for all we know. Moreover, the rest of the book gave detailed examples of where Jesus' influence was in fact significant. I follow the same general procedure here.

However, we should reiterate that we cannot simply assume that Jesus must *necessarily* have been the most important factor in the emergence of the new movement. Indeed, Burton Mack has argued that assuming the importance of Jesus in the historical process is in fact misguided.[92] There is nothing implausible about this suggestion in the abstract because influence has to be shown rather than assumed and so, throughout this study, there will be an implicit assessment of the influence of the earliest Jesus tradition. This stands in contrast to another recent approach by K. L. Noll which has emphatically tried to downplay the influence of the historical Jesus, or indeed a reconstruction of the historical Jesus at all.[93]

Noll writes from 'a Darwinian perspective' which 'treats religious ideas as memes, as defined by Richard Dawkins . . . A religious meme that is fit for survival and replication is one that is sufficiently simple to be understood and inculcated by the average human mind, yet can appeal to human perceptions of religious need'.[94] He argues that if this perspective as applied to Christian origins is correct, then 'it is reasonable for historians to dismiss all quests for a historical Jesus from discussion about the process by which the religion of Christianity emerged, evolved and survived'.[95] He argues that clusters of 'memes' (in a 'doctrinal mode') give a 'religion' a distinctive branding in competition with other 'religious ideas' and are defended by trained leaders over time and distance.[96] The Jesus tradition, he argues, continued in generic form and became part of competing Jesus-memes in earliest Christianity yet it became 'irrelevant' among the competitors and his own contribution disappeared when he died. After the crucifixion, the (hypothetical) historical Jesus (and other strands of Christianity) lost out in the Darwinian struggle. He concludes: 'To the extent that the Jesus of the canonical Gospels preserves any DNA from pre-Gospel stages of the religion's evolution, that DNA derives from Paul, not from the Jerusalem pillars . . . and certainly not from a hypothetical historical Jesus.'[97]

Aside from too many unsubstantiated statements concerning historical reconstruction, Noll's attempt to bring in the language of memes, evolution, and DNA to suggest that we know nothing of the earliest tradition or the historical Jesus fails for a number of reasons. The very approach is problematic as Noll's analysis works with the assumption that 'religion' is somehow natural.[98] This means it buys into the problematic assumption of 'religion' as a sui generis discourse[99] and thus, as Kenneth MacKendrick put it in his sharp and succinct analysis of cognitive approaches to 'religion', it 'would be more accurate to say that the strong naturalist thesis is actually a religious theory of cognition . . . a *religious* re-description of cognition'.[100] It may have been more helpful, though potentially further undermining his argument, if Noll had discussed competing discourses *and* material conditions. From the outset, then, Noll's very assumptions are flawed. Moreover, the language of DNA and memes is presumably in part responsible for his far too rigid notion of identity feeding into the Gospels and Christian origins:

a Darwinian struggle for survival among competing Jesus-memes invented by variant presuppositions. These were sometimes Jewish presuppositions (e.g. those of the Jerusalem pillars) or Jewish-Gnostic (perhaps those Paul opposed in 1 Corinthians?). In some cases they were Cynic presuppositions, or Platonic, or Stoic, or a variation of one of the many Greco-Roman mystery religions...[101]

History and society does not work in such clearly defined ways and, in terms of Christian origins at least, identity (at least in the sense of how individuals identified themselves and were identified by others) could differ from context to context and categories such as 'Jewish' and 'Cynic' may easily be overlapping and intersecting, possibly indistinguishable at times.[102] To impose the language of memes seems to give them some kind of natural quality that somehow exists apart from human society and culture. In terms of Christian origins and the historical Jesus, there is no reason why overlapping and intersecting ideas were part of cultural context rather than the rigid and simplified model provided by Noll.

There is, of course, a lot of creative work currently happening in cognitive studies of Christian origins and 'religion' and no doubt there will be many advances but, as the example of Noll shows, it is difficult to see how downplaying broader historical and social processes will be possible. Like certain cognitive approaches to 'religion', Noll's analysis is far too removed, at least in its presentation and rhetoric, from the intersection of intellectual genealogies (which may be dormant, hidden, implicit, explicit, and so on) with material, political, social, particular, and ideological aspects of historical processes. To take a simple example of Noll's problematic results: he argues that 'Early post-Pauline writings transmit favourite Pauline doctrines (such as a declaration that *kashrut* need not be observed; Mk 7:19b)...It is Paul's doctrinal DNA that survives in the Jesus who undermines Torah (Mk 2:23–3:5)...'.[103] But these are only favoured Pauline doctrines if we believe they are. Unfortunately, Noll is simply following outdated scholarship on such matters and does not consider recent scholarly arguments which have suggested that Mark 7.19b is part of the debate over hand-washing in the rest of the chapter and that the Sabbath disputes in Mark 2 and 3 show no indication of any biblical Sabbath law being undermined, and that both these purity and Sabbath disputes echo what is known about early Jewish Sabbath disputes over the specifics of interpretation.[104] Alternatively, why could these not be remnants of earlier tradition? Why could earlier tradition not survive more generally in a more complex social world? Why could such potentially earlier tradition not be useful? What about Ebionites or groups dedicated to Law, the Sabbath, or Passover which did not die out so quickly? Noll's failure does not mean we have to reinstate an influential figure of Jesus as the most significant point of origin but it does mean that Noll's analysis does not mean that there is *necessarily* such a disjunction.

Back to the future

An extreme example of making unexpected connections across time would be our opening quotations from Badiou and Žižek about Jesus plus Paul equals Lenin plus Marx. From what we have discussed so far, there are hints that this anachronistic formula has something to it. After all, the earliest Jesus tradition does seem to point to the hope for a better world and Paul comes along controversially reinterpreting the Master's message (Žižek, incidentally, embraces the idea of the betrayal of Judas in relation to Paul's 'betrayal' of Jesus' message[105]), carrying out the hard work, and establishing the communities. And now, as is increasingly apparent, the eye-opening use of Paul among thinkers such as Badiou and Žižek has Paul doing just this and more: Paul is a thinker pushing for a radical universality in implicit or explicit opposition to Rome and its empire. This reading has obvious affinities with the recent, though not new, trend in more conventional New Testament studies that reads Paul as an explicitly or implicitly, or even indifferent, anti-imperial figure.

However, what we also see is a tendency all too familiar to the universalism of Marxism (and Christianity): a new power to replace the old. And so, there is something else which we should be wary of in the Marx/Lenin analogy by turning the analogy on itself in the form of a historic (and often liberal and crude) critique of Marxism: it leads to totalitarianism. Of course, we should also be wary of hagiographical readings of figures of origins in that this classic criticism of Marxism should not mean the Great Leader is exempt from critique, as if it were the deluded power-hungry followers who just 'misinterpreted' what came before. Here we might return to the nineteenth century and a criticism of Marxism which, I think, has more validity than the liberal critique of Marxism, which owes more to a fear of challenging its power structures. Mikhail Bakunin prophetically saw one potential future of Marxism as a 'red bureaucracy'. In one scathing criticism of the implications of Marxism, he added:

> The reasoning of Marx ends in absolute contradiction. Taking into account only the economic question, he insists that only the most advanced countries... are most capable of making social revolution... This revolution will expropriate either by peaceful, gradual or violent means, the present property owners and capitalists. To appropriate all the landed property and capital, and to carry out its extensive economic and political programs, the revolutionary State will have to be very powerful and highly centralized. The State will administer and direct the cultivation of the land, by means of salaried officials commanding armies of rural workers organized and disciplined for that purpose. At the same time, on the ruins of existing banks, it will establish a single state bank which will finance all labour and national commerce... For the proletariat this will, in reality, be nothing but a barracks: a regime, where regimented workingmen and women will sleep, wake, work, and live to the beat of a drum; where the shrewd and educated will be granted government privileges... There will be slavery within this state, and abroad there will be war without truce, at least until the 'inferior' races, Latin and Slav, tired of bourgeois civilization, no longer resign themselves to the subjection of the State, which will be even more despotic than the former State, although it calls itself a Peoples' State.[106]

This remarkable analysis was, of course, before the rise of the Soviet Union.

Unlike Bakunin, we now have the benefit of hindsight and we can see similar processes at work with reference to what we call 'religion' in forms where it echoes Marx's 'sigh of the oppressed creature, the heart of a heartless world, and the soul of soulless conditions'. Certain influential forms of evangelical Christianity in America may well be the sigh of the oppressed, being part of a cultural context of wage decrease or stagnation, increased working hours, and indebtedness.

The related Tea Party may be as much a product of the economic crises as the Occupy Movement but it, and key strands of evangelical Christianity, has become a significant part of certain hegemonic discourses in contemporary American politics with its calls for extreme freedom from the state often becoming a support for corporate power. An equally striking manifestation of what we might loosely call a Bakuninist understanding of history is in that peculiar marriage of Marxism and religion: influential strands of revolutionary Islam. The revolutionary or highly politicized sorts of Islam—from the Iranian revolutionaries to al-Qaeda—are in many ways, though not unprecedented, thoroughly modern, developing throughout the twentieth century and associated with pivotal figures such as Hassan al-Banna (1906–49), Sayyid Abul Ala Maududii (1903–79) and Sayyid Qutb (*c.*1906–66) and movements such as the Muslim Brotherhood. As is often pointed out, underlying the quranic and general Islamic rhetoric are clear influences from strands of Marxism (e.g. revolutionary vanguard, anti-imperialism, terror, internationalism, and popular justice—even the aggressive splintering and internecine disputes so often associated with Marxist groups), hardly a surprise given the prominence of intellectual Marxism in universities and the nationalist and socialist movements in colonial, postcolonial, and neocolonial contexts, including the Middle East, India, and North Africa. Furthermore, this sort of politicized Islam had an appeal well beyond the universities as it began to flourish among the urban lower classes in North Africa and parts of Asia and so, just as we find in left-wing and even hard-right thought, there is an attempt, crucially, to deal with serious socio-economic problems, with further reference to cultural, 'spiritual', and moral issues.[107]

Bakunin's critique of Marxism is also applicable to a reading of Christian origins and its views on theocracy and the readings of Paul by Badiou and Žižek (though Žižek has been particularly sensitive to the implicit totalitarianism in Marx and Lenin).[108] Whereas the imposition of Marxism *did* become a 'red bureaucracy', did not Paul's letters and Christian theology become empire? The radical transformation of the past, the shaking off of particular identities, the idea of neither Jew nor Greek, male nor female, slave nor free *in Christ* (Gal. 3.28) meant that everyone could now be placed under the umbrella of a Christian empire. Rome effectively developed, rightly or wrongly, these ideas and Christianity became central to a theocracy. And if we take this one step further and were to follow Badiou's line of fidelity to the 'event', even when everything seems to be going wrong, are we not on the slippery slope to the defences of Stalin's mass murders or the Inquisition, both in the name of loyalty to the revolution in testing times?

This is not simply an abstract reading of Christianity, as if the misguided and power hungry somehow hijacked the 'original' meaning, as the implication of the seemingly benign Gal. 3.28 would already suggest. On the contrary, and as postcolonial studies of Mark and Revelation have shown, critiques of imperial power in earliest Christian texts were done through absorbing and mimicking the language and structures of power.[109] We likewise see this in our 'Lenin' figure, Paul. It is more than likely that Paul looks forward to some kind of theocracy. In the famous passage from Phil. 2.6–11 we learn that the crucified one will be exalted above all names 'so that at the name of Jesus every knee should bend, in heaven and on earth and under the earth and every tongue should confess that Jesus Christ is Lord' (Phil. 2.10–11). And what is also significant about this is that New Testament scholars, including famous historical Jesus scholars, can accept Paul's rhetoric and, if anything, intensify it. For example, Wright, one of the most vocal proponents of the view that Jesus was declared in mocking contrast to Caesar by Paul and the early Christians, may see the proclamation of resurrection as a 'politically revolutionary doctrine'.[110] However, even when discussing anti-imperialist rhetoric he likewise discusses (and presumably endorses) imperialist language as a replacement: 'his people are now a "colony of heaven", an advance guard of the project to bring the whole world under the sovereign and saving rule of Israel's god'.[111] We will return to such issues in Chapter 3.

Of course, what is possible for later texts is also possible for the earliest Jesus tradition, which looks as if it does point to a theocracy that could later be picked up for imperial uses here on earth. Or maybe not. It still remains an option that there was a complete disjunction between the earliest Palestinian tradition and what followed. What the rest of this book does is to look at whether there are a range of connections with or disjunctions from the traditions and whether this tells us something about the socio-economic upheaval, structures, trends, and long-term developments which fed into the rise of Christianity. This sort of thinking will underpin the more exegetical chapters that follow, even when it is not explicit. In the concluding chapter I will tackle the ways in which people may or may not be trapped by the revolutions that failed, so to speak.[112]

2

Criteria, Historicity, and the Earliest Palestinian Tradition

In order to gain a picture of the earliest tradition for an understanding of historical change we will need to turn to the criteria for reconstructing the historical Jesus. It should become clear that I share the increasing disillusionment about their usefulness,[1] as well as sharing the view that we should be using the specific analysis of passages not to be precise in our historical reconstructions but to build up general pictures of plausibility.[2] However, this needs further qualification, namely, that I am aiming more at the general reconstruction of the earliest Palestinian tradition which may (or may not) reflect something of the early Jesus movement rather than promising a precise picture of the historical Jesus. In fact, this approach is just as useful for my overall approach because I am more concerned with the ways in which the general historical chaos of a specific time and place feeds into historical trends and change and the ways in which human beings engage with such changes while downplaying the centrality of Jesus the Great Man.[3] While the purpose of the first half of this chapter is to see how we might understand the earliest tradition, we should also assume throughout the negative argument that will become more explicit in the second half: the approach taken here can suggest material attributed to Jesus which does *not* reflect the historical Jesus or the earliest Palestinian tradition.

Dissimilarity, double dissimilarity, and embarrassment

It has long been recognized that the criterion of dissimilarity is of minimal use.[4] The idea that a saying (or action) is deemed more likely historically authentic if Jesus is different from his Jewish context and the early church raises the obvious counterargument: how, with sufficiently incomplete evidence, are we to make such a judgement? It also effectively assumes that Jesus must have been different from both Judaism and what came after him. Of course, such uniqueness is theoretically possible but a criterion which *assumes* it to be the case shows how loaded the criterion is before we even start. Put bluntly, what if he was *not* different from one or either? Why could someone *after* Jesus' death not have created something different from one or the other? That is, if it is assumed Jesus could say or do something so 'unique', then why not another person? The consensus view is right: dissimilarity is of minimal use, if that.

However, despite the consistent scholarly rhetoric about the uselessness of dissimilarity, it has not prevented it from getting a liberal makeover for a postmodern age or it being used for seemingly 'exceptional' cases. The most obvious repackaging for contemporary sensibilities would have to be that by N. T. Wright: 'when something can be seen to be credible (though perhaps deeply subversive) within first-century Judaism, and credible as the implied starting point (though not the exact replica) of something in later Christianity, there is a strong possibility of our being in touch with the genuine history of Jesus'. However, this is coupled with a watered down version of the criterion of dissimilarity. Thus when discussing Jesus' teaching, Wright claims, 'It is thus decisively *similar* to both the Jewish context and the early Christian world, and at the same time importantly *dissimilar*...'.[5] Put simply, the same criticisms of dissimilarity apply. Furthermore, if this sort of thinking is going to be applied, should we not be finding as much Jewish evidence as possible to show that Jesus was legitimately different? This is precisely what Wright does not do. As I have argued elsewhere, Wright and others regularly work with generalizations about Judaism without providing detailed examples to see if this or that saying of Jesus can be paralleled in early Judaism. The driving assumption is that Jesus *must* be different from the outset, no matter how 'very Jewish' Wright claims this difference is.[6]

It is noticeable how much closer to dissimilarity this supposedly different criterion gets in its reception, whether used implicitly or explicitly. According to Roland Deines:

> He can be compared with other healers and charismatics, but again, the analogies are only partial and at their heart leave as much unexplained as they explain . . . Jesus cannot be placed in a single category only, or, whenever this attempt is made, Jesus stands out as somehow 'unique-ish'. He cannot be understood without the analogies provided by the Jewish world he lived in but at the same time he is not fully encapsulated by them . . . all attempts to narrow down Jesus into one particular tradition simply failed to convince . . . It is indeed essential that the person Jesus of Nazareth is to be understood within the Jewish traditions of his time, but at the same time it is equally true that he cannot be fully captured by any or even all of these traditions.[7]

But again, we can question the necessity of the driving narrative. What if it were the Gospel writers or the post-Jesus tradition constructing Jesus as a 'unique-ish' figure (assuming for the moment that they all did)? What if some or all of the other healers and charismatics were slightly more complex individuals—maybe 'unique-ish' themselves!—and were likewise not fully captured by these traditions either? If so, where does that leave the historical reconstruction of a 'unique-ish' Jesus? What if the suspiciously essentializing static and fixed types for Jesus might also be more complex rather than merely providing a background to make Jesus superior?[8]

The apologetic function of this criterion is clearer in a number of presentations. Paul Barnett, for instance, likes what he calls the 'criterion of similarity *and* dissimilarity' because it recognizes 'that as a Jew many of Jesus' words are "similar" to Jewish thought while also observing that Jesus' radicalism will often subvert or overturn Jewish thought'.[9] But who said Jesus must have been 'radical'? What if he was not? What is 'radical' anyway? Does 'radical' mean proto-Christian and an overturning of the somewhat large 'Jewish thought'? Or, again, notice how sort-of-difference from Judaism and sort-of-difference from Christianity can so easily become difference from Judaism and similarity to Christianity. In a more sophisticated analysis, Darrell Bock acknowledges the similarity with the older criterion and, implicitly, the methodological assumption that Jesus must be different from Judaism: 'I am appealing to Tom Wright's variation of the criterion of dissimilarity, what has come to be called double dissimilarity, which means close to but not quite like Judaism or the early church expression'. But when Bock completes his argument concerning the phrase 'Son of the Blessed One' (Mark 14.61–2) in relation to Jesus, Judaism, and similarity/dissimilarity, he effectively claims that it is in fact a Christian sentiment: 'The NT reflects such usage in Eph 1:3 and 1 Pet 1:3.'[10] This rescuing of double dissimilarity from being 'too Jewish', thus rescuing it for Christianity, occurs elsewhere in the same volume, which Bock co-edited and to which he contributed. Probably the most explicit example of this tendency is in Grant Osborne's contribution on the resurrection accounts, where it appears he has simply given up on aspects of dissimilarity from Christianity and replaced them with complete continuity: 'Here Wright's criterion of "double similarity and double dissimilarity" is relevant, for this mission was instituted by Jesus in Jewish ministry and yet transcends that setting by moving here to the Gentile mission. The mission command as such provides a bridge from the life of Jesus to the mission of the church.'[11] In what useful sense is this dissimilar from Christianity?[12]

The most obvious exceptional case of dissimilarity in practice would probably be the parallel passage in Matt. 8.21–2 and Luke 9.59–60, 'let the dead bury their own dead'. The typical argument, as presented influentially by Martin Hengel, E. P. Sanders, and N. T. Wright, would be something like this: the sentiment is shocking in the context of early Judaism (and indeed the ancient world more generally), where burial of parents was regarded so highly (e.g. Gen. 23.3–4; Tobit 6.13–15; *m. Ber.* 3.1; *m. Nazir* 7.1), and therefore we should attribute it to the historical Jesus.[13] But a basic reading of the passage itself would already show how problematic this common argument is. There is no indication in the passage, or in the immediate narrative contexts, that this saying was deemed to be shocking, and Matthew and Luke were not sufficiently shocked to omit the saying. The Gospel tradition is happy to present a number of disputes between Jesus and various opponents, as well as questions from puzzled disciples; so why not here, particularly if the saying were as outrageous as scholars sometimes tell us? Moreover, what does it say about the reliance on the Hengel-Sanders-Wright tradition when we see long-available evidence concerning debates about avoiding corpses beyond biblical commandments (e.g. cf. Luke 10.29–37; Philo *Spec. Leg.* 1.113–15, 250; *m. Nazir* 7.1)? Is there not a problem that none of the sources cited by Hengel have the high priest or Nazirite exempted to bury parents (cf. *Spec. Leg.* 1.113–15, 250)?[14] Could not these latter two questions suggest or imply that this saying might indeed be said to be less shocking in the context of early Judaism than is often suggested?

Perhaps more useful than the different forms of dissimilarity is the criterion of embarrassment. At first sight, the reasoning seems valid: anything that might be deemed to embarrass Jesus and yet makes it into the Gospels is more likely to be historically 'authentic'. It might be thought that the following goes against the grain of early Christian conceptions of Jesus as an elevated figure: 'And he could do no deed of power there. Except that he laid his hands on a few sick people and cured them. And he was amazed at their unbelief' (Mark 6.5–6). Furthermore, Matthew feels the need to alter the emphasis of this comment by claiming that the lack of healing was Jesus' *choice*, revealing that at least someone had issues with it (Matt. 13.58). Similar examples might be the different accounts of Joseph of Arimathea (Mark 15.43–47; Matt. 27.57; Luke 23.50–1; John 19.38) or the different accounts of Jesus' baptism (Mark 1.9; Matt. 3.13–15). Clearly these examples show that there were problematic or embarrassing accounts of Jesus which some figures within the early church felt the need to change.

It seems, then, that we might be onto something with the criterion of embarrassment. There are still problems, however. If a saying or deed is embarrassing, why does it have to be Jesus who created the embarrassing moment? Why not someone else earlier in the tradition? Or, that which is embarrassing to one need not necessarily be embarrassing to another.[15] How do we judge what is embarrassing? Might not embarrassment be a matter of perspective? Such questions suggest a general problem with this criterion. John's Gospel, for instance, removes Jesus' association with 'sinners' and removes the stories of Jesus as exorcist. The reason may well be that he found these themes embarrassing. But it is equally clear that the other Gospel writers who did include these themes did *not* find them embarrassing. Obviously, then, what we might be establishing is what John found embarrassing and not necessarily an argument in favour of material about the historical Jesus.[16] As with dissimilarity, there is something counterproductive: why would Matthew and Luke be prepared to include the saying 'let the dead bury their own dead' if it were both shocking and (presumably therefore) embarrassing? In the case of the lack of power in Nazareth, it could simply be that we have found something Mark did *not* find embarrassing, or that we are dealing with a context which might not have elevated Jesus as highly as others. This makes it more difficult to assess the value of embarrassment for the historical reconstruction of Jesus. However, we might be able to form the basis of an argument (requiring further evidence) that Mark 6.5–6 represents an earlier tradition in that it does not seem to be in line with typical Markan redaction and that it is less likely to have been created by the early church. Embarrassment may be limited in reconstructing the historical Jesus but if we could locate a passage such as Mark 6.5–6 in a context which reflects early Palestinian tradition then that might be something. But whether we still call this 'embarrassment' is moot.

Historical plausibility, Aramaisms, and multiple attestation

Perhaps, at best, we can generalize a variant of embarrassment a little more: it may, *ideally*, be deemed strongest if we can make an argument that the passage or theme in question might share the cultural assumptions of Palestine or Galilee around the early or mid-first century, or at least be plausibly part of such contexts, and lack interest in the influence of later developments in the early church. Here we might make connections with the criterion of historical plausibility, developed in particular by Gerd Theissen and Dagmar Winter.[17] Some of its strength is basic common sense: Jesus' life and teaching ought to be compatible with, or understandable within the context of, the Judaism of Jesus' time and place, and Jesus must emerge as a recognizable figure within that context while still remaining a figure who influenced what came after him in earliest Christian history. Some qualifications need to be made. Again, Jesus could, *theoretically*, have been a truly revolutionary figure of his time and done things beyond what is known about early Judaism. However, this qualification could be used to our advantage. If Jesus' teachings start to look as if they are an integral part of what is known of his time and place then this would, obviously perhaps, suggest they were indeed from his general time and place. Another qualification should, however, be made. What if parts of Jesus' teaching had no influence in earliest Christianity? Theoretically, this too must be an option, not least because the earliest Christians faced different situations to those of Galilee and Palestine in the early and mid-first century. As Dale Allison put it, 'We cannot ascribe everything in early Christianity to its founder. We can no more praise him for all that went right than we can blame him for all that went wrong. His followers sometimes reaped where he did not sow.'[18]

Purity, an issue to which we will return in Chapter 4, might be a good example of this because it involves a practice which in specifically Jewish purity was not believed to concern Gentiles and was of minimal interest to the early church as far as we know, yet coheres with practices which were the subject of intense debates in Palestinian Judaism, including those which involved the role of purity in relation to the Temple (see e.g. Luke 10.31–7). Similarly we could bring in the sometimes unfairly maligned criterion of 'Aramaic influence'; unfair at least in the sense that equal scepticism has not always been applied to the other criteria.[19] As with historical plausibility, it is possible that an understanding of Aramaic contexts may give us a more nuanced view of the early Palestinian tradition. However, the scepticism towards the use of 'Aramaisms' as a means of establishing historicity is well known and important. For example: there could have been additional Semitic influences on the tradition at a post-Jesus stage; there could be influences from overlapping scriptural versions and translations; there could be influences from one language to another (especially in the case of Aramaic, Greek, and Hebrew); there could have been 're-Semitization' of tradition; and so on.[20] John Meier's sceptical argument against Aramaisms, namely that they provide only additional support for historicity only after indications of authenticity on other grounds,[21] might even be too generous according to Loren Stuckenbruck.[22] But perhaps we could go further still and simply add that the other criteria are no better as a guiding principle either and we should, as Stuckenbruck rightly points out, simply be thinking in the following terms: 'each potential case has to be examined on its own merits'.[23]

So how might Aramaic be of use? Let me give an example which the reader may for now treat as hypothetical. In Mark 2.23–8 we have a dispute over plucking grain on the Sabbath which concludes with a 'son of man' (ὁ υἱὸς τοῦ ἀνθρώπου) saying. The son of man saying is part of a general literary context: 'Then he said to them, "The Sabbath was made for humankind, and not humankind for the Sabbath; so the son of man is lord even of the Sabbath"' (Mark 2.27–8). Elsewhere, Mark certainly uses 'the Son of Man' as a title for Jesus alone and even alludes to Dan. 7.13, which he reinterpreted as the second coming

(Mark 13.26; cf. Mark 14.62). But 'son of man' was not really a Greek term but a Semitic one and in the case of Mark 2.27–8 it reads much more like the form of the Aramaic idiom (בר [א]נש[א]), which has a generic frame of reference as well as a reference to the speaker, hence the general contextualization in 2.27.[24] This reading is supported by Matthew and Luke dropping the general frame of reference in Mark 2.27 and making sure that 'the Son of Man' is a title for Jesus alone (Matt. 12.8; Luke 6.5). As we will see, it is important to make arguments of collective weight, or at least provide supplementary arguments. In this instance, we have a number of additional cultural details which would support Mark 2.23–8 as being part of an early Palestinian tradition. The sentiment of justifying Sabbath practice in terms of being made for humanity was something known in, and associated with, Palestinian Judaism (e.g. Exod. 16.29; *Jub.* 2.17; *Mek. Exod.* 31.12–17; *b. Yoma* 85b). Prior to Mark 2.27–8 we have a dispute over plucking (*τίλλοντες*) grain on the Sabbath (Mark 2.23). Plucking grain was not prohibited in biblical law but disputes or rulings over related issues were again known in Palestinian Judaism (e.g. CD 10.22–3; *m. Pesah.* 4.8). From what we know, these sorts of discussions over what can and cannot be done on the Sabbath were not a major issue for the church as described outside the Synoptic tradition and, where the issue does turn up, it concerns whether the Sabbath should be observed at all (Gal. 4.10; Rom. 14.5–6; Col. 2.16; cf. John 5.1–18). In this context, it is notable that Matthew and Luke make Mark's assumptions explicit by explaining that Jesus' disciples were not going to break a commandment and carry the grain; they make it clear that they ate it there and then (Matt. 12.1; Luke 6.1). This sort of reasoning—even if we take it as a hypothetical example—would therefore suggest that it is possible to see what sort of ideas might have come from early Palestinian tradition.

But we should not think that any of this necessarily takes us directly to the historical Jesus. While we do not know the details of any Christian group with such a keen interest in the specifics of Sabbath and purity who might have been responsible for developing such a story after Jesus' death, this does not mean that no such group existed.[25] There is, we must always acknowledge, a lot we do *not* know about first-century Christianity. Given the existence of (say) the parable of the Good Samaritan (see below) or the story of plucking grain on the Sabbath, someone at least must have known the details of purity and Sabbath.[26] Or, someone could, theoretically, have written up a creative fiction in Aramaic in the late 30s, or, for all we know, during Jesus' lifetime. As the extensive work of Roger Aus has shown, haggadic traditions about Jesus were likely to have been compiled in Aramaic or Hebrew before the compilation of the Gospels (but, given the approach of this book, certain haggadic traditions could still, of course, give useful information about the earliest Palestinian tradition or Jesus, irrespective of 'historical accuracy').[27] Of course, it is possible that Aramaisms and historical plausibility does in fact reflect something of the historical figure of Jesus but we must accept there are limits on just how certain we can be, at least when using such criteria alone.

What this discussion should show us so far is that the criteria cannot be applied mechanically to the Gospel sources when evaluating historical accuracy, if they can even be applied as 'criteria' at all. One way to make the case stronger would be to combine different points within the criteria to provide an argument of collective weight. If we take the parable of the Good Samaritan, we could add that debates over the issue of purity were discussed in traditions presumably pre-Lukan (e.g. Mark 7.1–23; Matt. 23.25–6//Luke 11.39–41) and so such disputes are potentially early, an issue which was not deemed to concern Gentiles, and possibly a non-issue for those outside the perceived boundaries of Israel.[28] We could then add that disputes and conflicts over issues of the Law are common in the Synoptic Gospels but were also culturally plausible. There are plenty of disputes attested between different groups and individuals over points of Law and purity (for the general point see *Ant.* 13.297–8). Again, such disputes over the details of interpretation were not, as far as we know, typical of earliest Christianity, where disputes tended to be over whether the Law should be observed at all. We could further add that explanations were clearly added for puzzled audiences unfamiliar with local practices (e.g. Mark 7.1–5), which may suggest that they were explanations of inherited tradition. It may well be the case that conflict traditions were 'fictional' but collectively this would make a stronger argument for some of the earliest Palestinian tradition being concerned with conflicts between Jesus and his opponents over the details of interpretation.

It might be thought that the criterion of multiple attestation would further help here, that is, multiple attestation understood as involving an idea or saying of Jesus found independently in different sources. According to the standard model of the Synoptic Problem this would involve Mark, Q, M, and L. However, if we took the Farrer-Goulder-Goodacre hypothesis (or variations on the model that Matthew and Luke used Mark and that Luke additionally used Matthew), or a combination of the standard Two or Four Source hypothesis and the Farrer-Goulder-Goodacre hypothesis, this might instead involve using Mark and material particular to Matthew and/or Luke.[29] To this, scholars have added sayings from (for instance) *Thomas* and parts of John's Gospel, a point to which we will return in the case of the latter.[30] Multiple attestation is, of course, sometimes expanded to include forms such as parables and pronouncement stories and so if a saying, idea, or theme is found across sources and forms, so the logic goes, the more likely it is to be 'authentic'. But multiple attestation is hardly without its difficulties. What the criterion of multiple attestation can tell us is whether a tradition is early and/or pre-Gospel. This problem is perhaps highlighted best by the multiple attestation of miracle stories. It is hardly proof that miracles 'really happened' because they are attested independently, as has been argued,[31] but it *is* a good indicator that the earliest people responsible for the pre-Gospel tradition thought Jesus was quite special and it still tells us something potentially important about the earliest Palestinian tradition. Given the understanding of the criteria I have advocated so far, *independent* multiple attestation has its uses (establishing early, pre-Gospel material is not without merit) but it obviously only takes us so far, if indeed independence can be shown to any significant degree.

Arguments of collective weight

Rafael Rodriguez has argued that with at least some criteria (especially dissimilarity), and attempts to establish basic 'facts' about Jesus, *interpretation* is implicitly occurring, whether or not a given scholar realizes interpretation is occurring.[32] We might push this further still and emphasize that interpretation is always going to be the case when trying to reconstruct early traditions (or indeed anything else). But we can also embrace this. Emerging from under the rubble of the criteria, we are left with an old-fashioned view of interpretation, argument, and the combining of arguments for collective weight to make a general case. As another hypothetical argument, we might take the famous prayer in Matthew and Luke (Matt. 6.9–13; Luke 11.2–4; cf. *Didache* 8) to illuminate the point. I leave to one side the question of whether it is a Q passage or Luke using Matthew (and possibly other sources) because we are still probably dealing with one source and the following analysis would work with either hypothesis (or some combination of the two). But taking some key themes in this prayer and locating them in the context of recurrent themes in the Gospel tradition allows us to make some provisional conclusions about the contents of some of the earliest Palestinian tradition (which may or may not go directly back to the historical Jesus).

So, for instance, in both versions Jesus tells his disciples to call God 'our father' or 'father'. The use of the language of 'father' for God is well attested in the sayings of Jesus (e.g. Mark 14.25, 36; Matt. 5.16; Matt. 5.44–7//Luke 6.27–8, 33, 35–6; Matt. 6.26//Luke 12.24; Matt. 6.2–8, 16–18; Matt. 6.31–2//Luke 12.29–30; Matt.7.9–11; Luke 11.13; Luke 23.34) and clearly implied in parables (e.g. Mark 12.1–12; Matt. 21.28–32; Luke 15.11–32), all of which are found across the Gospel tradition. By the conventional use of the criterion of multiple attestation of sources and forms, the use of such language would suggest that it is early. We also know of similar language used in the Hebrew Bible/Old Testament and early Palestinian Judaism before, during, and after the time of Jesus (e.g. Deut. 32.6; 2 Sam. 7.4; Isa. 64.7; Ps. 89.26–8; Sirach 51.10; 4Q372; 1QH 9.34–5; *Ant.* 5.93; *m. Abot* 5.20; *Tg. Ps.-J.* Lev. 22.28), including prayers (e.g. *m. Ber.* 5.1; *b. Taan.* 23b) such as the famous Jewish prayer, the *Qaddish*, a close Aramaic parallel to the Lord's Prayer ('their father who is in heaven').[33] Moreover, there are instances where we get the distinctive use of the Aramaic *abba* in the Gospels and the early church (e.g. Mark 14.36; Gal. 4.6; Rom. 8.15) and so this usage, long recognized, is most likely to have originally derived from, or been influenced by, Palestinian tradition (cf. *Tg. Neof. I* Gen. 27.31; *b. Taan.* 23b). Overall, even if the prayer in Matt. 6.9–13 and Luke 11.2–4 is a post-Jesus creation in its wording, the general use of 'father' is culturally plausible in, and probably developed from, an early Palestinian context.

In both Matt. 6.9–13 and Luke 11.2–4, Jesus refers to 'your kingdom come'. The coming of the kingdom is a common feature of teaching attributed to Jesus and has multiple attestation of sources and forms (e.g. Mark 1.15; 4.30–2; 9.1; Matt. 5.3//Luke 6.20; Matt. 13.33//Luke 13.20–1; Matt. 25). Hopes for the coming kingdom, or at least a great divine intervention, of God were also known in early Judaism. Again there is a famous parallel in the *Qaddish*: 'May he establish his kingdom in your life and in your days and in the life of all the house of Israel, speedily and in a short while!' We also know that there was enthusiastic expectation of something dramatic in the decades immediately after Jesus' death (e.g. 1 Thess. 4.13–5.13; cf. 1 Cor. 16.22), an enthusiasm which dampened down towards the end of the first century (John 21; 2 Pet. 3). The probable explanation for this was that someone very early on predicted something dramatic such as the establishment of the kingdom of God (see Chapter 3).[34]

In both versions of the prayer, we have talk of forgiveness but the language is subtly different. Matthew talks about debts whereas Luke talks about sins. It is possible that both could equally be a fair translation of an Aramaic idiom. In Aramaic, 'debts' and 'debtors' (from חוב) was a known way of talking about 'sins' and 'sinners' (see Chapter 4; cf. Matt. 18.23–35; Luke 7.36–50; 16.1–9) so, while we may well have a case of Matthew and Luke making what would both be reasonable judgements about translation if there was an independent source, Matthew gives us a potentially more precise example of earlier tradition. Moreover, a concern for the forgiveness of sins is also found possibly independently and in a context where the assumptions are not so obviously those of the post-70 CE Christian movement: 'So when you are offering your gift at the altar, if you remember that your brother or sister has something against you, leave your gift there before the altar and go; first be reconciled to your brother or sister, and then come and offer your gift' (Matt. 5.23–4).

There is, of course, much more to be said about Matt. 6.9–13 and Luke 11.2–4 but, again, it shows that we can say, at least hypothetically, something general about early Palestinian tradition when we try to make arguments of collective weight. Of course, this does not necessarily mean that we have found the actual words of the historical Jesus. Again, what I am suggesting is that by taking such an example we can detect some broad themes most likely to have been associated with the early Palestinian tradition. Amidst the cautious language, readers may by now have expected that my repeated use of phrases such as 'earliest tradition' or 'early Palestinian tradition' should be explained. It may well be that such traditions were generated from the Jesus movement whilst Jesus was alive. It is increasingly common in recent scholarship to talk about ways in which Jesus was 'remembered' and how memory might retain the 'gist' of a given saying or action, or that memory preserves, refracts, impacts, adapts, modifies, or can be generated by older ideas or community memories, even when reused for the present.[35] While individual specialists working with 'memory' may dispute details, these emphases broadly complement (with qualifications below) my argument that we should be content with generalizations about the early tradition that we might reasonably associate with the social upheavals of Galilee and Palestine roughly around the time Jesus was growing up. Whilst the study of memory looks set to provide an important development in reconstructing lives of Jesus, we should also not forget (and a number of those working in this area regularly point this out) that memory can distort, omit, mislead, reinterpret, or misinterpret,[36] and we will return to a potential overreliance on Bauckham's 'gist' when discussing the 'negative' implications.

More generally, it may be possible to build up a general picture of Jesus according to the earliest tradition. Some of it may seem banal enough, such as he was born and active in Galilee, attracted followers, clashed with people over interpretation of the Law, gained a reputation as a (sometimes) successful healer and exorcist, preached the coming of the kingdom, often spoke in parables, and went to Jerusalem where he died. This is more or less the Gospel outline but it is also fair to say that it can be found in the earliest tradition, and further development of some of these points will occur in the following chapters. It is hopefully clear, then, that I am making claims about the earliest traditions which are likely to have been in proximity to where Jesus was said to be active. Beyond this, who knows what actually happened? [37] But this sort of speculation is not necessarily a major issue for my approach, which is less about finding the 'real man' finally behind the tradition and more about how historical chaos generates ideas and historical change. So much for the 'positive' element of historical reconstruction in my approach; I now want to focus on what cannot be said to have come from the historical Jesus. In particular, I now want to critique some recent high-profile attempts using John's Gospel in the reconstruction of the historical Jesus.

Narrative, theology, and John

Thomas Thompson has looked at the figure of Jesus presented in the Gospels, who he views as comprehensible in terms of ancient Near Eastern traditions about royalty and the 'Messiah myth'.[38] It may indeed be the case that some or all of the Gospels are immersed in such narratives. However, we should, of course, be cautious in developing this line of thinking in the direction of arguments that go like this: narrative or theological tropes mean that we are dealing with pure literary fiction or narrative or literary tropes are not a part of the world of historical actors themselves in their everyday lives. For a start, and as much as some literary critics might like to abandon notions of history, the literary and the historical actor are, obviously, part of historical and material processes and whatever historical 'event' we write about, speak about, or imagine has to be constructed in some form or other. Wright may have got many things wrong about the historical Jesus but he was at least correct to stress the importance of received narratives for understanding human actions, a point which has long been made by historians.[39] To twist a phrase, everything may indeed be a text but we should equally be prepared to historicize everything.[40]

But there is another justification for discussing this sort of reasoning: a use of John's Gospel which comes perilously close to arguing that because the Gospel tradition is so 'theological', then so John's Gospel might likewise be a useful source for the historical Jesus (or, in my terms, the early Palestinian tradition). Whereas *Thomas* became embedded in historical Jesus scholarship by the end of the last century, a case is now being made for John's Gospel which I consider less than convincing.[41] Over the past ten years, at the annual Society of Biblical Literature meeting, the John, Jesus, and History Project has been discussing issues of historicity and John's Gospel. One of the most prominent figures in the group, Paul Anderson, has become increasingly vocal in his advocacy of John's Gospel to be used in reconstructions of the historical Jesus, even to the extent of inventing a 'Fourth Quest' for the historical Jesus.[42] An underlying feature of the Project is the idea that theology does not necessarily equal historical inaccuracies.[43] Anderson argues that the 'assumption that theologization and spiritualization necessarily imply ahistoricity' is a 'fallacy' and to say that 'symbolization, spiritualization, or theologization displaces originative history is terribly flawed as a historiographic procedure'. Anderson qualifies this and claims, 'equating John's spiritualization of events in the ministry of Jesus cannot be considered a solid proof of its ahistoricity'.[44] Anderson is, of course, correct but I am not sure that the approach critiqued by Anderson is pushed by many, if any, contemporary scholars. However, a more precise target is mentioned in the same volume, namely, in D. A. Carson's critique of the work of Maurice Casey on Johannine theological and Christological development over against the historical Jesus: 'one thing that stands out in Casey's work is the way he pits history against theology. By contrast, Marianne Meye Thompson constantly endeavours to show the ways in which history and theology should not be pitted against each other'.[45]

I am not sure this is a useful critique. The late Maurice Casey could easily have defended himself and I would add that the general issue in his work is not a simple one of pitting theology against history but rather the historical location of a given type of theology. To take a comparison to which we will return, a theology which has Jesus cast as being equal with God in a Sabbath dispute (e.g. John 5.1–18; cf. John 10.30–9) is highly likely to be theological reflection some time after the death of Jesus, whereas a theology which defends what is deemed a correct legal interpretation with reference to an idiomatic Aramaic saying in another Sabbath dispute (e.g. Mark 2.23–8) has more chance of being from the historical Jesus or earlier Palestinian tradition. Of course, things, including theology, do not necessarily develop and grow in precise and neat chronological order (and 'low' Christology alone did not die out so quickly and can be invented too) but the question here, it should be stressed, is dating, contextualizing, and locating theology and *not* pitting theology over against history.

The critiques of Anderson, Carson, and Thompson, and the Project as a whole, are part of an increasingly vocal group of scholars who have tried to rescue John for the historical Jesus. One of the most important advocates of the use of John's Gospel in areas relating to historical Jesus research is Richard Bauckham.[46] While he accepts that 'the finished Gospel has a high degree of highly reflective interpretation',[47]

Bauckham argues that the Beloved Disciple is claiming to be a witness to the thrust of the sword into Jesus' side which produced flows of blood and water, to the resurrected Jesus preparing breakfast, and to a huge catch of fish. As Bauckham puts it, 'these details do help to give readers the impression that the Gospel portrays the Beloved Disciple as an observant witness of what happened'.[48] There is also a similar suggestion about eyewitnesses to the wedding at Cana where, according to John, Jesus famously turned water into wine (John 2.1–11).[49] These arguments made by Bauckham seem to come close to implying that these miraculous events can be established historically, thereby going beyond traditional mainstream views on John's Gospel.[50]

Bauckham's arguments are related to other recent studies of memory which have called into question the language of 'authentic' and 'inauthentic'.[51] Again, this is not to suggest that the recent challenges to such categories are without merit; on the contrary, they are assumed throughout this book. To take a clear example hinted at earlier, even if we do not think miracles really happen/happened, we could theoretically learn something about the impact of Jesus and early understandings of Jesus which may assist us in understanding ideas associated with the historical Jesus. However, I am not convinced we should entirely dismiss concepts of 'authentic' and 'inauthentic'. For a start, we might indeed accept that memory and gist play a crucial role in reflections on the historical Jesus but at what point do we get out of touch with Jesus, or too abstractly related to Jesus to be of significant use in the study of the historical Jesus? This is where understanding John's Gospel becomes particularly important.

If Bauckham and others are along the right lines, what do we do with a passage such as John 5.1–18? This text presents Jesus as divine in an exceptionally strong sense and as a figure who endorsed the breaking of *biblical* Sabbath commandments in accepting that a burden may be carried ('For this reason the Jews were seeking all the more to kill him, because he was not only breaking the Sabbath, but was also calling God his own Father, thereby making himself equal to God'). In John's Gospel we have further high Christological sentiment, as we see in John 5.1–18, such as Thomas' exclamation 'My Lord and my God' (John 20.28) and 'the Jews' claiming that 'It is not for a good work that we are going to stone you, but for blasphemy, because you, though only a human being, are making yourself God' (John 10.33). If we were to follow Bauckham and others, this retelling of a Sabbath dispute by one eyewitness stands in sharp contrast to another person deemed to be an eyewitness, namely Peter, assumed to be a key eyewitness for Mark's Gospel according to Bauckham. Again, Mark's Gospel did not see fit to mention the monumental claims of explicitly high Christology in (say) his retelling of Sabbath disputes in Mark 2.23–3.6, which do not endorse the breaking of a single *biblical* commandment.[52] Instead, Jesus defends his disciples plucking grain on the Sabbath against criticism from Pharisees.

Theoretically, it is possible that both the Sabbath traditions in the Synoptic Gospels and John's Gospel were fictional creations of the early church. However, if one tradition were more obviously representative of the historical Jesus, it is the Synoptic tradition. The Synoptic disputes are fairly typical halakhic disputes, which do not seem to have been of interest to the early church outside of the Gospel tradition, and Jesus provides justification of the disciples' actions, at least in the earliest tradition, in terms of a known Aramaic idiom ('son of man'/ בר [א]נש[א]), and with conflict being with defined groups (Pharisees and Herodians). The Johannine dispute justifies non-observance of the Sabbath commandment, something we know was happening already in mid-first-century Christianity (e.g. Rom. 14.5–6), and justification comes through Christianized claims in distinction from 'the Jews'. Whatever we make of the historicity of the Synoptic tradition, that the Johannine material, with its justification of Christian practice and extremely high Christology, is particular to John and not found in the Synoptic tradition suggests at the very least that such ideas were not available in the Synoptic tradition. Otherwise, why leave such hugely relevant material out? Is not the explanation that the Johannine material is largely the product of either a later Christian dispute or a creative mind (or both) the most plausible one?[53]

This brings us back to questions which have haunted some Christian thinkers from early on. Some of the major Johannine problems will not go away. The Synoptic Gospels have Jesus' action in the Temple as the immediate cause of Jesus' death (Mark 11.15–18) while John puts the Temple action at the beginning of his narrative and has the raising of Lazarus as the immediate cause of Jesus' death (John 11). A standard explanation in terms of issues of historicity is that the Synoptic tradition is more historically plausible than the highly distinctive Johannine tradition. Based on his work on eyewitnesses, Bauckham provides counterarguments to the most prominent scholarly views on the (non-)historicity of the story of the raising of Lazarus:

> the occurrence and nonoccurrence of names in stories in the Gospels may be partially explained by supposing that the named characters were members of the early Christian communities and themselves told the stories of the events in which they had been participants. So long as they were known figures, their names remained attached to their stories as indications of eyewitness sources of these stories. The same explanation easily fits the case of Lazarus, Martha, and Mary.[54]

Bauckham admits that the 'weightiest argument against the historicity of the raising of Lazarus (apart from the naturalistic objections to the miraculous) has always been its absence from the Synoptics'. Bauckham rightly points out that the presence of a given tradition in one Gospel only is not necessarily an argument against historicity and that there may have been reasons why the Synoptic writers did not feel the need to include another 'resuscitation miracle', like that of Jairus' daughter, and he adds that the raising of Lazarus is 'an especially impressive miracle and also gives it a key role in the sequence of events that led to Jesus' death'. To deal with such issues, Bauckham suggests that this could be something like a theological evaluation of historical events and that the raising of Lazarus is the culmination of conflict against a backdrop of Jesus' popularity. Bauckham argues that this is a '*historical* form of explanation, which is arguably more convincing than Mark's, in which it seems to be Jesus' demonstration in the temple alone that provokes authorities to plot his death (Mark 11.18)'.[55] An explanation for Mark leaving out the Lazarus story could have been, Bauckham suggests, due to 'protective anonymity' where figures such as Lazarus were not named (or discussed at all) in a passion story originating in Jerusalem in the 40s.[56]

I am not convinced this provides a satisfactory counterargument to the view that the raising of Lazarus has limited connection with the earliest tradition. The supernatural is glossed over too quickly by Bauckham. The raising of Jairus' daughter is subtly different. The girl is, after all, not dead but 'sleeping' (Mark 5.39) and it has long been noted that such resuscitations are paralleled cross-culturally, so in themselves do not have the conventional barriers to historicity that we face with the miraculous. The story of the raising of Lazarus, however, makes it perfectly clear that Lazarus is not sleeping but is, in fact, very, very dead and in the tomb for four days (John 11.13–14, 17), with the fourth day being the time required to establish the certainty that a person be deemed well and truly dead so that the soul cannot return to the body according to a later rabbinic tradition (*Lev. R.* 18.1). This now means we have, on the one hand, a Markan-based tradition where authorities want to put Jesus to death because he did something particularly provocative in the Temple during a major festival; on the other hand, we have a Johannine tradition where the demonstration in the Temple is pushed to the beginning of the Gospel and the direct cause of Jesus' death is replaced with a supernatural miracle.

It seems to me that, irrespective of what we make of the historicity of the Markan story, the conventional explanation is perfectly reasonable: the idea that someone overturning tables of moneychangers and dove sellers at Passover could lead to a less direct means of securing his arrest (a more direct arrest there and then might have led to disorder) is far more believable than a supernatural miracle, particularly when we recall that the more mundane action in the Temple has been pushed to the beginning of John's Gospel. At this point the argument that the raising of Lazarus occurs only in John becomes more significant. Not only was John written up around the late first century at the earliest, but the fact that the story of a stunning miracle is missing in Luke and Matthew, not to mention non-Christian sources, is very suspicious and 'protective anonymity', which may work in other instances, only gets us so far here. Why would no other source include this spectacular miracle to explain Jesus' death, especially as we move further and further away from the 40s CE? And is there not a profound problem in suggesting that a man who had previously been dead was walking around Jerusalem but was being protected through anonymity?[57] In terms of conventional historical judgement at least, should we not stick with the obvious and suggest that the idea of a formerly dead man walking around Jerusalem is too problematic for understanding why Jesus was put to death?

Bauckham suggests that 'As with any other historical source, what needs to be assessed is its general reliability... If the Gospel is judged trustworthy so far as we can test it, then we should trust it for what we cannot verify. That is ordinary historical method.'[58] This seems reasonable enough but this is precisely what has led so many scholars into believing that John's Gospel is of minimal value for reconstructing the life and teaching of the historical Jesus. I have already given old and supplementary reasons but more general points ought to give collective weight. Let us take the story of Nicodemus (John 3). Even if we were to assume that there was a historical Nicodemus active around the time of Jesus,[59] this story contains the only two Johannine references to the 'kingdom of God' (John 3.3, 5). This is, of course, in sharp contrast to the Synoptics where the phrase is famously common. Not only that, but these two references stand in stark contrast to the predictions of the imminent kingdom in Mark and Matthew because the Johannine verses speak of entry into the kingdom in terms of being 'born again'/'from above'. In addition to removing all the kingdom of God sayings, John 21 shows that there were obvious problems with predictions of the second coming of Jesus not happening, whereas the Synoptics still expect the second coming within a lifetime of Jesus' audience (Mark 13; Matt. 24; Luke 21). Notice that John's Jesus can also speak of 'my kingdom' not being of this world (John 18.36). This is not 'the kingdom of God' of the earlier traditions and we can already observe the development from 'the kingdom of God' to *Jesus'* kingdom in the development of Mark's tradition (compare Mark 9.1 with Matt. 16.28). Again, John's wording presumably points away from the earliest tradition.[60]

We might further add that the Nicodemus dialogue looks like a classic case of Johannine replacement theology where Jewish ethnicity is replaced with some kind of Christianizing practice (baptism?), hence Nicodemus asks quizzically about being literally born again (John 3.4). Again, such dramatic claims are not found in the Synoptic tradition. So, once more, we are left with, on the one hand, the Synoptic tradition expecting the imminent coming of the kingdom, alongside the return of Jesus within a generation; on the other hand, we have a removal of the imminent kingdom, which is substituted with what is effectively a theological replacement for Jewish ethnicity at a time when other Christians were clearly experiencing problems with eschatological predictions not materializing. Ironically, there may actually be some use for John here in terms of the development of the earliest Jesus tradition because the Nicodemus story and the problems with imminent eschatology in John obviously suggest that there were earlier predictions concerning end times. But it is extremely difficult to avoid the conclusion that the Nicodemus story has, at the very least, been written to reflect later first-century (or later) issues.

Eyewitnesses, historicity, and John

It might be countered that a Bauckham-style reading of memory works with the idea of eyewitnesses providing a generally accurate recollection of Jesus. While Bauckham accepts the storyteller's licence, he argues that eyewitness testimony retains the 'gist' of the story through memory and with fidelity to past events: 'the "gist" of an event that is remembered even when details are inaccurate . . . Those who recall the past really do intend to recall the past, not to create it to suit present needs and purposes.'[61] Though certainly not without qualification, much of Bauckham's methodology seems to be geared towards general historical accuracy and, more specifically, the Gospels as recalling unique, unusual, memorable, and salient *historical* events, echoing a notable strand running through the diverse studies on memory and the historical Jesus over the past decade. Generally speaking, Bauckham may well have a point but, when applied to John's Gospel, his approach encounters some problems. We have already seen issues concerning 'high' Christology, Nicodemus and the kingdom of God, and Sabbath disputes which are significantly different from the Synoptic Gospels. To this we might ask: why are there no 'I am' sayings, with all their replacement theology and with obvious implications of high Christology (John 8.12 [cf. 7.2]; 10.7, 9; 11.25; 14.6) in the Synoptic tradition and does not this John-only appearance suggest later theological creation? Moreover, what about the farewell discourses, the teaching on 'the world', the promise of the 'paraclete' (John 14.16–26; 15.26–7; 16.7–15), and so on? It is very difficult to see how these were missed out in the earlier Jesus tradition and, even if there are connections with and developments from earlier memories, the explanation that these themes were Johannine creations is forceful.[62] If significant differences are accepted as such, then the negative side of Bauckham's take on 'gist' has the potential to be expanded indefinitely to include almost anything as a kind of 'natural' development. So where does 'gist' end? And can people not simply invent things which are significantly discontinuous with the historical Jesus or anything that came before?

It ought to be added that even if we assume that eyewitnesses underlie John's Gospel and Mark's Gospel, the old problems of different sources telling us different things remain and thus the same questions of historical accuracy remain. Can we say that the Beloved Disciple invented material or got a little too creative in his recollections? Or do we have to suggest that this material was always implicit in Jesus' teaching, that it was not really made so explicit in the other canonical Gospels and it took the Beloved Disciple to make it so? These are serious problems which remain for historical Jesus scholars wanting to use John's Gospel as a source, irrespective of whether such sources are eyewitness testimony. Even if we were to accept that an eyewitness wrote John's Gospel, it seems more plausible that we would have a highly creative eyewitness who wrote creative fiction concerning Jesus, with minimal use for understanding early tradition.[63]

If we follow Bauckham on the importance of general reliability, then we would have to suggest that things do not look hopeful for those wishing to use John's Gospel to reconstruct the life and teaching of Jesus. However, the John, Jesus, and History Project (especially Paul Anderson) are more systematic in their treatment of issues surrounding John's Gospel and historicity, unsurprisingly given the scope and nature of the different projects. In a lengthy essay in the first edited volume of the Project, Paul Anderson assesses the big issues, including those discussed above, and accepts that some of the criticisms against historicity have a degree of strength. However, Anderson argues, they also have significant weaknesses. On the virtual absence of 'the kingdom of God' in John's Gospel, Anderson makes the following counter:

> [D]o we have a Johannine representation of the essential kingdom teaching of Jesus, even as represented in the fuller Synoptic accounts? After all, the spiritual workings of God's active and dynamic reign are indeed contrasted with the human scaffoldings of the religious quest in the Synoptics and the truthful and penetrating activity of God's present-and-ultimate reign is contrasted to all worldly powers—political and otherwise. In that sense, rather than leaving out Jesus' teachings on the kingdom, it could be said that John *summarizes* them.[64]

This may be fair as a (very broad) generalization but if we were to push this further in terms of use for the study of the historical Jesus then the generalization would not work well because the future aspect of the kingdom in John does not have the crucial issue of the imminence of the kingdom we find in Mark and Matthew at least. It is well known that John keeps the future kingdom but it is presumably not thought to be coming in power within the lifetime of Jesus' audience (cf. Mark 9.1) and this is why John removes the precise phrase 'the kingdom of God' and, for not unrelated reasons, why we get John 21. To refer back to the arguments made against Bauckham, there may be general similarities between John and the Synoptics but once the specifics are mentioned the most obvious explanation is that the predictions of the imminent kingdom are early and the avoidance of these predictions is late and more obviously secondary. If we refer back to the argument that the discussion of the kingdom in John 3 has implications which appear to replace Jewish ethnicity as a means of belonging to the 'in-group', then, on this topic at least, John's Gospel tells us much more about Christianity at the turn of the first century than it does about the historical Jesus. There is certainly nothing John adds to help in the quest for the historical Jesus on this issue, if it is in this direction that we wish to take Anderson's argument.

Anderson also tackles other issues but there is again the problematic tendency to make the arguments too generalized so that crucial details are omitted. To use an example already discussed, Anderson suggests that 'Jesus' healing on the Sabbath and challenge of religious authority is presented as clearly in John as it is in the Synoptics, despite its many distinctive features.'[65] But the distinctive features are crucial. John may agree with the Synoptics over healings on the Sabbath but the example of John 5, at least, takes it in directions that are much more obviously reflective of the early church and the Johannine situation (the acceptance of the breaking of biblical law by carrying a burden and claiming equality with God) and has less chance of telling us anything significant about earlier tradition. As with Mark 3.1–6, the Lukan Sabbath healings are not constructed against any biblical law, and are disputes over whether the healing activity itself is permitted on the Sabbath and if life is at risk (Luke 13.10–17; 14.1–6). Once specifics are properly noted, we can again see why John is deemed suspect for some in historical Jesus studies, at least in the instance of healing on the Sabbath.

The generalizing becomes a further problem when Anderson turns to historical Jesus scholarship. Based on Marcus Borg's summary of the different possible portraits of Jesus, Anderson suggests that John's Gospel is coherent with the different models and that John's Jesus is a 'noneschatological prophet... the prophet-like-Moses'. The Johannine Jesus fits 'within the portraiture of a wisdom-imparting sage' and an 'institution-challenging Cynic, in that Jesus cleanses the Temple at the beginning of his ministry, heals on the Sabbath, confronts religious authorities in Jerusalem prolifically, and is willing to challenge the Roman governor in the name of God's transcendent truth and reign'. Anderson adds that Jesus 'comes across with spiritual power, as a holy man in John. While he does not perform exorcisms, the Johannine Jesus is encountered by people epiphanically... Jesus as a holy man cannot be said to be incompatible with the Johannine presentation of Jesus'. Adding to Borg's list, Anderson suggests John's Jesus also comes across as 'an apocalyptic messenger... and the entire ministry of Jesus is presented eschatologically'.[66]

Assuming for the moment the validity of using such a range of disputed categories from historical Jesus scholarship, it is questionable whether Anderson's points help us in any significant way in terms of the quest for the historical Jesus. The idea of an apocalyptic and eschatological Jesus in John may well give a general insight into Jesus and the earliest Palestinian tradition (as well as earliest Christianity, of course) but, as we have pointed out, it potentially gives us a distorted insight in that the imminent predictions of 'the kingdom of God' are not included. Furthermore, is it really any surprise that images of Jesus as a prophet, an eschatological prophet, and of a wisdom-related figure turn up in earliest Christianity, irrespective of whether Jesus generated such images of himself? In its struggle with identity in relationship to Jewish groups, it is no surprise that the Christian movement (or whatever we want to call it) tried to monopolize Jewish ideas for the figure of Jesus. After all, as Anderson points out, 'Jesus not only brings light to penetrate the darkness of the worldly thought; he *is* the Light of the world (John 1:4, 5, 8, 9; 3:19; 8:12; 9:5; 12:46)'.[67] This could, of course, be plausibly explained as later Christian theology with only a very general connection to the historical Jesus.

The description of a Cynic Jesus highlights well the problems in working with such generalities. None of the features described by

Anderson are exclusively Cynic, or at least in the sense that numerous non-Cynic people could have been likewise cited. The Bible, the Dead Sea Scrolls, Josephus, and rabbinic literature, for instance, give plenty of examples of institution-challenging figures. Many of the portraits of the Gospel contexts, including the Johannine contexts and the contexts of the earliest Christians, suggest institution-challenging figures and groups, perhaps inevitably given that a new movement was to emerge. It is difficult to see how this very general parallel means we should be including John in historical Jesus discussion. Much more precise and detailed evidence is needed. One point is worth re-emphasizing in response to Anderson: putting the cleansing of the Temple at the beginning of the ministry in John means putting the raising of Lazarus as the immediate cause of Jesus' death instead and again, if anything, this detracts from using John as a source for understanding the cleansing of the Temple in relation to the historical Jesus. In all these portraits of Jesus, and against Anderson, we *cannot* say that 'One might even make the case that any of these portraits might be sketched *more clearly* from Johannine material than from any of the other Gospels'.[68]

Similarly, when Anderson points out that 'In all four Gospels, Jesus comes across as a Jewish prophet healing the sick, challenging the religious institutions, speaking with prophetic urgency, and suffering death at the hands of the Romans in Jerusalem', we miss out on the key distinctive features of John versus the Synoptics and how the Johannine version is clearly building on and altering earlier versions. Anderson, however, adds further Johannine contributions to the quest for the historical Jesus:

1. Jesus' simultaneous ministry alongside John the Baptizer and the prolific availability of purifying power
2. Jesus' cleansing of the temple as an inaugural prophetic sign
3. Jesus' travel to and from Jerusalem and his multiyear ministry
4. Early events in the public ministry of Jesus
5. Favourable receptions in Galilee among Samaritans, women, and Gentiles
6. Jesus' Judean ministry and archaeological realism
7. The Last Supper as a common meal and its proper dating
8. Jesus' teaching about the way of the Spirit and the reign of truth.[69]

Certainly we may grant potential specifics. It may be the case that there was a simultaneous ministry with John the Baptist, as has also been noted in analysis of material particular to Luke and Matthew.[70] While some of us are not convinced, arguments in favour of Johannine chronology will no doubt continue on the dating of the 'Last Supper'. While there are other aspects, such as Jesus' prediction of a rebuilt Temple (John 2.13–22),[71] which may reflect early tradition, we are still dealing with arguments which effectively assume historical Jesus 'results' based on the analysis from the *Synoptic* tradition and then corrected or modified using John's Gospel.[72] This may be an important point to emphasize but the implication is that if we used John's Gospel as *the* source then we would have a view of the historical Jesus which was far more reflective of *later* Christian theology and lacking useful connections in earliest tradition.

Some points raised by Anderson (and others) are too general to warrant a precise response, though this is partly because Anderson understandably wants to foreground the issues and similarities in historical Jesus and Johannine scholarship. The 'multiyear' ministry and numerous visits to Jerusalem may have been the case, but we could work that out by looking at first-century cultural contexts. If it were the case that it is more likely Jesus visited Jerusalem more than once, then it may simply be assumed in Mark (cf. Mark 11.2–6; 14.12–14) and not worthy of mention because it was supposed, perhaps, that nothing particularly interesting happened in other visits. If this is the case then we are back to John being the less useful Gospel.[73]

We might develop such ideas to include the Passion chronology and the trial in John's Gospel compared to Mark, a common issue raised in the publications of the John, Jesus, and History Project. Mark's trial scene may well contain historical inaccuracies (Mark 14.53–15.1; cf. *m. Sanh.* 4.1) that cast strong doubts on the validity of its overall historical accuracy and it may well be a fictional polemic designed to persuade people that Jesus was unjustly killed. But this does not mean John is necessarily more helpful. If John provides a more plausible outline of chronology and procedure then this only need mean, like John's geographical knowledge, that he knows the right details, in this case procedural. John's trial and crucifixion narratives still contain all sorts of issues which may be motivated more by Johannine interests than fidelity to earlier theological tendencies and historical realities, such as a revelation of Jesus' 'true identity' (compare John 18.19 with 13.36–8) and a theological construction of superiority over against the high priest.[74] We might also observe that another disciple, in addition to Peter, managed to get in on the act of Jesus' trial, and indeed into the court of the high priest as Peter stood by denying Jesus (John 18.15–17). Is there reason not to be a little suspicious of this Johannine addition, written, perhaps, to explain how a reliable Johannine source got into the heart of the trial, and that it is thus not a remnant of an earlier tradition?

Some of this is, of course, speculative but we have little to go on and so little can actually be said. Elsewhere, Anderson points out that 'Mark mentions only one Passover, the one at which Jesus was killed, implying that Jesus' ministry and opposition were all mounted within a relatively short period of time rather than over a period of several years' and argues that 'This could have been the case, but John's rendering here seems more plausible'.[75] But there is still no reason why John should be more plausible. Why would it be less plausible for Jesus to have done something provocative in the Temple once and then be killed for it? Why is it less plausible that there was a relatively short ministry (assuming Mark is implying this)? Is it not plausible that John's Gospel introduced extra visits to Jerusalem for theological reasons (e.g. replacement theology) which had no grounding in actual visits to Jerusalem and which only happen to reflect the very general point that some Jews went to Jerusalem more than once?[76] Further problems arise when we note that the Johannine conflicts, in contrast to the Synoptic conflicts, involve the raising of Lazarus, disputes over Jesus being equal with God, and the displacement of the Temple scene to the beginning of his ministry. In this light, it is not difficult to see why scholars have been so sceptical in using John as a source for historical Jesus studies.

Similarly, John may record earlier events but these include things like the wedding at Cana which are not especially helpful in reconstruction of the historical Jesus or earliest tradition, and earlier events may simply be legendary additions of minimal use in reconstruction, as we usually imply from Luke's story of Jesus as a youth. Archaeological realism tells us little other than details of the place. These details may be helpful in understanding the physical world but fictional stories can, of course, be crafted in very real settings and all that such Johannine material really shows us is familiarity with Jerusalem.[77] Some suggestions raised by Anderson are also confronted with old problems. The idea of an 'inaugural prophetic sign' in the cleansing of the Temple again faces the massive historical issue of the location of the raising of Lazarus. The idea that Jesus found favourable receptions in Galilee, 'among Samaritans, women, and Gentiles', poses big problems. It may have been that Jesus had female followers but this is mentioned in the Synoptics (e.g. Mark 15.40–1; Luke 8.1–3) and the argument is again too general as we know that in a later context Celsus looked down on Christianity partly through tying it in with an unfortunate lure for women (e.g. Origen, *C. Cels.* 3.10, 44).

Johannine illumination of early Galilean tradition in general is certainly possible, perhaps with reference to Bethsaida, even if the tradition has been heavily reworked and we only have the idea that, say, Bethsaida was initially a significant centre (cf. John 1.43–51; 12.20–2).[78] However, the notion of favourable receptions by the Gentiles and Samaritans is most likely Christian fiction, or at least faces the problem that earlier material did not present Jesus facing such favourable receptions or interactions, at least not in any enthusiastic way. Mark 7 provides the explicitly exceptional example of the Syro-Phoenician woman, while Matt. 10.5–6 has Jesus saying, 'Go nowhere among the Gentiles, and enter no town of the Samaritans, but go rather to the lost sheep of the house of Israel'. Given that the debates in earliest Christianity were about *how* non-Jews were to be incorporated, not *if* they were to be incorporated, then it is much more difficult to see how the favourable reaction among non-Jews and Samaritans is to be deemed more likely to go back to the historical Jesus than Matt. 10.5–6. Moreover, if material concerning a favourable reaction among non-Jews and Samaritans were available, is this not exactly the sort of thing Mark would have craved (cf. Mark 6–8; 13.10)?[79]

Concluding remarks

It is clear, then, that the traditional position viewing John's Gospel as of minimal use in reconstructing the life of Jesus must remain in place despite recent challenges. It is significant that the arguments have to work at a level of such generality because only by downplaying the serious differences between John and the Synoptics can John be allowed back into play. In this sense, John's Gospel may have similarity with the 'gist' of earlier outlines of Jesus' teaching but this only works at a general level. It is telling that serious differences are downplayed by Anderson and this is highlighted by comparing John and the Synoptics. Of course, in light of the discussion about the limited usefulness of the criteria, it remains that we have to be content working with a degree of generality, even if we must appreciate the differences from obviously later Christianized tradition in John's Gospel.

More positively, the hypothetical examples used in the discussion of the criteria show that we can potentially make some important general comments about early Palestinian tradition which was generated or modified in the contexts of social upheaval, and the following chapters will prove a number of more developed examples.[80] While focusing on early Palestinian tradition is more methodologically useful for the purposes of an argument de-emphasizing the idea of Jesus the Great Man, there is also a degree of necessity in this approach because it seems that the criteria are of limited use and only some of the general approaches embedded in the criteria remain of use. Realistically, it is difficult to see how we can move beyond the usual ways human beings make basic arguments, including those of collective weight. Perhaps, after all, Geza Vermes had a point when establishing some general and pragmatic 'guide-lines ... to assist in the search, along a very rough path' in the quest for Jesus. 'It would be quite inappropriate, however,' he added, 'to attach to these guide-lines the grandiloquent, but highly fashionable, label of methodology. In my opinion, research aiming to be innovative should not be bound by strict, predetermined rules'.[81]

3

The Dictatorship of God?

Kingdom and Christology

Peace, prosperity, egalitarianism, force, power, and dominance are claims we might associate with any number of empires, theocracies, dictatorships, and totalitarian regimes, as well as any number of revolutionaries who were involved in the process. Perhaps the most obvious case of issues surrounding social upheaval, millenarianism, power, and imperialism in the Gospel tradition—and especially susceptible to this Bakuninist view of history—involves eschatology and the kingdom of God.[1] The Gospel kingdom tradition has all the key elements: challenging the dominant world power from below while implicitly or explicitly putting in place a system that likewise uses imperial language in its replacement of kingdom with kingdom, or empire with empire. After all, the kingdom of God would, in the long run, become the empire of Rome and, of course, it helped to have imperial teaching which was ultimately compatible with Roman power. The cliché that Constantine was a betrayal of Jesus' teaching may be true to some extent but it is not the full story. The earliest teaching in Jesus' name does seem to have envisaged him as having a prime position in the impending kingdom of God, as did the developing Christology in his name. It should be stated from the outset that the analysis in this chapter concerns the development of monarchical and imperial language and ideology rather than extended discussions of the specifics of Jesus' teaching on the kingdom or the development of Christology and Christian monotheism, though touching on such issues will be necessary.[2]

Living in the end times?

First, some comments are required on Jesus' teaching in relation to eschatology and the kingdom of God and the idea that Jesus was an 'apocalyptic prophet'.[3] The more recent post-Sanders–Meier cases made by scholars who may likewise be located somewhere in the Weiss–Schweitzer tradition (e.g. Edward Adams, Dale Allison, Maurice Casey, Bart Ehrman, and Paula Fredriksen), that Jesus (or the earliest tradition) predicted that something dramatic would happen, and that this should be taken somewhat literally, are persuasive and do not require me to add to their work other than to lay out a general scenario.[4] This is not, of course, to rule out the importance of a 'present' kingdom in the earliest tradition either; such understandings of the kingdom may simply complement the future kingdom (e.g. Mark 4.26–32; cf. Dan. 4.34–7).[5] Or, as Stephen Patterson's recent arguments might be developed, a present kingdom could have been emphasized alongside or in distinction from, or even in flat contradiction to, the imminent predictions and from early on in the tradition (cf. Luke 17.20–1; *Thom.* 113).[6] As we will see in Chapter 5, simultaneous transmission of chaotic or incompatible ideas cannot be ruled out. Patterson's focus was on Jesus but his proposal gains more strength if we spread this out wider and think in terms of early Palestinian tradition. Indeed, the overall argument of this chapter involving the implicit imperialism in kingdom and eschatological sayings remains, irrespective of present or future emphasis. Nevertheless, the long scholarly tradition of those who argue that Jesus or the earliest tradition expected end times to come within the lifetime of some of their audience appears to be a dominant and favoured feature of the Gospel tradition. After his latest detailed analysis of the Gospel tradition and earliest eschatological and apocalyptic beliefs, Dale Allison concluded that

> the materials gathered into the Synoptics, however stylized and otherwise distorted, descend from narratives and sayings that were widely in circulation and widely valued from early times . . . taken together, [the tradition and the earliest churches] produce more than a faint image . . . while the Synoptic Jesus often appears to be an apocalyptic prophet, we can infer his status as such from the foundational beliefs of the early churches . . . Although barnacles cover the rock, we can still see the rock's shape.[7]

For all the modifications, nuances, and scholarly differences, the case is clear enough. Here I lay out a general case that others have presented in far more detail and which continues to prove convincing in scholarly circles despite its obvious problems for contemporary Christians and despite regular challenges, apologetic or otherwise.[8] The Gospel tradition has predictions of the kingdom, judgement, and end times as imminent (e.g. Mark 1.15; 9.1; 13.30, 33–7; Matt. 10.23; Matt. 25.1–13; Matt. 6.10//Luke 11.2; Matt. 23.34–5//Luke 11.49–51; Matt. 24.42–4//Luke 12.39–40; Matt. 24.45–51//Luke 12.42–6; Luke 12.35–8; 21.34–6; cf. Mark 15.43; Luke 2.25; *Thom.* 21, 111), including those passages concerning John the Baptist (e.g. Matt. 3.1–2, 9–12; Luke 3.7–9, 17; cf. Mark 1.7–8). As Mark 9.1 bluntly put it, 'Truly/Amen I tell you, there are some standing here who will not taste death until they see that the kingdom of God has come with power.' This may not have been as precise a prediction of end times or dramatic future events as found in the mistaken predictions of 1QpHabVII 1–14 or even Dan. 12.11–12 but it is clearly a prediction that the kingdom will come sometime very soon (cf. 4 Ezra 4.26; 2 Bar. 82.20; 85.10). Paul would continue to believe that end times were imminent (e.g. Rom. 13.11–12; 16.20; 1 Cor. 7.29; 1 Cor. 10.11; 1 Cor. 15.51; Phil. 4.5) and, in one of the earliest 'Christian' texts we have, the Thessalonians seem to think end times and the return of Jesus were even overdue as Paul has to give an explanation about those who have already died, and those currently living, who will see the return of Jesus (1 Thess. 4–5). By the end of the first century or beginning of the second century, it is clear that there were problems. According to 2 Peter,

First of all you must understand this, that in the last days scoffers will come, scoffing and indulging their own lusts and saying, 'Where is the promise of his coming? For ever since our ancestors died, all things continue as they were from the beginning of creation!' They deliberately ignore this fact, that by the word of God heavens existed long ago and an earth was formed out of water and by means of water, through which the world of that time was deluged with water and perished. But by the same word the present heavens and earth have been reserved for fire, being kept until the day of judgement and destruction of the godless. But do not ignore this one fact, beloved, that with the Lord one day is like a thousand years, and a thousand years are like one day. The Lord is not slow about his promise, as some think of slowness, but is patient with you, not wanting any to perish, but all to come to repentance. But the day of the Lord will come like a thief, and then the heavens will pass away with a loud noise, and the elements will be dissolved with fire, and the earth and everything that is done on it will be disclosed. (2 Pet. 3.3–10)

John's Gospel likewise had to deal with the problem. John eliminates almost all references to the kingdom of God and when the phrase does occur (John 3.3, 5) the discussion is about being born again/from above. Dealing with the second coming, John 21 makes a similar case to 2 Peter:

Peter turned and saw the disciple whom Jesus loved following them; he was the one who had reclined next to Jesus at the supper and had said, 'Lord, who is it that is going to betray you?' When Peter saw him, he said to Jesus, 'Lord, what about him?' Jesus said to him, 'If it is my will that he remain until I come, what is that to you? Follow me!' So the rumour spread in the community that this disciple would not die. Yet Jesus did not say to him that he would not die, but, 'If it is my will that he remain until I come, what is that to you?' (John 21.20–3)

The evidence is clear cut: very early on there were predictions of end times and, later on, Christians realized that these predictions were not being fulfilled and so attempted to explain why.[9]

The anti-imperial kingdom

The idea that Jesus, certain Gospels, Paul, or most of the New Testament writers were anti-Rome may be a popular scholarly fashion and such arguments are hardly without support.[10] Obviously, if there were a coming kingdom and a coming reign of God on earth, Rome would not be ruling forever, and certainly not in Israel. From a first-century perspective, Daniel would seem to have clear implications for Rome: 'And in the days of those kings the God of heaven will set up a kingdom that shall never be destroyed, nor shall this kingdom be left to another people. It shall crush all these kingdoms and bring them to an end, and it shall stand for ever' (Dan. 2.44).[11] Josephus gave some insight into how Daniel's take on the history of world powers was understood and retold in the first century (*Ant.* 10.209–10, 268, 272–7). The following especially shows how politically sensitive a reading of Daniel 2, and the interpretation of the smashed statue and growing stone, could be:

The head of gold represents you and the Babylonian kings who were before you. The two hands and shoulders signify that your empire will be brought to an end by two kings. But their empire will be destroyed by another king from the west, clad in bronze, and that this power will be ended by still another, like iron, that will have dominion for ever through its iron nature, which, he said, is harder than that of gold or silver or bronze. And Daniel also revealed the meaning of the stone, but I have not thought it proper to relate this, since I am expected to write of what is past and done and not of what is to be; if, however, there is anyone who has so keen a desire for exact information that he will not stop short of inquiring more closely but wishes to learn about the hidden things that are to come, let him take the trouble to read the Book of Daniel, which he will find among the sacred writings. (*Ant.* 10.209–10)

Clearly, the destruction of the iron rule by the stone was not going to be good news for Rome and the emperor. And Josephus knew it.

We have other types of 'radical' statements of dramatic role reversal related to eschatology in the Gospel tradition, including economic reversal (e.g. Luke 6.20; but cf. Matt. 5.3). One of the most explicit passages in this respect, and with direct reference to the kingdom of God, is Mark 10.17–31, a passage I have discussed in more detail elsewhere.[12] Here, the rich man has observed those commandments listed (Mark 10.17–22) but is told to give to the poor the proceeds from selling his possessions or properties and follow Jesus. The addition to the commandments (10.19) is a prohibition of defrauding (*μὴ ἀποστερήσης*), a phrase not in the Decalogue (cf. Exod. 20.17/Deut. 5.21). Other uses of the phrase would further suggest that this involves not withholding workers' wages or engaging with economic exploitation (e.g. Deut. 24.14–15; Mal. 3.5; Sir. 4.1; 1QapGen 20.11; *Tg. Onq*. Lev. 5.21; *Tg. Ps.-J.* Lev. 5.23; *Tg. Neof.* and *Ps-J.* Deut. 24.14; *Tg*. Mal. 3.5; *Lev. R.* 12.1; Pesh. Mk 10.19; Pesh. Deut. 24.14–15; Pesh. Mal. 3.5). No doubt this additional commandment is given to suit the specific case of the rich man who might be expected to exploit poorer people. However, even with the addition, the rich man has behaved himself. Yet the idea that he should give his possessions away would suggest that 'many possessions' (10.22) are not proof of reward for observing the commandments. Instead, the idea of wealth in the here and now as a reward for observing commandments is rejected (Mark 10.23–5) and this is presumably why the disciples are amazed (Mark 10.26).[13] Mark 10.27 should not be seen as a qualification of a difficult saying because it would contradict Peter's words in 10.28 and Jesus' words in 10.29–31. Instead, this is more likely to have been an attempt at explaining a rethinking of reward theology and placement of reward sometime in the future (Mark 10.29–31). Arguments along these lines are found elsewhere, whether precise discussions of the perils of wealth or how an eschatological reward awaits those who have died observing the commandments (e.g. 1 *En.* 96.4; 103.5–8; Dan. 12; 2 Macc. 7). Mark 10.17–31 stands in the tradition of equating wealth with wickedness (e.g. CD 4.15–19; 1QS 11.1–2; *Ps. Sol.* 5.16) and a more detailed expression of the point that you cannot serve God and Mammon (Luke 16.13//Matt. 6.24). From this perspective it would be no more possible for someone like the rich man to enter the kingdom than a camel to pass through the eye of a needle.

Another explicit exposition of this principle appears in Luke 16.19–31, where rich and poor are in stark opposition.[14] The rich man dressed in the colour associated with wealth, royalty, and power (purple; cf. Prov. 31.22; Judg. 8.26; Esth. 8.15; 1 Macc. 8.14; 1QapGen 20.31; *1 En.* 98.2; Rev. 18.12), ate well and presumably did not have to pray for his daily bread (cf. Jas. 5.5), while the poor man, Lazarus, was at the rich man's gate, hungry and covered in sores, an expected sign of divine punishment (Exod. 9.10–11; Deut. 28.35; Rev. 16.2). The burial treatment, or lack of it, is also significant as the parable continues to critique certain assumptions of reward. According to some views, a decent burial is a reward a good person should expect (e.g. Deut. 29.26; Jer. 8.1–2; 16.1–4; Ezek. 29.5; Tob. 1.16–2.10; *Apion* 2.211).[15] By way of contrast, in the case of Lazarus, a lack of a burial could be seen as a sign of divine displeasure (e.g. Jer. 7.33; 22.19; Ezek. 29.5; *1 En.* 98.13; *War* 4.317, 331–2, 359–60, 381–2), and could even be linked with the punishment of boils (Deut. 28.27, 35). It may be significant that one of the parallel stories of stark opposites claims that the Torah scholar of Ashqelon 'was not properly mourned' in contrast to the tax-collector bar Maayan (*y. Sanh.* 6.23c; *y. Hag.* 2.77d). The rich man and Lazarus are clearly constructed as being at the complete opposite ends of the social scale and receiving the rewards one reading of reward theology would suggest each deserved. But this stark opposition is to highlight the dramatic role reversal in the afterlife. As Richard Bauckham has pointed out, the reasons for the reversal are not because of a misuse of wealth or immoral behaviour in the case of the rich man, nor is it a case of particularly good behaviour in the case of Lazarus; rather, the only reason given in the parable is given in Luke 16.25: 'Child, remember that during your lifetime you received your good things, and Lazarus in like manner evil things; but now he is comforted here, and you are in agony.'[16] The rich man realizes the problem in the afterlife and tries to warn his brothers but the parable stresses that this should not be required because, with the authoritative support of Abraham, it should be obvious from the Law and the Prophets.

While Luke has a clear interest in issues of rich and poor, this economic take on eschatological reversal of rich and poor is also likely to reflect views found in the earliest Palestinian tradition, even if we cannot always be sure about the details of specific passages. Ideas about the stark opposition of wealth and poverty, God and Mammon, are found across the Synoptic tradition, including independent tradition (a point which stands irrespective of whether we accept some form of Q or not) and different forms (e.g. Mark 10.17–31; Luke 6.20–6// Matt. 5.3–12; Matt. 6.24//Luke 16.13; Luke 14.12–24//Matt. 22.1–14; Luke 4.18; 12.13–21; cf. *Thom.* 64). We can also point to interrelated concerns across the Synoptic tradition, such as: the recurring theme of debt (e.g. Luke 12.57–9//Matt. 5.25; Luke 6.35; 16.1–8; Matt. 5.40–2; 6.12; 18.23–35); concern for those without food, clothing, drink, and community (Matt. 25.31–46; Luke 6.20–1); opposition to wealth, fine clothing, and eating well (e.g. Matt. 11.8//Luke 7.25; Matt. 6.25–34//Luke 12.22–31; Luke 6.24–5; cf. *1 En.* 98.2; 102.9–11); and the theme of stark difference between rich and poor (Luke 6.20–6//Matt. 5.3–12; Luke 14.12–24// Matt. 22.1–14; cf. *Thom.* 64). Again, this is not to say that concerns for rich and poor could not be created at any point in the tradition or from a range of cultural contexts. It is also not to say that clichéd language could not have been imported into the tradition. But the sheer amount and concentration of such themes in independent sources and forms strongly suggests that this was a theme inherited by the Gospel writers and that such a serious concern is most likely to have been generated by the perceptions of what was happening as a result of the social upheavals in Galilee, with the rebuilding of Sepphoris and the building of Tiberias, and what was happening more broadly in Palestine as a result of the extensive additions to the Jerusalem Temple (see Chapter 1).

In the case of Luke 16.19–31, there are hints that the passage comes from an earlier tradition, even though it is of particular interest to Luke.[17] The parable, for instance, is lacking in Lukan vocabulary.[18] Furthermore, the conclusion to the parable, which is sometimes taken as explicit evidence of Lukan or later editing,[19] actually suggests a lack of Lukan interference:

> 'Abraham replied, "They have Moses and the prophets; they should listen to them." He [the rich man] said, "No, father Abraham; but if someone goes to them from the dead, they will repent (μετανοήσουσιν)." He said to him, "If they do not listen to Moses and the prophets, neither will they be convinced even if someone rises from the dead."' (Luke 16.29–31)

Despite Luke 24.27, 44, there is no working of this parable to reflect issues of Jesus and the resurrection and the only person who might potentially return from the dead is Lazarus: 'father, I beg you to send him to my father's house—for I have five brothers—that he may warn them, so that they will not also come into this place of torment' (Luke 16.28). Sending someone back from the afterlife to warn the living was a known belief (cf. 1 Sam. 28.7–20; *Eccl. R.* 9.10.1–2), as Bauckham points out.[20] Moreover, the notion of repentance here is tied up with the Law and Prophets and, understood this way, almost always refers to exclusively Jewish repentance of Jews or Israelites returning to the Law (see Chapter 4).[21] Lacking overt indications of concern for Gentile inclusion, this assumption of Jewish repentance is more likely to have come from an earlier tradition.

The imperial kingdom

It seems, then, that a more 'revolutionary' or 'subversive' attitude towards empire, wealth, and inequality is an integral part of the earliest Palestinian tradition and a product of socio-economic changes in Palestine as Jesus was growing up. However, this new kingdom hardly escaped imperial ideology; it reinscribed it. In some ways this idea is nothing new. Yet it is not difficult to get the impression that this theocratic imperialism of Jesus is hidden in plain sight in scholarship which has not typically focused on the imperialism of Jesus' anti-imperialist rhetoric (see below). It is worth, then, repeating some of the general statements made in scholarship concerning the kingdom of God. Most obviously, the language of 'kingdom' (*βασιλεία*/מלכות) is said to be about God's rule or kingship as well as a more spatial dimension, that is, God's territory and rule over all peoples. Some of the ideas and texts cited as key background material are likewise imperial in nature. God's kingdom in heaven consists of a throne or chariot where he is surrounded by countless warrior-like angels, while an earthly kingdom of God language can work with the assumption of a Davidic king (cf. 1 Chron. 28.5). Language of God's kingdom on earth, or language associated with early kingdoms more generally, is imperial, theocratic, and territorial, all familiar enough ideas from the ancient world and ancient kingdoms and empires. The sentiments of the following passages are standard fare:

> Those of the Negeb shall possess Mount Esau, and those of the Shephelah the land of the Philistines; they shall possess the land of Ephraim and the land of Samaria, and Benjamin shall possess Gilead. The exiles of the Israelites who are in Halah shall possess Phoenicia as far as Zarephath; and the exiles of Jerusalem who are in Sepharad shall possess the towns of the Negeb. Those who have been saved shall go up to Mount Zion to rule Mount Esau; and the kingdom shall be the Lord's. (Obad. 19–21)

> And the Lord will become king over all the earth; on that day the Lord will be one and his name one. (Zech. 14.9)

> For the Lord, the Most High, is awesome, a great king over all the earth. He subdued peoples under us, and nations under our feet. (Ps. 47.2–3)

> The kingship and dominion and the greatness of the kingdoms under the whole heaven shall be given to the people of the holy ones of the Most High; their kingdom shall be an everlasting kingdom, and all dominions shall serve and obey them. (Daniel 7.27)

As Casey says of Daniel, 'If this was reapplied to the time of Jesus . . . it was bound to mean that the Romans would be driven out of Israel and made subject to the Jewish people,'[22] a point we have seen, particularly with reference to the stone that will replace the iron in Josephus' received understanding of Dan. 2 (*Ant.* 10.209–10; cf. *Ant.* 10.268, 272–7). Allison has further argued (with reference to LXX Exod. 12.25; Lev. 19.23; Num. 15.2; 20.24; Deut. 1.8; 4.1, 21; 6.18; 16.20; 27.3; Judg. 18.9; Ezek. 13.9; 20.38; *T. Mos.* 2.1; *T. Levi* 12.5) that the language of 'inheriting the kingdom' in the Gospel tradition 'is like taking possession of the land' in his cited Jewish tradition.[23] The examples given by Casey and Allison highlight clearly that ideas of the coming kingdom frequently had imperialist implications.

But there are explicit examples in the Gospel tradition. One of the most explicit passages suggesting power and dominance in relation to the kingdom of God is found in Matt. 19.28 and Luke 22.29–30:

> Jesus said to them, 'Truly I tell you, at the renewal of all things, when the Son of Man is seated on the throne of his glory, you who have followed me will also sit on twelve thrones, judging the twelve tribes of Israel.' (Matt. 19.28)
>
> 'and I confer on you, just as my Father has conferred on me, a kingdom, so that you may eat and drink at my table in my kingdom, and you will sit on thrones judging the twelve tribes of Israel.' (Luke 22.29–30)

While both presumably are developed by Matthew and Luke, the trope of followers being sat on thrones judging the twelve tribes of Israel is common to both, and a good case can be made for this reflecting an earlier tradition, irrespective of whether we work with the Q hypothesis or an alternative. For instance, the idea of judging the twelve tribes of Israel does not concern Gentiles and concerns only Israel in end times. And this saying does, of course, give Jesus, and his followers, power, authority, and pride of place in the eschatological hierarchy. There are other examples of the kingdom in relation to power, authority, and dominion. In Mark 11.10 we have the exclamation, 'Blessed is the coming kingdom of our ancestor David! Hosanna in the highest heaven!' Clearly, this take on the kingdom of God implies replacement of Roman rule over the land with an alternative king. In terms of establishing early tradition, it is perhaps significant (and I put it no stronger than that) that Matthew and Luke feel obliged to work this over by proclaiming Jesus the king and the son of David (Matt. 21.5, 9; Luke 19.38). Indeed, we might tentatively suggest that there is a similar view implicit in Bartimaeus' exclamation which, in turn, would point to a Semitic context: Bartimaeus may be implying that Jesus is a 'son of David' like the self-proclaimed descendants of David in Mark 11.10. In Mark 11.10, this does not seem to be a developed title but an identification of Jesus as a Jew in relation to King David, or akin to the labelling of the 'daughter of Abraham' in Luke 13.16. I cannot prove this argument but the text can certainly be read as I suggest.

While the equation of kingdom with the church is common enough in the history of Christianity, this is not to say that the kingdom would necessarily become equated with an earthly realm before the end times.[24] However, this imperial language replicates, re-inscribes, and buys into imperialism, domination, and authority. Such confusion and blurred lines can be found, for instance, in the kingdom language in Jesus' exorcisms. Jesus is said to have brought the kingdom by exorcizing with the power of God (e.g. Matt. 12.28//Luke 11.20) but it is striking that some of Jesus' opponents do not deny Jesus' abilities. Instead, it is claimed that they said his power was from the satanic kingdom which itself implies similarities between kingdom and authority on both sides (Mark 3.22–7).

Arguments concerning replication and mimicry of pre-existing systems similarly apply in the case of reward theology where the reward gets pushed to the future or the afterlife (see e.g. *1 En.* 92–105; cf. Job 42.10–17). As we saw, the reason given for the stark reversal in the parable of the rich man and Lazarus is given by Abraham: 'Child, remember that during your lifetime you received your good things, and Lazarus in like manner evil things; but now he is comforted here, and you are in agony.' The expected rewards may be reversed but, ultimately, the same hierarchical structure of privilege remains and is not, ultimately, dismantled. Mark 10.17–31 is more explicit. Rich people may have about as much chance of entering the kingdom of God as a camel has of passing through the eye of a needle but the system of reward replicates the existing system, even in 'this age' and not just 'the age to come':

> Peter began to say to him, 'Look, we have left everything and followed you.' Jesus said, 'Truly/amen I tell you, there is no one who has left house or brothers or sisters or mother or father or children or fields, for my sake and for the sake of the good news, who will not receive a hundredfold now in this age—houses, brothers and sisters, mothers and children, and fields, with persecutions—and in the age to come eternal life. But many who are first will be last, and the last will be first.' (Mark 10.28–31)

This Jesus predicts a reversal of fortune for those who follow him and his message, but in describing the kingdom in this way he also reveals the limits of an imagined alternative. Far from advocating a world that removes imperial power, these descriptions of the kingdom of God champion little more than a changing of the guard. This replication of critiqued ideas also includes passages which have more explicit implications for human relations in the present and with reference to the kingdom. This general sort of thinking is found in the development of the kingdom sayings. For instance, in Matt. 16.19 (which presumably does not come directly from the historical Jesus), Jesus says to Peter: 'I will give you the keys of the kingdom of heaven, and whatever you bind on earth will be bound in heaven, and whatever you loose on earth will be loosed in heaven.' Luke 22.29–30 provides a telling addition to the twelve tribes saying: 'I confer on you, just as my Father has conferred on me, a kingdom, so that you may eat and drink at my table in my kingdom, and you will sit on thrones judging the twelve tribes of Israel.' Again, a strong case could be made for this sort of human ownership or stewardship of the kingdom being a Lukan note in Luke 22.29–30, but it is the sort of thinking implicit in the Gospel sayings about the present and growing kingdom (e.g. Mark 4.26–32; Luke 13.20–1//Matt. 13.33; Matt. 13.44; Luke 17.20–1; *Thom.* 113). The dispute about casting out demons (Mark 3.22–30), including the words 'If a kingdom is divided against itself, that kingdom cannot stand,' works with the assumption of connections with a powerful kingdom in the present, as seen also in Matt. 12.28//Luke 11.20 (see 'Christology: revolutionary or imperialist?'; cf. Mark 10.14–15; 12.34). While these sorts of sayings are not as obviously later developments like Matt. 16.19, this does not prove they go back to the historical Jesus of course, though dealing with the problematic memory of Jesus being thought to be in league with the satanic (Mark 3.22–30) may imply an earlier tradition. Nevertheless, this idea of a present imperial kingdom would have no doubt been assumed in the earliest Palestinian tradition, particularly in light of Daniel and its popularity.[25] Daniel did look to the future coming kingdom but the basic assumption was that even Nebuchadnezzar could recognize who was really in charge: 'I, Nebuchadnezzar, lifted my eyes to heaven, and my reason returned to me. I blessed the Most High, and praised and honoured the one who lives for ever. For his sovereignty is an everlasting sovereignty, and his kingdom endures from generation to generation' (Dan. 4.34).

It is worth re-stressing an earlier point. These problems establishing historicity and early tradition based on specific sayings are partly why thinking about the Synoptic tradition in more general terms becomes helpful. This, as we saw, has been most recently recognized in different ways by, for instance, Sanders (if he still counts as recent), Allison, and the memory studies associated with Schröter, Le Donne, Keith, Rodriguez, and others. We may not be able to establish a precise context for any of the sayings discussed above but we can make an argument with some degree of plausibility, as we did above, that there were predictions about the kingdom and end times from the early Palestinian tradition, that they generated eschatological enthusiasm, and that when the kingdom or end times failed to materialize fully then the predictions had to be explained. And any thinking about end times in the earliest tradition would presumably have involved all those elements discussed above. Domination, subjugation, imperialism, and theocracy are part of both the Synoptic tradition and the relevant contextualizing sources, and are perhaps the only way people could realistically conceive an alternative to the present world powers. Moreover, Paul may have used different language but clearly he inherited these sorts of imperial ideas, as we saw in Chapter 1. As Paul put it, one who humbled himself would become so exalted 'that at the name of Jesus every knee should bend, in heaven and on earth and under the earth and every tongue should confess that Jesus Christ is Lord' (Phil. 2.10–11).

Christology: revolutionary or imperialist?

Christopher Rowland has argued that the more he looks at millenarian movements the more he finds figures who went beyond a sense of mere prophetic vocation but also believed themselves to be indwelt by the divine in ways that makes the Jesus of John's Gospel seem relatively tame. Rowland, notably, points to the various texts collected in Christopher Hill's *The World Turned Upside Down*, and the sorts of contexts of social upheaval discussed in Chapter 1. Such contexts, Rowland suggests, have the potential to refocus the traditional questions, such as the origins of Christology.[26] Dale Allison has similarly compared Jesus the apocalyptic prophet with millenarian movements, both cross-culturally and in early Judaism. Allison points out that such millenarian movements can, among other things, 'address the disaffected in a period of social change that threatens traditional ways', 'depict reversal as imminent and ultimate', 'promote egalitarianism', 'break hallowed taboos associated with religious custom', 'demand an intense commitment and unconditional loyalty', and 'focus upon a charismatic leader'.[27] Again, the potential for making connections between social upheaval, eschatology, exalted perceptions of individuals, and Christological development ought to be clear, as Allison goes on to show.[28]

But this also brings us to the highly contentious and complex area of reconstructing Christological changes and developments in the early traditions and Christian origins. We can certainly make some basic and uncontroversial statements. Despite Trinitarianism eventually winning the day in orthodox Christianity, it was hardly without a fight and the range of competing understandings of Jesus in the first few Christian centuries already implies how unclear the New Testament could be concerning the deification of Jesus. Yet, from a very early date (at the very least within twenty years of Jesus' death), speculation about, or elevated understandings of Jesus, were rife, whether the various claims made about Jesus as Lord, Messiah, or eschatological Son of Man, which, in different ways, can be found in Paul, throughout the Synoptic Gospels, and, whatever their historical worth, the early chapters of Acts. We might add that there was a wide range of speculations about various elevated figures (e.g. angels, Enoch, Moses, Melchizedek) and divine emanations (e.g. Wisdom, Word) which would have provided a readily available context for any speculations concerning Jesus in the earliest Palestinian tradition. However, that this was a major feature of first-century Christianity only makes it more difficult to establish how the earliest Palestinian tradition perceived Jesus because they clearly could not stop thinking and writing about him. Conceivably the earliest Palestinian tradition could have developed dramatic claims, perhaps chaotically and inconsistently, over a period of weeks or a few years in the 30s for all we know.

The debates over where and when Jesus was fully equated with God in a 'binatarian' sense, or deemed worthy of worship in the way the god of Israel was, requires far more attention than can be offered here.[29] Nevertheless, we can make some general claims. One of the clearest examples was one we saw in the previous chapter. Jesus, according to John 5.1–18, appears to endorse a man carrying a 'burden' on the Sabbath (and thereby overriding a biblical concern not to do so; Jer. 17.19–22) but also makes a close connection between himself and his

'Father'. 'The Jews' want to kill Jesus because this is taken to mean 'he was also calling God his own Father, thereby making himself equal to God' (John 5.18). Similarly, in John 10.30–3, Jesus claims that 'the Father and I are one' for which 'the Jews' want to stone Jesus for blasphemy 'because you, though only a human being, are making yourself God'. Given the range of speculations about elevated figures in early Judaism, the Johannine Jesus must be reflecting some extremely elevated claims about Jesus for this to be written in terms of wanting to kill him. As we saw in Chapter 2, these sorts of disputes are not in the Synoptic tradition which, although concerned with Sabbath issues, is only concerned with debating what can and cannot be done on the Sabbath (rather than supporting an outright violation, as in John 5.1–18) and certainly does not make claims about Jesus being equal with God. Quite simply, this would presumably suggest that the earliest tradition did not make or discuss claims such as 'the Father and I are one', or that Jesus made himself equal with God, otherwise we would have had earlier claims and more explicit conflicts.

We can perhaps make some comments about the nature of the eschatology in the earliest tradition. It is possible that a more fully blown idea of the second coming was a later development in the tradition, even if still early, as shown by 1 Thess. 4–5 and the Aramaic *maranatha* exclamation (e.g. 1 Cor. 16.22; *Didache* 10.6). For instance, Mark 9.1 predicted the coming of the kingdom of God within the lifetime of Jesus' audience whereas Matthew's use of Mark in Matt. 16.28 heightens the eschatological expectation by a slightly different emphasis: 'Truly I tell you, there are some standing here who will not taste death before they see the Son of Man coming in his kingdom.'[30] There is also evidence of this development in the Markan tradition because the two key examples of Jesus as the Danielic Son of Man with the clouds of heaven are in Mark 13.26 and Mark 14.62. Mark 14.62 occurs in the historically dubious trial scene where it is not entirely clear how it would have been possible to pass on a tradition of Jesus as the Danielic Son of Man. Mark.13.26 not only discusses the return of the Son of Man on the clouds of heaven, but it is located in a text which looks as if it includes significant issues that are clearly not from the historical Jesus.[31]

For instance, that Mark 13 is a lengthy eschatological discourse but does not mention the 'kingdom of God' should raise some suspicions.

And there are further clues that Mark 13 reflects developments as the movement spread. For example, being beaten in synagogues and being brought before governors and kings (Mark 13.9) is something attested elsewhere (e.g. 2 Cor. 11.32–3; Acts 12.1–3; 18.12–16; 23.23; 25.6, 23). Taking the Gospel to the nations (Mark 13.10) is likely to be a development after the historical Jesus and the very earliest Palestinian tradition. Elsewhere, meetings with Gentiles are exceptional (Mark 7.24–30) and Matthew has Jesus claim that the twelve should go to the lost sheep of Israel and avoid Gentiles and Samaritans (Matt. 10.5–6; cf. Mark 2.15–17; 7.27; Matt. 6.7, 32; 10.23; 18.17; Luke 15). As such sentiments appear unlike concerns with a Gentile mission (cf. Gal. 1.16; Acts 8.26–40; 9.15) and avoiding Gentiles is not entirely supportive of Matthew's theology (cf. Matt. 2.1; 4.15–16; 5.14; 8.5–13; 10.17–18; 12.18–21; 21.33–41; 24.14; 28.19), Mark 13.10 is more likely to reflect later concerns. The prediction of the abomination of desolation in Mark 13.14 is not found elsewhere in the Synoptic tradition (other than the Matthean parallel), which we might expect had the historical Jesus, or indeed earlier tradition, made such a claim.[32] The Markan Jesus' reference to himself as 'the Son' (Mark 13.32) is likewise only used in self-reference in Mark 13 (Mark 12.6 and 14.62 are not explicit) and its use as self-reference is only found once in a Matthean and Lukan parallel (Matt. 11.27//Luke 10.22). John's Jesus, by contrast, uses the term twenty-three times of himself, and notably in contexts of highly elevated Christological claims (cf. John 5.18–26; 10.30–9). Matthew also heightens the Christological significance of the term 'Son' in his use of Mark (Mark 6.52//Matt. 14.33; Mark 8.29//Matt. 16.16; Mark 15.30// Matt. 27.40; Mark 15.32//Matt. 27.43). The use of the term 'the Son' in Mark 13.32 looks, then, like it belongs to a developing tradition and not from the historical Jesus. These arguments carry some collective weight and would suggest that the parousia and the Son of Man coming with the clouds of heaven are part of a rapidly developing tradition. Conversely, a better case can be made for those traditions which mention the more generic 'kingdom of God' being more likely to reflect the very earliest tradition than an extensive passage such as Mark 13, which does not. This is not to say that the second coming is unconnected with the idea of the kingdom of God; indeed in some ways it may well be one logical development of the kingdom (cf. Mark 14.25; Matt. 16.28 using Mark 9.1) and the prominent role Jesus is said to play within it (see below).

Nevertheless we can say one important thing about the earliest tradition: the first followers had visions of Jesus very shortly after he died. This is in the tradition Paul received and is as good a piece of evidence for early tradition as could be hoped:

For I handed on to you as of first importance what I in turn had received: that Christ died for our sins in accordance with the scriptures, and that he was buried, and that he was raised on the third day in accordance with the scriptures, and that he appeared to Cephas, then to the twelve. Then he appeared to more than five hundred brothers and sisters at one time, most of whom are still alive, though some have died. Then he appeared to James, then to all the apostles. Last of all, as to someone untimely born, he appeared also to me. (1 Cor. 15.3–9)

These appearances must have been vital in the development of Christology. Acts describes Saul's vision of Jesus on the way to Damascus as involving a 'light from heaven' that flashed around him (Acts 9.3). Whatever the historical value of Acts, we still have 2 Cor. 12.2–4 where Paul describes his experience in a way generally familiar from early Jewish visions of heaven:

I know a person in Christ who fourteen years ago was caught up to the third heaven—whether in the body or out of the body I do not know; God knows. And I know that such a person—whether in the body or out of the body I do not know; God knows—was caught up into Paradise and heard things that are not to be told, that no mortal is permitted to repeat.

Worth comparing here is 4Q405 frag. 23 col. II 8–12 because of how this understanding of heaven could also be related to kingdom and kingship:

In their wonderful stations there are spirits (with) multi-coloured (clothes), like woven material engraved with splendid effigies. In the midst of the glorious appearance of scarlet, the colours of the light of the spirit of the holy of holies, they remain fixed in their holy station before [the k]ing ([מ]לך), spirits of [pure] colours in the midst of the appearance of the whiteness. And the substance of the spirit of glory is like work from Ophir, which diffuses [lig]ht. All their decorations are mixed purely, artful like woven material. These are the chiefs of those wonderfully clothed for service, the chiefs of the kingdom (ממלכות) <of the kingdom> of the holy ones of the holy king (למלך) in all the heights of the sanctuaries of the kingdom (תמלכות) of his glory.

In the case of Paul, and with this sort of background in mind, we have good evidence for thinking that the resurrection appearances were part of the earliest Palestinian tradition which generated sustained Christological speculation.[33]

It can be further argued that the early exaltation of Jesus involved, or even assumed, an understanding of some sort of enthronement.[34] Two of the more useful passages in this respect are Mark 10.35–45 and Matt. 19.28//Luke 22.28–30. In the case of Matt. 19.28//Luke 22.28–30, we have seen that it has a good chance of being generated in early Palestinian tradition on the grounds that it is Israel-focused with no indication of a concern for Gentiles. It is also clear that this passage envisages Jesus and the twelve to have a prominent role in the kingdom (judging Israel, no less). This sort of thinking appears to be implied in Mark 10.35–45 where the sons of Zebedee ask to sit at the right and left of Jesus 'in your glory' (Mark 10.37). Mark 10.35–45 looks like it is tied in with Maccabean martyr theology of dying for Israel (e.g. 2 Macc. 7; 4 Macc. 17.20–2), which is likewise tied up with ideas of glorification after death (Dan. 12.2–3). The 'son of man' saying similarly works, potentially, as a generic idiomatic Aramaic saying with reference to the speaker and dying for 'the many', which may again imply a limited group, perhaps Israel (cf. the more limited sense of 'the many', in 1QS 6.1, 7–25; CD 13.7; 14.7).[35] As ever, this does not 'prove' historicity but such arguments concerning Mark 10.35–45 suggest that we are dealing with something at least compatible with the earliest Palestinian tradition.

Coming from rural Galilee, these would be striking claims attributed to Jesus.[36] Here Gerhard Lenski's classic cross-cultural analysis of the 'priestly class' (with echoes in the arguments of Rowland and Allison) in agrarian societies can be helpful. Lenski's 'priestly class' is broadly conceived (rabbis, imams, temple priests, monks, etc.) as figures who mediate between humanity and the divine. On the one hand, they may indeed be drawn from, or depend upon, privileged social strata and official lines of divine authority and support the status quo. On the other hand, there are figures outside the official system who can support a redistribution ethic and the needs of those at the lower end of the social structure.[37] Lenski's model is too definite, at least in the abstract, and would need nuancing in terms of details on both 'sides'. Such is the problem, of course, with macrosociological analysis. Nevertheless, the idea of direct access to the divine from outside the 'channels of salvation' of the ruling classes has historically posed conflict and tensions (again, the English Civil Wars come to mind) because if authority comes directly from the divine then who needs justification from the official channels of ruling classes? This is a useful way of understanding the Jesus tradition because clearly his authority is presented as charismatic authority directly from God and there are questions of his authority raised in the Gospels, notably in relation to healing and exorcism and John the Baptist (e.g. Mark 1.23–7; 2.10; 11.27–33).

Perhaps the clearest case of an early Palestinian tradition reflecting such ideas is Matt. 12.28//Luke 11.20:

> But if it is by the spirit of God that I cast out demons, then the kingdom of God has come to you. (Matt. 12.28)
>
> But if it is by the finger of God that I cast out the demons, then the kingdom of God has come to you. (Luke 11.20)

The finger/spirit difference is not problematic for present purposes as both concern ideas about divine power. Irrespective of whether this could be attributed to Q, there are arguments which would suggest its placement in early Palestinian tradition. The combination of exorcism, possession, and Jesus' power is well attested across the Gospel tradition in different sources, stories, and forms (e.g. Mark 1.23–7; 3.11–12, 14–15, 22–9; 7.24–30; 9.17–29; Matt. 4.23–5; 9.35; 15.30–1; Matt. 12.43–5//Luke 11.24–6; Luke 8.2; Luke 13.10–11), and we should note the related issue of the lack of power that Mark claims Jesus had in Nazareth (Mark 6.5–6), which is one of the less obvious creations of the early church (see Chapter 2). This combination of exorcism (and healing more generally), authority, and power is presumably a strong memory from early tradition (and one that John's Gospel did not like). While this does not prove historicity, recent discussions of Jesus' healings and exorcisms in terms of cross-cultural psychosomatic healing, healers, and shamans at least shows that we are not necessarily dealing with the problematic issues of the miraculous.[38] Moreover, as Geza Vermes famously showed, Jesus' healings and exorcisms would have been familiar in a Palestinian context, so, again, this tradition is at least culturally plausible.[39] And even if we cannot precisely locate specific traditions, something like the logic of Matt. 12.28//Luke 11.20 would no doubt have been assumed throughout healings and exorcisms. A comparison with the use of the 'present' kingdom in Dan. 4 is again instructive.[40] Nebuchadnezzar is said to have been 'driven away from human society, ate grass like oxen, and his body was bathed with the dew of heaven, until his hair grew as long as eagles' feathers and his nails became like birds' claws' (Dan. 4.33) but 'when that period was over', Nebuchadnezzar lifted his eyes to heaven, and his 'reason returned' (Dan. 4.34). He then gave his speech, blessing the 'Most High', and praising his 'everlasting sovereignty' and his enduring kingdom (Dan. 4.34–5). The early Gospel tradition has Jesus closely associated with, and possibly channelling, this sort of divine power.

A good case can, then, be made for Jesus being perceived in elevated terms or in terms with the potential for elevation and the development of Christology (as in the case of Matt. 12.28//Luke 11.20). As we have seen throughout this book, and now with reference to the reading of Jesus as a millenarian prophet by Rowland and Allison, this is partly a product of a time of social upheaval and change and could have a distinctly non-elite, 'subversive', or counter cultural twist. However, as we have seen throughout this chapter, movements and leaders in times of social upheaval can also have agendas of power too. As bandits could be remembered as a product of social upheaval (e.g. *Ant.* 17.270–84; *Ant.* 18.269–75; *War* 2.57–65; *War* 2.585–8; *Life* 35, 66), attacking power, wealth, and Rome (*War* 2.427–8; *Ant.* 18.269–75; *War* 2.228–31; *Ant.* 20.113–17; *Life* 126–7), and mimicking the world of kings and kingship (*War* 2.57–62; *Ant.* 17.273–8; Tacitus, *Hist.* 5.9), so can Jesus in the earliest Palestinian tradition, where he seems to have a prime role in the kingdom—might we even say, perhaps, leading the vanguard of the dictatorship of God? This is clearly the case in traditions about judging the twelve tribes and being given a place next to Jesus in his glory but also in the connection between authority, power, exorcism, and healing. Furthermore, we get the familiar theme of eschatological reversal in Mark 10.35–45. We could add to this that irrespective of whether Jesus was identified or self-identified as 'the Messiah' (and whatever that may have meant to a first-century audience), kingly and 'messianic' traits are indeed attributed to Jesus across the earliest tradition, and arguments have been made for this being among the *earliest* traditions.[41] One of the more important individual examples is 'king of the Jews', which runs throughout the build-up to Jesus' crucifixion in Mark 15 and is a mocking inscription on his cross in Mark 15.26. This title given by his executioners is not directly in line with early Christology and so a strong case can be made (and, of course, has been made[42]) that it reflects an early memory of Jesus and it certainly makes sense as a parody of the ideas with which Jesus was associated.[43]

Given all the above, the following texts may or may not provide a precise fit for the earliest Jesus tradition but they give us some of the flavour of what we might expect if Jesus and the twelve were to rule and judge:

> Lord, you are our king forevermore . . . the kingdom of our God is forever over the nations in judgment. Lord, you chose David to be king over Israel, and swore to him about his descendants forever, that his kingdom shall not fail before you . . . sinners rose up against us, they set upon us and drove us out . . . With pomp they set up a monarchy because of their arrogance, they despoiled the throne of David with arrogant shouting. But you, O Lord, overthrew them, and uprooted their descendants from the earth . . . The lawless one laid waste our land, so that no one inhabited it . . . See, Lord, and raise up for them their king, the son of David, to rule over your servant Israel in the time known to you, O God. Undergird him with the strength to destroy the unrighteous rulers, to purge Jerusalem from gentiles who trample her to destruction; in wisdom and in righteousness to drive out the sinners from the inheritance; to smash the arrogance of sinners . . . He will gather a holy people whom he will lead in righteousness; and he will judge the tribes of the people that have been made holy by the Lord their God. He will not tolerate unrighteousness . . . any person who knows wickedness shall not live with them . . . He will distribute them upon the land according to their tribes; the alien and the foreigner will no longer live near them. He will judge peoples and nations in the wisdom of his righteousness . . . And he will have gentile nations serving him under his yoke, and he will glorify the Lord in a place prominent above the whole earth . . . And he will be a righteous king over them, taught by God. There will be no unrighteousness among them in his days, for all shall be holy, and their king shall be the Lord Messiah. (*Ps. Sol.* 17)

> He will be called son of God, and they will call him son of the Most High . . . Until the people of God arises and makes everyone rest from the sword. His

kingdom will be an eternal kingdom, and all his paths in truth. He will jud[ge] the earth in truth and all will make peace. The sword will cease from the earth and all provinces will pay him homage. The great God is his strength, he will wage war for him; he will place the peoples in his hand and cast them all away before him. His rule will be an eternal rule ... (4Q246 II 1–9)

The first battalion will be equipped with a shield and a sword, to fell the dead by the judgment of God and to humiliate the enemy line by God's might, to pay the reward of their evil towards every people of futility. For kingship belongs to the God of Israel and with the holy ones of his nation he will work wonders. (1QM VI 4–6)

While Israel has the dominion, there [will not] be cut off someone who sits on the throne of David. For <<the staff>> is the covenant of royalty, [and the thou]sands of Israel are <<the standards>>. Until the messiah of righteousness comes, the branch of David. For to him and to his descendants has been given the covenant of the kingship of his people for everlasting generations ... (4Q252 V, 1–4)

[for the heav]ens and the earth will listen to his anointed one ... For the Lord will consider the pious, and call the righteous by name, and his spirit will hover upon the poor, and he will renew the faithful with strength. For he will honour the pious upon the throne of an eternal kingdom, freeing prisoners, giving sight to the blind, straightening out the twis[ted] ... he will proclaim good news to the poor ... enrich the hungry. (4Q521 2 II 1–13)

But, Melchizedek will carry out the vengeance of Go[d's] judgments, [and on that day he will fr]e[e them from the hand of] Belial and from the hand of all the sp[irits of his lot.] (11Q13 2.13)

... when the nations are in confusion, and the time of my Messiah is come, he will call all the nations together, and some of them he will spare, and some of them he will destroy ... And when he has brought low everything that is in the world, and sat down in peace forever on the throne of his kingdom, then joy shall be revealed ... And shall healing descend as dew, and disease shall disappear ... And gladness shall spread through all the earth (*2 Syr. Bar.* 72.2–73.2)

Note throughout how promises of peace and prosperity are intertwined with power, force, and dominance; all these themes are found throughout the Gospel tradition. And, put another way, could not such claims equally be made of Rome?

Jesus becomes Caesar

Obviously, one way we could develop an understanding of the Christological material in the earliest tradition would be to examine how it fed into the development of 'high' (and ultimately Trinitarian) Christology, though the 'lower' view of Jesus can also be found in the earliest tradition and would, of course, have its own influences. But, as I pointed out, I want to take this sort of thinking in a different direction and look at the connections between the development of 'high' Christological thinking and imperialistic thinking. Again, the idea that Jesus was proclaimed in contrast to Caesar is commonplace in contemporary New Testament studies but I want to look more at the idea that this sort of Christological thinking mimicked and replicated imperial power to the extent that it became part of imperial power on earth. What we have seen so far suggests that there was something far more hierarchical and less egalitarian about the earliest thinking about Jesus than Crossan's famous 'brokerless kingdom' would suggest.[44] Yet Crossan's thinking has similarities to certain advocates of an 'apocalyptic Jesus'. Bart Ehrman, for instance, claimed the following of Jesus' eschatological teachings:

> In the Kingdom there would be no more war. Jesus' disciples were not to engage in acts of violence *now*... Jesus' disciples were to treat all people equally and fairly *now*—even the lower classes, the outcasts, the destitute; even women and children... [Jesus' disciples] had experienced a foretaste of the glories that lay ahead, in a world in which there would be no demonic powers, disease, or death, a world in which no one would suffer from poverty or oppression, where no one hurt another, hit another, or hated another... No wonder that Jesus saw this kingdom as good news and invited his hearers to join him in preparing for it...[45]

While Ehrman is probably correct in his assessment of some of the behaviour attributed to Jesus and his disciples concerning present behaviour in relation to the kingdom, I wonder if, in this and other such cases, scholars have implicitly bought into the rhetoric of Jesus too much and have not been suspicious enough of the violence involved in such theocratic thinking. But even in the unlikely possibility that the earliest Jesus tradition did not also contain non-egalitarian and imperialist-theocratic potential (it seems that we do have, after all, a promise of a king and judge, no matter how benign), we do know that the development of imperialistic Christology was well under way.[46] As we saw above, Paul clearly envisaged Christ playing an extremely elevated role in this alternative imperial system (e.g. Phil. 2.10–11) and in a different, seemingly more benign way, the removal of particular identities in Christ (Gal. 3.28). Echoing and expanding the Gospel tradition of judging, Paul (1 Cor. 6.2) is clear about eschatological change in power relations:

When any of you has a grievance against another, do you dare to take it to court before the unrighteous, instead of taking it before the saints? Do you not know that the saints will judge the world? And if the world is to be judged by you, are you incompetent to try trivial cases? Do you not know that we are to judge angels—to say nothing of ordinary matters?

However, one of the features of New Testament scholarship which has focused on the early Christian proclamations of Jesus in contrast to Caesar has also suggested a non-imperial or non-monarchical alternative.[47] This seems highly unlikely to me but in the spread of early Christian ideas it might also be irrelevant as these texts are very easy to read imperialistically and dominance is often implicit even if we do not always see this as obvious, as Stephen Moore has shown in the case of John's Gospel,[48] a text which has also been read *against* Caesar and empire.[49] I want to make a slightly different point to Moore's concerning a more recent reception of John's presentation of Jesus in John 5.1–18. Here, John's Jesus is in dispute with 'the Jews' who, it is claimed, want to persecute and kill him because of his view of the Sabbath and because he was 'calling God his own Father, thereby making himself equal to God' (John 5.18; cf. John 10.30–3). It may or may not be the case that John's Christology was the language and product of a relatively powerless Christian group who may or may not have experienced troubles and persecution for their high Christological beliefs (cf. John 16.2). It may or may not be the case that John envisaged a peaceful future once Jesus took full control. Tom Thatcher, who has thought about the potential imperial ramifications of anti-imperialism more than most Gospel scholars, has claimed the following:

Time and again—so often that it seems to be the rule rather than the exception—rebel leaders with high ideals become oppressive dictators once their movement has disposed the old regime. This observable fact of history is a surface manifestation of the many hidden hierarchies of power that operate within the communities of the oppressed before the revolution begins—the rebel leader was already a king of sorts and simply begins to act like one once he officially takes charge . . . Viewed in this light, the genius of the footwashing lies in the fact that Jesus anticipates and precludes the emergence of anything like a new imperial order within his eschatological community. No one steps in to take the throne once the ruler of this world is cast out. In fact, there are no thrones, only footstools, and masters find themselves in place of slaves, washing the filthy feet of the people over whom they have authority.[50]

But even in this attempt, Thatcher cannot escape the language of 'authority' and we should not underestimate the significance of reversal in propping up the structure of an existing ideological system. Thatcher is aware of and sensitive to the idea that intentions do not necessarily control receptions. As he points out, 'there can be little doubt that the Gospel of John has been read in support of imperial politics—Roman, European, and, more recently, American'.[51] And once the conflicts between Jesus and 'the Jews' over Christology in John 5.1–18 are placed in a context of Christian power, it ought to be clear how issues of power and imperialism are present in the story of Jesus changing established ways of understanding God. In general terms, re-reading this story in light of the history of European Jews clearly shows how narrative power relations can be strengthened when understood in certain contexts of social and material power relations.

The particular reception I have in mind is a striking example of a reading of John 5.1–18, where Christianity is seen by the colonized to represent imperialism and which has been discussed by Mary Huie-Jolly.[52] Huie-Jolly shows that after the Anglo-Maori wars of the 1860s and early 1870s some indigenous Maori in New Zealand's Bay of Plenty region started to identify themselves with 'the Jews' of John 5, the hostile enemy of Jesus, and by association Christianity. In earlier missionary activity, while some people would profess Christianity, others identified themselves as 'Jews' or 'unbelievers' and similar reactions were found later among those previously deemed converted. This was done as a response to colonial practices which undermined traditional ways of life and land rights. This also led to another aspect of the identification with 'the Jews' because of the connotations of Israelites as the real chosen people entitled to the land over against the Canaanite settlers, that is, the European settlers. According to Huie-Jolly's postcolonial reading, John 'constructs a dominating Christology which has affinities with the universalizing claims of later colonialist Christianity'. While John 5 may have once been designed to give the group's authority to the Son in the context of a split from synagogue authority, John 5, in the context of a politically dominant Christianity, can be used to make claims of cultural and religious superiority. In this respect, note the shift in John 5 from Jesus as one 'the Jews' sought to kill (5.18) to the all-powerful judge (5.19–23). In the context of the colonization of New Zealand, the decision to identify with 'the Jews' of John 5 was part of 'a decision to "leave the way of the Son" and to resist colonial domination'.[53]

Whatever the intentions of the earliest tradition or various New Testament authors, the domineering, monarchical, and imperialistic aspect of Christology would prove crucial to the long-term survival of Christianity. For centuries, there were developing what we might broadly call 'monotheizing' or universalizing tendencies in the ancient world which could be brought into the service of empire.[54] Macro-sociologically speaking, it is notable that ancient agrarian societies produced Buddhism, Christianity, Judaism, and Islam which owed something to developments in technology, transportation, and trade which came about with empire-building.[55] The greater connections across human society, as well as defeating rival gods on what was then a global scale, meant that the divine world could reflect the human in different ways,[56] such as an emperor and his lackeys in heaven reflecting life as it is on earth.[57]

Whether this is an argument that can be made on a broad scale over centuries is not one I take up here. I do not use this macrosociological argument to say that there is a precise match between empire and 'monotheizing' or universalizing tendencies. Nor is there the space to discuss the development of Christian monotheism or the extent of 'pagan monotheism' or the extent to which it had an impact on the development of Christian monotheism in the Roman empire. Rather, I want to make a much more basic point that the 'monotheizing' and universalizing in the earliest Christian claims of kingdom, kingship, and elevated Christology always had the potential to be developed imperialistically. One important point of comparison comes from the emergence of the Persian empire where there were some explicit claims of something we might loosely label 'monotheizing' or universalizing alongside its monetary system, legal administration, communication networks, and the spread of Aramaic as a common language. Within 'Zoroastrianism' Ahura Mazda was emerging as the major deity and as its foremost creator and ruler (cf. e.g. Naqsh-e Rostam A 1–8; *ANET* 316).[58] Herodotus claimed that it is not the custom of the Persians

> to make and set up statues and temples and altars, but those who do such things they think foolish, because, I suppose, they have never believed the gods to be like men, as the Greeks do; but they call the whole circuit of heaven Zeus, and to him they sacrifice on the highest peaks of the mountains. (Herodotus 1.131)

The famous Persian dualism should be qualified in that there was a belief that good would ultimately triumph: such dualism is not greatly incompatible with Jewish 'monotheizing' or monotheistic tendencies observable in the Dead Sea Scrolls. Plutarch, citing an earlier source, notes of this imbalance between the opposing forces (e.g. Plutarch, *On Isis and Osiris* 46–7) that there were two sides, but one would win. The connections with empire are found, for instance, in a fifth-century BCE inscription:

> Ahuramazda is the great god who gave us this earth, who gave that sky... who made Xerxes, the great king, the king of kings, the king of (all) countries (which speak) all kinds of languages, the king of this (entire) big and far (-reaching) earth... These are the countries—in addition to Persia—over which I am king under the 'shadow' of Ahuramazda, over which I hold sway... May Ahuramazda protect me, my family and these countries from all evil. (*ANET* 316–17)[59]

Bruce Lincoln has provided a detailed analysis of Achaemenian inscriptions and politics in which he argued that a range of 'religious' topics, now familiar from the earliest Palestinian and Christian tradition, were embedded in the imperial enterprise. As Lincoln puts it of his own work, he explores 'how certain Achaemenian religious constructs that resemble those found elsewhere—reverence for a benevolent creator, a theology of election and vocation, a dualistic ethics, eschatological expectations, and a sense of soteriological mission—helped inspire the project of empire and informed even its most brutally violent aspects'.[60]

We can make more general comments about the compatibility of 'monotheizing' and empire. There were, of course, Hellenistic 'monotheizing' and universalizing tendencies, particularly in philosophical traditions and discussed by philosophical elites. In the long term the most influential 'monotheizing' ideas were found in Plato, though there are other philosophical developments in the long term (cf. Plutarch, *De comm. not.* 1051e–f, 1052a; 1077e), as Michael Frede has shown and whose work I develop here.[61] For instance, Aristotle identified the first 'unmoved mover' with 'God' and makes a number of statements that might be described as 'monotheizing' (e.g. *Metaphysics Λ*; 7, 1072b 13–14, 25–30; 8, 1074a 36–7; 10, 1075a 11). 'Monotheizing' tendencies can also be found in Xenophanes of Colophon (e.g. B 1, 15–16, 24–6), concerning which Aristotle noted: 'But Xenophanes, the first exponent of the Unity... gave no definite teaching, nor does he seem to have grasped either of these conceptions of unity; but regarding the whole material universe he stated that the Unity is God' (Aristotle, *Metaphysics* 986b, 20). Elsewhere, even Zeus could be understood in 'monotheizing' terms. Aeschylus, for instance, can closely associate Zeus with Fate (*Eumenides* 1044) and present Zeus as follows: 'Lord of lords, most blessed among the blessed, power most perfect among the perfect, O blessed Zeus, hear! And from your offspring ward off in utter abhorrence the lust of men, and into the purple sea cast their black-benched madness' (*Supplicant Women* 524–30; cf. 599, 823; *Agamemnon* 160–6; 1487–8).

Again, I make no bold claims about the extent of 'monotheizing' in Hellenistic thought and certainly not the Hellenistic world more broadly. Nor is it to say that 'monotheism' was always consciously developed imperialistically. My point is again a basic one: these 'monotheizing' ideas could be compatible with imperialistic thinking. Walter Burkert described the rise of Greek philosophical-theological speculation in relation to more materialist expansion, adding that 'Greeks have conquered the Mediterranean, new colonies springing up, trade and industry are on the increase, and Greek forms are being imitated everywhere. Possibilities for development are offered to the individual which are no longer confined to family, city, or tribe.'[62] We might also compare the connections between Greek-inspired ideas and forms of imperialism which might be seen in the assimilation of local gods. Isis, for instance, could be identified with other goddesses who were deemed manifestations (Apuleius, *Metamorphoses* 11.5). Zeus the supreme god could be viewed by different names. We can find this in, for instance, 2 Macc. 6.1–2, which writes about the appropriately named 'Zeus-the-Friend-of-Strangers' and the pollution of the Jerusalem Temple, calling it 'the temple of Olympian Zeus, and to call the one in Gerizim the temple of Zeus-the-Friend-of-Strangers, as did the people who lived in that place'. These assimilating and universalizing ideas are clearly part of a broader human interaction in that Zeus is identified as the friend of the stranger, a great unifying figure. It is worth pointing out the different perspective on Hellenism found in the *Letter of Aristeas* where Aristeas claims that Jews worship the God who is 'the creator and overseer of all' while Gentiles refer to this divine figure as 'Zeus or Dis' (*Aristeas* 16; cf. 140).

Whatever the extent of 'monotheizing' or universalizing tendencies in the ancient world, the emerging Christian movement had to negotiate related tendencies in an area prominent in contemporary New Testament scholarship: the emperor cult. Again, whether or not the emperor cult is compatible with scholarly definitions of ancient 'monotheism' is not the question here but there were certainly universalist features which were familiar and potentially problematic for Jews and Christians, notably the emperor's world-rule and divine authority. In terms of the similarities and competition between Christ-devotion and Caesar-devotion, Gerd Theissen noted that 'in both connections one found forms of solidarity which transcended the regions, a promise of a change of life, a cohesion which transcended classes, and a certain privilege which others who lived without such a relationship to the "ruler of the world" did not have'.[63] Moreover, outsider perceptions of the Jewish and/or Christian god were not always convinced that there was any difference from other views of the divine, in much the same way as the view attributed to Aristeas. Of Jewish views of god, Celsus claimed 'that it makes no difference whether you call the highest being Zeus, or Zen, or Adonai, or Sabaoth, or Ammoun like the Egyptians, or Pappaeus like the Scythians' (Origen, *C. Cel.* 5.41). Justin Martyr knew his opponents would perceive that similar ideas of the divine could be found in Plato: 'For while we say that all things have been produced and arranged into a world by God, we shall seem to utter the doctrine of Plato' (Justin, *Apology* 1.20). Even concepts of multiple gods could be compared to views of angels and intermediary figures. The philosopher referred to by Macarius Magnes claimed:

At any rate, if you say that angels stand before God who are not subject to feeling and death, and immortal in their nature, whom we ourselves speak of as gods, because they are close to the Godhead, why do we dispute about a name?... The difference therefore is not great, whether a man calls them gods or angels, since their divine nature bears witness to them... (*Monogenes* 4.21)

This was not a difficult move to make given that the language of divinity (e.g. *theos*, *El*, *Elohim*) could be applied not only to God but also to angels and elevated figures such as Moses or Melchizedek (e.g. Philo, *Moses* 1.155–8; 4Q405 20 ii 7b–9; 11Q13 2.10–11).[64] The general point should be clear: Christians had to negotiate claims of similar conceptions of the divine world which, for outsiders at least, were certainly compatible with life under Rome.

And, of course, Christianity and Christ did become integral to the empire by the fourth century CE. But what is further significant about this was the attempt by the emperor Julian ('the Apostate') to change this after he renounced his Christian past in an attempt to turn the Christian tide.[65] Whether Julian's discussion stands up to contemporary definitions of 'monotheism' in late antiquity is again debated but it looks as if Julian thought the many gods and local cults were emanations of the creator:

The sun which is visible to our eyes is the likeness of the intelligible and invisible sun, and again the moon which is visible to our eyes and every one of the stars are likenesses of the intelligible. Accordingly Plato knows of those intelligible and invisible gods which are immanent in and coexist with the creator himself and were begotten and proceeded from him. Naturally, therefore, the creator in Plato's account says 'gods' when he is addressing the invisible beings and 'of gods' meaning by this, evidently the visible gods. And the common creator of both these is he who fashioned the heavens and the earth and the sea and the stars, and begat in the intelligible world the archetypes of these. (*Against the Galileans* 65b–c)

Indeed, it seems that Julian attempted to challenge Judaism and Christianity in terms of the validity of their universalizing and 'monotheizing' for the empire. He therefore has to compare Moses with Plato in order to establish who presents the better divine system for the empire. Different peoples have different gods with local kingly authority but, Julian argued, they are dependent on the overarching imperial god (e.g. *Against the Galileans* 143a–b). This meant he could argue that there was a problem with Moses' god being a universal god because of the connection with a specific group of people and this was not suitable for the empire. As Julian would claim, 'it is natural to think that the God of the Hebrews was not the begetter of the whole universe with lordship over the whole, but rather, as I said before, that he is confined within limits, and that since his empire has bounds we must conceive of him as only one of the crowd of other gods' (*Against the Galileans* 100c; cf. 143a–e). Christians, however, could not even match Moses' seemingly low standards of universalism or 'monotheism' (*Against the Galileans* 290b–e; cf. 146a–b) and contradict Moses by worshipping two or three gods:

> Moses, therefore, utters many sayings to the following effect and in many places: 'you shall fear the Lord your God and him only shall you serve' (Deut. 6.13; 10.20). How then has it been handed down in the Gospels that Jesus commanded: 'Go therefore and teach all the nations, baptising them in the name of the Father, and of the Son, and of the Holy Spirit' (Mt. 28.19), if they were not intended to serve him also? (*Against the Galileans* 290e–291a)

As with Judaism, Julian wanted to prove that the god of Christianity was simply not suited to empire. The flip side of this is, of course, that Christian monotheism and its universalizing concept of god really was compatible with imperialism. And this was already implicit in the earliest Palestinian traditions which gave Jesus pride of place in the kingdom and made him a conduit of the rule of god. There were all sorts of hurdles to get to the fourth-century manifestation of Christian monotheism but imperialism was hardly an insurmountable one.

Imperial Christology and kingdom

Of course Christianity would win and become the religion of the empire. But what the example of Julian shows is that there could be connections made between universalism, 'monotheizing', and empire. To stress yet again, this is not to make a case for or against what was 'inherently' the most compatible divine system in relation to empire. Nor is this to suggest that Christianity was always consciously developing imperial Christology. Yet it is clear that any movement with universalist claims of its god would eventually have to reckon with imperialist ideology and that Christian monotheism was potentially compatible with empire. And, while some might go down the Ebionite path, it was those who went the imperial road who became history's 'winners'.

Again, it is not good enough to claim that this imperial thinking was a 'betrayal' of Jesus' teaching, though no doubt Jesus and the earliest tradition (or even Paul, John, or Revelation) would not have been happy to see their vision of theocracy become so closely identified with Rome. Yet intentionality only gets us so far. Imperialism, theocracy, and empire were as integral to the earliest tradition as were promises to the poor and overthrowing the rich and Rome. With the reinterpretation of Daniel in mind, the future kingdom would have envisaged the overthrowing of the Romans but with the rule of the Jewish god being fully realized. The earliest Palestinian tradition contained the ideas that the world to come and the afterlife would overthrow the rich and the poorest would take their place and be rewarded, but the rewards kept the pre-existing structure of privilege. Likewise, the social upheavals may well have generated 'anti-establishment' Christological claims but they would very quickly, indeed simultaneously, be taken up in the direction of Jesus' authoritative place in the kingdom. While Christianity would hardly lose its concern for inequality, it would not lose its interest in imperial thinking either, notably in the case of the long-term understanding of the development of Christian monotheism in the empire. What we have in the eschatological material is arguably the clearest case of what Roland Boer has often noted as 'the tension between reaction and revolution that one so often finds with Christianity'.[66] The history of Christianity obviously bears out Boer's suggestion and we can get seemingly irreconcilable trends from radical readers of the Bible to Church of England bishops taking a privileged place in the House of Lords. Yet, we should not perhaps be so surprised to find the emerging British Labour movement using 'apocalyptic' language to promote radical social change being transformed by Tony Blair to justify the invasions of Afghanistan and Iraq, or Church of England bishops confronting a government over economic inequality, for these apparent 'tensions' exist simultaneously in the earliest Palestinian tradition and were taken up in the Christian movement that followed.[67]

4

'Sinners', Law, and Purity

What I want to do in this chapter is to look at another aspect of the reversal of rich and poor, a theme we saw was partly generated by, and interacted with, the socio-economic changes in Galilee. Here, I will focus on the group labelled 'sinners' and the call for their repentance and return to the Law.[1] In particular, I will focus on the role of purity and morality in the earliest Palestinian tradition because of the ways in which the language of the behaviour of 'sinners' was constructed in relation to purity concerns. Some consideration will be given to the kinds of contexts that could have contributed to the interest in the related concerns of purity and 'sinners'. Overall, it should become clear that the interest in such 'sinners' in the earliest Palestinian tradition provided a connection (whether consciously or unconsciously) to ideas about inclusion of Gentiles and the process in which morality could become separated from purity. This also meant that texts about purity disputes would survive simultaneously in the first century. As we will see, the importance of purity was assumed in the earliest Palestinian tradition but once these memories were present in contexts of Gentile inclusion in the Greco-Roman world, where such issues were of minimal concern, 'morality' becomes heightened as a boundary marker and purity no longer remains a focus, and so it could then be reinterpreted metaphorically, or simply forgotten.

'Sinners'

In a recent essay Craig Blomberg argued that Jesus' association with 'sinners' was a 'countercultural association with the outcast in the intimacy of his table fellowship', that such people were 'on the fringe of first century society', and that the female 'sinner' in Luke 7.36–50 could 'theoretically' have been the wife of someone with a dishonourable occupation, a woman in debt, an 'adulteress', or someone who was 'ill, disabled or in regular contact with Gentiles', or, as Blomberg ultimately prefers, a 'prostitute' as 'the most probable "occupation" from which she would have incurred this stigma . . . we dare not deny the probable reference to literal harlots as well'.[2] For Blomberg, such deeds of Jesus were 'precisely to enhance the possibilities of genuine repentance for those alienated by standard Jewish separatism and to show the results of the new way he brings, Jesus "mixes it up" with the notorious and riff-raff of this world' and 'notorious sinners and outcasts of society'.[3] There are a number of problems with Blomberg's essay but we might focus on his discussion of 'riff-raff' or 'the outcast' as being those regarded as 'sinners'. Even a basic critique of Luke 7.36–50 should begin to show why Blomberg's view is problematic. As has been pointed out time and time again, and as Blomberg is aware, the woman is not identified as a 'literal harlot' and, in an earlier chapter (Luke 5.8), Peter claims to be a 'sinful man (ἀνὴρ ἁμαρτωλός)', which is not, presumably, to be understood as a reference to prostitution. The sinner of Luke 7.36–50 might have been a sex worker for all we know but we cannot work it out from the text. Nor are there any indications that she might be understood as 'riff-raff', whatever that vague term may actually mean. We may be able to deduce some details. She has an alabaster jar of ointment (Luke 7.37) and from elsewhere in the Gospel tradition, and in a similar story, this is an indication of wealth (Mark 14.3). Of course, it might be possible to talk of wealthy people who were despised (cf. Luke 16.19–31), on the fringes of society, and associated with Gentiles but this is not how Blomberg appears to understand 'riff-raff' and 'the outcast'.

Nevertheless, the little information that Luke 7.36–50 provides does cohere with some of the wide-ranging references to 'sinners' in Jewish literature.[4] In the Greek version of the Hebrew Bible/Old Testament (LXX), the term for 'sinner' that we find in the Gospels (ἁμαρτωλός) typically translates the precise Hebrew equivalent (רשע), frequently found in the Psalms, with the English translation 'wicked'. Whenever anything relating to socio-economic status is mentioned, such people are referred to as oppressive, unjust, and rich (Pss. 9.24

[10.3]; 9.17–18; 36[37].21; 72[73].3–12; 81[82].2, 4; 93[94].3–5; 111[112].10),[5] as the following example shows:

For I was envious of the arrogant; I saw the prosperity of the wicked (רשעים/ *ἁμαρτωλῶν*). For they have no pain; their bodies are sound and sleek. They are not in trouble as others are; they are not plagued like other people. Therefore pride is their necklace; violence covers them like a garment. Their eyes swell out with fatness; their hearts overflow with follies. They scoff and speak with malice; loftily they threaten oppression. They set their mouths against heaven, and their tongues range over the earth... Such are the wicked (רשעים/ *ἁμαρτωλοὶ*); always at ease, they increase in riches. (Ps. 72[73].3–12)

Such 'sinners' were perceived to be acting as if they were outside the covenant and were thus seen as law-breakers (e.g. Ps. 49[50].16–23; see also 93[94].13; Ezek. 33.8, 19; Prov. 15.8; Dan. 12.10). As Ps. 119.118(119) put it, 'All the wicked of the earth you count as dross; therefore I love your decrees' (see also Ps. 119.53, 61, 95, 110, 155). From this perspective, 'sinners' were structurally similar to the nations and it is a label which can be synonymous with Gentiles (as it is in Gal. 2.15): 'The wicked shall depart to Sheol, all the nations that forget God' (Ps. 9.17; see also Pss. 9.15–16; 9.36 [10.15]; 83[84].10). Other general notions of what 'sinners' were flow fairly naturally from this logic. So, for instance, 'sinners' could act as if 'there is no God': 'the wicked say, "God will not seek it out"; all their thoughts are, "There is no God"' (9.25 [10.4]; Ps. 57[58].3–5). In language which should also be familiar from the Gospel tradition, 'the sinners' are placed in binary opposition to the 'righteous (צדיק/*δίκαιος*)'.[6] Ps. 36[37].21, for instance, claims that, 'The wicked borrow and do not pay back, but the righteous are generous and keep giving.' Unsurprisingly, punishment of 'sinners' is commonly found.[7] As Ps. 36[37].34 promises, 'Wait for the Lord, and keep to his way, and he will exalt you to inherit the land, you will look on the destruction of the wicked.' We might add that the Greek 'sinner' (*ἁμαρτωλός*) is used to translate other Hebrew words (namely חנף, חרש, רע, and especially חטא) and the similarities with the above are clear enough (e.g. Gen. 13.13; Num. 16.38; 32.14; 1 Kgs 1.21; Isa. 1.4, 28; Amos 9.8, 10; Prov. 23.17; 13.31; Pss. 1.1, 5; 103[104].35).

Other early Jewish literature shows very similar patterns, though 'sinner' (*ἁμαρτωλός*) appears to be absent from Philo and Josephus.

Again, whenever socio-economic status is mentioned it involves 'sinners' as rich people who are powerful, oppressive, abusing justice, and unjustly successful (e.g. Sir. 9.11; 11.9, 21; 27.30; 28.9; 29.19; 35[32].17; 39.26–7; *1 En.* 100.2–3; 103.5, 11, 15; 104.5–7; 106.18; *Ps. Sol.* 17.5; cf. Sir. 10.23; *1 En.* 97.7). The following example is typical:

Now I tell you, sinners, you have satiated yourselves with food and drink, robbing and sin, impoverishing people and gaining property, and seeing good days. Have you seen the righteous, how their end comes about, for no injustice is found upon them until their death? (*1 En.* 102. 9–11)

Again, this line of thinking is connected with the idea of 'sinners' as law-breakers acting as if they are outside the covenant (e.g. Sir. 15.7, 9; 1 Macc. 1.34; 2.44, 62; *1 En.* 104.10; *Ps. Sol.* 1.1; 2.1; 4.8; 14.6; 15.5, 8). James Dunn noticed a more specific nuance to some of the legal references in early Jewish sources, namely that 'sinner' (ἁμαρτωλός) was used as a polemical label to be attributed to rival Jewish groups, as the following examples show:[8]

And the devout will prove their God's judgement to be right when sinners are driven out from the presence of the righteous, those who please men, who deceitfully quote the Law. (*Ps. Sol.* 4.8)

And now I know this mystery: For they [the sinners] shall alter the just verdict [or: words of truth] and many sinners will take it to heart; they will speak evil words and lie, and they will invent fictitious stories and write out my scriptures on the basis of their own words... (*1 En.* 104.10; cf. 99.2)

There are also plenty of references to 'sinners' as synonymous with Gentiles (e.g. Tob. 13.6; Wisd. 19.13; *1 En.* 99.6–7; 104.7–9). Compare the following example, which brings together a number of associations in the term 'sinner':

And Matthias and his friends went around and tore down the altars; they forcibly circumcised all the uncircumcised boys that they found within the borders of Israel. They hunted down the arrogant and the work prospered in their hands. They rescued the law out of the hands of the gentiles and kings, and they never let the sinner gain the upper hand. (1 Macc. 2.45–8)

And it should be no surprise that Antiochus IV was the epitome of the 'sinner' (1 Macc. 1.10) and, after 63 BCE, the Romans would get similar treatment (e.g. *Pss. Sol.* 1.1; 2.1; cf. *Sib. Or.* 3.304). More general statements about sinners acting as if there were no God are also found,[9] as is the contrast with the good, the wise, and the righteous.[10] Such sinners should be avoided as they are a malignant influence (e.g. Sir. 12.14). A common theme is that these sinners should expect judgement and an unpleasant end, often an eschatological punishment.[11] The following should give some flavour of what was expected to happen to sinners:

The punishments did not come upon the sinners without prior signs in the violence of thunder, for they justly suffered because of their wicked acts . . . (Wisd. 19.13)

Famine and sword and death shall be far from the righteous; for they will retreat from the devout like those pursued by famine. But they shall pursue sinners and overtake them, for those who act lawlessly shall not escape the Lord's judgment. (*Ps. Sol.* 15.7–8)

You, sinners, are accursed forever; there is no peace for you! (*1 En.* 102.5)

In the Dead Sea Scrolls, the main Hebrew and Aramaic terms for 'sinner' (רשע along with חטא) continue the emphases of the Psalmist, though with particular reference to the issues faced by the writers of the Scrolls (e.g. polemics concerning 'the House of Judah' or the Wicked Priest). Once more, whenever socio-economic status is mentioned (and there are plenty of such references), it involves issues of oppressive and powerful rich people who are unjustly successful.[12] This, it should be observed, is tied in with issues of Law and the importance of the Psalms is clear:

'And the poor shall possess the land and enjoy peace in plenty [Ps. 37.11].' Its interpretation concerns the congregation of the poor who will tough out the period of distress and will be rescued from all the snares of Belial. Afterwards, all who shall po[sse]ss the land will enjoy and grow fat with everything enjoy[able to] the flesh. 'The wicked (רשע) plots against the just person (לצדיק) . . . [Ps. 37.12–13].' Its interpretation alludes to the ruthless ones of the covenant who are in the House of Judah, who plot to destroy those who observe the law, who are in the Community Council. (4Q171 2.9–16; cf. 4Q169, frags 3–4, 1.11–12)

The princes of Judah are those upon whom the rage will be vented, for they hope to be healed but the defects stick (to them); all are rebels because they have not left the path of traitors and have defiled themselves in paths of licentiousness, and with wicked wealth (ובהון רשעה), avenging themselves, and each one bearing resentment against his brother, and each one hating his fellow. Each one became obscured by blood relatives, and approached for debauchery and bragged about wealth and gain. Each one did what was right in his eyes and each one has chosen the stubbornness of his heart. They did not keep apart from the people and have rebelled with insolence, walking on the path of the wicked ones (רשעים), about whom God says: 'Their wine is serpents' venom and cruel poisons of asps.' (CD 8.3–10)

The interlinked themes of non-observance (including Dunn's emphasis on rival interpretations of the Law) and wealth are also present elsewhere. In 1QpHab it is claimed that the Wicked Priest (הכוהן הרשע) abandoned the Law (no doubt as interpreted by 1QpHab) for riches. The Wicked Priest is further accused of robbing, hoarding wealth, and being violent to the poor, and will thus face judgement (e.g. 1QpHab 8.8; 9.9; 11.4; 12.2; 12.8–9). Judgement on 'sinners' is another common theme which is frequently connected with observance of the Law.[13] Other familiar themes recur in the Scrolls, including: generic bad behaviour and acting as if there were no God;[14] contrasts with 'the righteous;[15] those outside the Law and covenant, including those outside the covenant understood by the writers of the Scrolls;[16] and Gentiles and idolaters.[17] It is worth adding that the standard Hebrew term (רשע) could also describe destructive evil spirits and the work of Belial (cf. 1QM 4.1–4; 1QS 2.5; 11Q13 1, 2.11; 4Q511 1.6).

Early rabbinic literature continues the now familiar uses of the standard Hebrew term for 'sinner' (רשע), though if anything it is typically more generic in its use (e.g. *m. Ned.* 1.1; *m. Abot* 1.7–8; *m. Sanh.* 10.6; *t. Sotah* 9.5; *t. Sanh.* 8.3–4; 13.1; 14.4). As ever, whenever the socio-economic status of 'sinners' is discussed it is, again, those deemed rich, powerful, comfortable, unjust, and oppressive (e.g. *m. Sanh.* 8.5; *m. Abot* 4.15; 5.1). There is one occurrence of 'sinner' (רשע) in the sense of someone who might not necessarily be perceived to be the oppressive rich in the conventional sense (*m. Qidd.* 4.14) but even this example concerns people who act like bandits and so, from this perspective, it is the same kind of idea as found in discussions of 'sinners' across Jewish literature, as well as being the language used polemically to describe those deemed wealthy and oppressive (e.g. Jer. 7.11; Mark 11.17). Telling texts which generated the extensive discussion of 'sinners' include: *m. Sanh.* 10.3, its reception in *b. Sanh.*

109a–b, as well as related discussions (e.g. *Gen. R.* 49.6). The *m. Sanh.* 10.3 passage discusses the sins of Sodom, and provides more close association between the main words translated as 'sinner' (רשע, חטא, and רע) by bringing together various connotations: sinners are lawless, idolatrous, violent, oppressive, rich, and hate the poor. While different sins are discussed, the overwhelming reason why the Sodomites are sinners is because of their wealth and oppressive behaviour at the expense of social justice. Later commentary (*b. Sanh.* 109a–b; cf. Deut. 15.9) develops this to comedic extremes. The miserly Sodomites brag about wealth, complain about having to be hospitable, want to abolish the possibility of travelling through their land, make the poorest do extra work for the richest, allow the starving to die while taunting them with money, make victims of violence pay money for the privilege of bleeding, charge even more money for wading or swimming across a river to the person who cannot afford to take the boat, smear a person in honey and set bees on her for carrying out charitable acts, and have judges called Liar, Awful Liar, Forger, and Perverter of Justice, and so on.

All the other uses of 'sinner' are found in rabbinic literature. It is used in relation to Law observance (e.g. *t. Ned.* 1.1; *t. Sotah* 7.4), including criticisms of different interpretations of the Law, as the following example shows: 'He who latches on to the lenient rulings of the House of Shammai and to the lenient rulings of the House of Hillel is an evil man/sinner (רשע)' (*t. Yeb.* 1.13//*t. Eduy.* 2.3; cf. *m. Eduy.* 5.6; *m. Neg.* 12.6; *t. AZ* 6.18). The contrast with 'the righteous' is present (e.g. *m. Sanh.* 6.5; 8.5; 10.5 [cf. *t. Sanh.* 14.4]; *m. Abot* 4.15; *t. Sotah* 10.2–3; *t. Sanh.* 8.4; 13.2, 6), as well as a contrast between the disciples of 'Balaam the wicked' and the disciples of Abraham (*m. Abot* 5.19). The connection with idolaters and Gentiles is also present (e.g. *t. Sanh.* 13.2; the variant in *m. Ned.* 3.11 is telling), as is a repeated theme of judgement on 'sinners' (e.g. *m. Eduy.* 2.10; *m. Sanh.* 10.6; *m. Abot* 5.1, 19; *t. Sotah* 10.2–3; *t. Sanh.* 13.1–3, 6). There is also a relatively rare concern for the future of 'sinners' which has echoes in the Jesus tradition. In *m. Sanh.* 6.5: 'Said R. Meir, "... If thus is the Omnipresent distressed on account of the blood of the wicked when it is shed, how much the more so on account of the blood of the righteous!"' (cf. *t. Qidd.* 1.16). We will return to similar views below.

It is worth looking at the possible Aramaic (and the closely related Syriac) words underlying the Greek in the Gospels, not least because Aramaic was the language of Jesus and presumably integral to the earliest Palestinian tradition. As E. P. Sanders stressed, and as we have already seen in the Dead Sea Scrolls, Aramaic uses the same root as the Hebrew equivalent (רשע).[18] Bruce Chilton looked at this Aramaic equivalent in the later Isaiah Targum, which again reveals a number of themes familiar from above.[19] I have added to this a variety of uses of this Aramaic equivalent in other Aramaic translations of the Old Testament/Hebrew Bible which translate a number of Hebrew words and likewise continue all the themes we have so far seen (e.g. 1 Sam. 30.22; 2 Sam. 7.10; 16.7; 20.1; 1 Kgs 21.10, 13).[20] These include the idea that the root can be connected with the oppressive rich (e.g. *Tg.* Jer. 7.11 [cf. Mk 11.17]; *Tg.* Jer. 12.1), Babylon (*Tg.* Jer. 50.31–2), judgement (e.g. *Tg.* 1 Sam. 2.9; *Tg.* Jer. 23.19; 25.31; 30.23), and constructed in antithetical parallelism with 'righteous' (e.g. *Tg.* 2 Sam. 4.11 [Heb. לצדיק /Aram. זכי]), a parallelism of course repeated in the Aramaic and Syriac translations of the Psalms. Echoing Dunn's emphasis on factionalism, the root can be used of opponents of prophetic words (e.g. *Tg.* Jer. 14.14; 23.16, 26; 43.2). The root also often translates בליעל ('Belial', 'worthlessness', 'base wickedness', 'ruin') in the Targumim (e.g. *Tg.* 1 Sam. 2.12; 25.25; 30.22; *Tg.* 1 Kgs 21.10, 13) which might have some significance given that 'Belial' was understood as a demonic force and tied in with the language of 'sinners' at the time of the earliest Palestinian tradition, most notably in the Scrolls (cf. 1QM 4.1–4; 1QS 2.5; 11Q13 1, 2.11; 4Q511 1.6; CD 4.15–19).

In the Syriac Peshitta Psalms and the Aramaic Psalms Targum the word for the frequent equivalent (רשיעא) of the standard Greek term (ἁμαρτωλός) in the LXX is again from the same root as the Hebrew term (רשע).[21] However, there are other words used in the Peshitta Psalms to cover the standard Greek and Hebrew terms (notably עולא[22] and חטיא[23]). What this means is that there must be added uncertainty as to what Aramaic words might have been used in the earliest Palestinian tradition. The following example from the Psalms shows how interchangeable the words can be:

Happy are those who do not follow the advice of the wicked (MT: רשעים; LXX: ἀσεβῶν; Pesh.: עולא) or take the path the sinners (MT: חטאים; LXX:

ἁμαρτωλῶν; Pesh.: חטיא) tread, or sit at the seat of the scoffers ... Therefore the wicked (MT: רשעים; LXX: *οἱ ἀσεβεῖς*; Pesh.: רשיעא) will not stand in judgment, nor sinners (MT: חטאים; LXX: *ἁμαρτωλοὶ*; Pesh.: חטיא) in the congregation of the righteous ... (Ps. 1.1, 5)

Nevertheless, it might not be of great significance what the Aramaic word or words may have been in the earliest Palestinian tradition because the semantic areas of these words are overlapping and very similar (e.g. Pesh. Gen. 13.13; 18.23; Num. 16.26; 32.14; Dan. 12.10), as we have already seen in the case of the Hebrew (e.g. Pss. 1.1, 5; 103[104].35; Prov. 23.17; Amos 9.8; Isa. 1.4, 28; 1 Kgs 1.21). Another word (עולא) is common enough in the Peshitta and, in addition to translating the standard Hebrew term (רשע), can translate Hebrew words such as עון ('iniquity'), חמס ('violence, wrong'), מעל ('unfaithful, treacherous'), פשע ('transgression') in a range of now familiar contexts and meanings (e.g. Pesh. Gen. 6.11, 13; Lev. 5.15; 16.22; 18.25; 20.17, 19; 26.39–43; Num. 5.12; 14.18–19, 34; 15.13, 31; 18.23; Ezek. 33.8; Prov. 24.19–20), as well as בליעל ('Belial', 'worthlessness', etc., e.g. Deut. 15.9).

But, as Chilton has shown, there is another important Aramaic word in the Isaiah Targum covering 'a variety of defects in the Masoretic text': חובא ('debtor' or 'sinner'). The meanings are again familiar, as 'debtors' can include: those punished by the Messiah (11.4); those destroyed by the Lord (14.4–5); wicked Gentiles (34.2); and an enemy of Jerusalem (54.17).[24] We might add to Chilton's collection that 'debtor' is used with reference to 'sin' throughout the Peshitta as well as in senses we have seen throughout this chapter (e.g. Pesh. Gen. 15.16; Exod. 20.5; Exod. 34.7, 9; Num. 14.18; Deut. 5.9). And, of course, traces of the Aramaic use of 'debtor' appear to be found in the Gospel traditions (e.g. Matt. 6.12//Luke 11.4; Matt. 18.23–5; Luke 7.36–50; 16.1–9).[25] To this we might add that the Aramaic root (חוב) is unsurprisingly in use by the time of the Gospels (e.g. 11Q10 21.5; 34.4). We cannot, then, dismiss the possible use of the 'debtor' language as perhaps underlying the Synoptic tradition on the grounds of it being commonly used in later texts.

What this sort of analysis shows is that there was a stable use of words relating to the Synoptic 'sinner' over a thousand-year period and that Blomberg's comments are not an entirely fair reflection of the different words in Greek, Hebrew, and Aramaic/Syriac. It is clear that whenever socio-economic status is mentioned, it refers to people of wealth and people who are perceived to be oppressive, cruel, and unjust. These people are deemed Law-breakers who act beyond the covenant and, as Dunn showed, this could be reapplied to factional interpretations of the Law. They are people who are often thought to act as if there were no God. From this logic, it also follows that Gentiles are 'sinners' by default. These meanings are not, of course, mutually exclusive, and they are often used together or different uses might be implied. None of this is a controversial reading of the Jewish sources and is relatively straightforward and clear cut.

The Gospel use of 'sinner' is in line with everything else we know about the words for 'sinner' in a wide range of Jewish texts. We have already raised the possibility that the 'sinner' in Luke 7.36–50 is connected in some way to wealth (Luke 7.37; cf. Mark 14.3). There is the implication that 'sinners' can be perceived to be violent and wealthy in the fairly vague Mark 14.41 (//Matt. 26.45; cf. Luke 24.7) and possibly incorporating a reference to Gentiles. There may be further indication of wealthy 'sinners', as well as the common contrast between 'sinners' and 'righteous', in Mark 2.15–17 (//Matt. 9.10–13// Luke 5.29–32) where Jesus reclines with Levi, tax collectors, and 'sinners'. The reference to 'tax collectors' may imply that these sinners were deemed rich and oppressive.[26] We might compare such views of tax collectors in Luke. In Luke 18.13 the tax collector in the parable self-identifies as a 'sinner' whereas the 'sinner' Zacchaeus is a rich chief tax collector who had defrauded people in the past (Luke 19.7). Similarly, Josephus claims that John the tax collector is extremely rich (*War* 2.287, 292), while rabbinic literature shows that tax collectors should be viewed alongside robbers and murderers (*m. Ned.* 3.4) and were known to overcharge (*b. Sanh.* 25b), and Cicero suggests that tax collector and usurer were taboo livelihoods which would only result in being hated (Cicero, *De officiis* 1.150). Matt. 11.19//Luke 7.34 has Jesus accused of being a glutton and drunkard who associates with tax collectors and sinners. In addition to the link with tax collectors, this sort of behaviour was associated with the rich (e.g. *1 En.* 97.8–10; 98.2; Matt. 6.25–34//Luke 12.22–32). There is one possibility of 'sinner' referring to a person who might have been deemed poor and that is Peter in Luke 5.8 ('I am a sinful man' [ἀνὴρ ἁμαρτωλός]). But this is probably the least likely use in the

Gospel tradition to reflect earliest Palestinian tradition because it is only in Luke and it is a word Luke particularly likes. Regardless, quite what kind of 'sinner' Peter was supposed to be is unclear and the association of 'sinners' with tax collectors and wealth has multiple attestation of sources and forms which would suggest that this theme is part of pre-Gospel tradition, even if it is one Luke in particular liked.

Moreover, none of this excludes the possibility of other, complementary meanings, as we have already seen in the case of the antithetical parallelism in Mark 2.15–17. There are other general uses of such language, such as the reference to this 'adulterous and sinful' generation in Mark 8.38 or the Galilean 'sinners' of Luke 13.2. In certain cases it may be implied that there are legal issues. In Luke 19.1–9, Zacchaeus' behaviour may have fitted the stereotypical role of rich sinners and tax collectors but it is also behaviour against the Law (Luke 19.7). As we will see, hand-washing before ordinary meals was practised by some Pharisees in order to prevent the transmission of impurity from hands to food to eater and it remains a possibility that related concerns are part of the criticism of Jesus and the disciples reclining with 'sinners'.[27] It is a possibility (and no more than that) that the text on the 'sinner' of Luke 7.36–50 may also be about table purity given that she is criticized in the context of eating in a Pharisee's house.

'I now repent'!

'Sinners' returning to the fold is one aspect of their role in the Gospel tradition, notably in Luke 15. It has long been noted that while the Greek terms for repentance (*μετανοέω/μετάνοια*) might suggest a change of mind, the idea of returning to the fold coheres with the Semitic *teshubah/tetubah*-repentance (Hebrew root: שוב; Aramaic root: תיב/תוב; Greek: *ἐπιστρέφω*), which has more precise connotations of a complete reorientation of behaviour that involves a return of Jews to God and the Law. This concept is abundantly attested in Jewish texts.[28] Despite an overwhelmingly negative attitude towards 'sinners' and an overwhelming positive attitude towards their judgement, there were traditions which are similar to the Gospel tradition in that they look to the possibility of 'sinners' returning. The most influential text in this respect was Ezek. 33:

So you, son of man, I have made a sentinel for the house of Israel; whenever you hear a word from my mouth, you shall give them a warning from me. If I say to the wicked (לרשע/τῷ ἁμαρτωλῷ), 'O wicked ones (רשע), you shall surely die,' and you do not speak to warn the wicked (רשע/τὸν ἀσεβῆ) to turn from their ways, the wicked (הוא רשע/αὐτὸς ὁ ἄνομος) shall die in their iniquity, but their blood I will require at your hand. But if you warn the wicked (רשע /τῷ ἀσεβεῖ) to turn (לשוב / ἀποστρέψαι) from their ways, and they do not turn (ולא־שב/μὴ ἀποστρέψῃ) from their ways, they shall die in their iniquity, but you will have saved your life... Say to them, And I live, says the Lord God, I have no pleasure in the death of the wicked (הרשע/τοῦ ἀσεβοῦς), but that the wicked turn (בשוב רשע/τὸ ἀποστρέψαι τὸν ἀσεβῆ) from their ways and live; turn back, turn back (שובו שובו/ἀποστροφῇ ἀποστρέψατε) from your evil ways; for why you will die, O house of Israel?... And when the wicked turn (ובשוב רשע/ἐν τῷ ἀποστρέψαι τὸν ἁμαρτωλὸν) from their wickedness, and do what is lawful and right they shall live by them. (Ezek. 33.7–9, 11, 19)

Some Pharisees may also have been in agreement with the sentiment that 'sinners' could potentially repent, as *t. Qidd.* 1.16 interprets Ezek. 33 to claim that it was acceptable for a 'sinner' to repent, even at the end of their life. Similar ideas are also found elsewhere:

And immediately a voice came down from heaven to the Commander-in-chief, speaking thus, 'O Michael, Commander-in-chief... Abraham has not sinned and he has no mercy on sinners (τοὺς ἁμαρτωλοὺς). But I made the world, and I do not want to destroy any one of them; but I delay the death of the sinner (τοῦ ἁμαρτωλοῦ) until he should convert (ἐπιστρέψαι) and live.' (*T. Abr.* [A] 10.13–15; cf. Tob. 13.6; Wisd. 19.13; *T. Ben.* 4:2; *Pr. Man.* 5–8).[29]

There was also the possibility that Aramaic 'debtors' might repent:[30]

Continually do the prophets prophesy to instruct, if by chance the ears of the guilty/debtors (חייביא) may be opened and they receive instruction. If the house of Israel would but set their faces to observe the law, would he not gather them again from among the nations? (*Tg.* Isa. 28.24–25)

As the idea of returning to the Law is central to ideas of repentance in biblical and early Jewish literature,[31] the threat of judgement is, unsurprisingly, an interrelated theme (e.g. Jdt. 5.17–21; *T. Iss.* 6.3; *T. Dan* 5.1–13; *T. Abr.* [B] 12.13; *Ps. Sol.* 9.10; Tob. 13.1–6; 14.5–11; Wisd.

16.5–13; Sir. 5.4–8; 17.25; 18.13–14, 19–23; 21.1–14; 49.1–3; 4 Macc. 13.1–18). The Dead Sea Scrolls likewise use the language of 'returning' (תוב/שוב) when discussing repentance and their particular interpretations of the Law (e.g. 1QS 3.1; 10.20; 4Q171 11.1; 4Q256 9.7; 4Q266 5.i.15; CD 6.5; 10.3; 11.5; 15.12; 16.1–5; 4Q375 1.1–4; 4Q378 11–13; 14–17; 4Q504 1–2.ii.13),[32] as the following interpretation of Ps. 37.8–9 illustrates: 'Its interpretation concerns all who converted to the law (כול השבים לתורה), who do not refuse to convert from their wickedness (לשוב מרעתם), for all those who resist to convert from their sin (לשוב מעונם) will be cut off (4Q171 2.2–4).' An eschatological focus is also present among the Scrolls, as in the following example: 'And we are aware that part of the blessings and curses have occurred that are written in the b[ook of Mos]es. And this is the end of days, when they will return in Israel to the L[aw] and not turn bac[k] (שישובו בישראל לת]ורה...]ולוא ישובו אחו[ר])...' (4Q398 11–13, 3–5). In rabbinic literature repentance again concerns returning to the Law and doing good deeds (e.g. *m. Git.* 5.5; *m. Abot* 4.11, 17; *m. Ned.* 9.3; *m. BM* 4.10; *y. Mak.* 2.6, 31d; *b. Yoma* 86a–b; *b. Yeb.* 105a),[33] and the following example is one of the better known:

> Sin offering and the unconditional guilt-offering effect atonement; death and the Day of Atonement effect atonement if there is repentance (התשובה). Repentance (תשובה) effects atonement for lesser transgressions against both positive and negative commands in the law; while for graver transgressions it suspends punishment until the Day of Atonement comes and effects atonement. If a man said, 'I will sin and repent (ואשוב), and sin again and repent (ואשוב)', he will be given no chance to repent (לעשות תשובה)... (*m. Yoma* 8.8–9)

As with the case of 'sinners', this concept of 'repentance' is, then, stable and consistent from the Old Testament/Hebrew Bible through to rabbinic literature.

All this is consistent with Gospel uses and the understanding of Law observance in the Gospel tradition is presumably tied in with repentance.[34] First, we should note that the theme of repentance is found across the Synoptic tradition in independent sources and forms (irrespective of whether we include Q or not), which is some indication that it is a pre-Gospel theme (e.g. Mark 1.14–15, 40–5; 6.12; Matt. 11.20; Matt. 11.21//Luke 10.13; Matt. 12.41//Luke 11.32; Matt. 18.12–14//Luke 15.3–7;[35] Matt. 5.23; Luke 13.1–5; 15;

19.1–9). Sanders was certainly correct in asserting that the Greek words for repentance (μετανοέω and μετάνοια) are relatively infrequent in Mark and Matthew when compared to Luke,[36] but the *theme* of repentance is found across the Synoptic tradition, even if the precise words are not.[37] This theme is found in passages which non-polemically assume the validity of Jewish institutions in relation to repentance and which would again point towards being understood to reflect a time when such institutions were normative (e.g. Mark 1.40–5; Matt. 5.23; Luke 19.1–9). Additionally, this may suggest that repentance in the Synoptic tradition could also work with the assumption that practising the commandments was expected for those who would return, possibly couched in language of the fruits of repentance (cf. Matt. 3.8–10//Luke 3.8–9 [cf. Sir. 5.5–8]; Luke 13.1–9; Matt. 7.15–20). But we also have an explicit example of *teshubah*-repentance in Luke 15.11–32 as the rebellious son leaves to work with pigs but returns to enjoy a kosher meal. Such assumptions point to a lack of interference where Gentiles are concerned and to a context where observing the Law is part of the repentance process and thus to a pre-Lukan emphasis.[38] We might compare a well-known rabbinic parallel which is clearly part of the same kind of thinking:

> Another explanation: You will return to the Lord your God (Deut. 4.30). R. Samuel Pargrita said in the name of R. Meir: this can be compared to the son of a king who took to evil ways. The king sent a tutor to him who appealed to him saying, 'Repent, my son.' The son, however, sent him back to his father [with the message], 'How can I have the effrontery to return? I am ashamed to come before you.' Thereupon his father sent back word, 'My son, is a son ever ashamed to return to his father? And is it not to your father that you will be returning?' Similarly the Holy One, blessed be He, sent Jeremiah to Israel when they sinned, and said to him: 'Go and proclaim these words, etc.' (Jer. 3.12) Israel asked Jeremiah: 'How can we have the effrontery to return to God?' ... But God sent back word to them: 'My children, if you return, will you not be returning to your father?' (*Deut. R.* 2.24)

Luke clearly likes the parables of return and repentance that we see in Luke 15 but, collectively, all the points above cohere with the idea that this theme was inherited from earlier Palestinian tradition.

Sanders also argued that repentance was not important for Jesus because 'no one would have objected if Jesus persuaded tax collectors to leave the ranks of the wicked: everybody else would have benefited.

If he were a successful reformer of dishonest tax collectors, Jesus would not have drawn criticism.'[39] But some creative thinking should illustrate the problems with this. What if a Pharisee repented and joined the people responsible for writing the Dead Sea Scrolls? What if a Sadducee turned to the Pharisees? If, say, the Jesus movement gained increasing numbers, might not some associated with a different group start to worry, as they seem to according to Luke 15.1–2, 25–32? We certainly do know that different early Jewish groups could be discussed and remembered in terms of conflict with one another (e.g. *Ant.* 13.296–8, 408–11; *War* 1.650–63; 1QpHab 11.2–8; 4Q171 4.8–9; Gal. 1.14).[40] If there is a legal element to understanding 'sinners', this context of conflict might be further reflected in the Synoptic tradition (cf. Mark 2.15–17; Matt. 11.19//Luke 7.34). We certainly do have a tradition with multiple attestation concerning conflict over the Law which adds further weight to repentance being potentially controversial in Palestinian Judaism (e.g. Mark 2.15–17, 23–8; 3.1–6; 7.1–23; Matt. 23.23//Luke 11.42; Matt. 23.25–6//Luke 11.39–41; Matt. 23.1–22, 24; Luke 13.10–17; 14.1–6).

Association with people deemed unpleasant outsiders could also have been a problematic aspect of repentance in the Synoptic tradition,[41] a view which has the most obvious textual support (e.g. Mark 2.16; Luke 15.1–2). Associating with 'sinners', who were regularly regarded as oppressive, unjust, violent, and rich, could easily be seen as siding with the very people representative of the economic injustices in (say) Galilee. Sirach also contains some common-sense sayings about the malignant influence of 'sinners' (e.g. Sir. 28.9; 41.5), such as the following: 'Who pities a snake charmer when he is bitten, or all those who go near wild animals? So no one pities a person who associates with a sinner (ἀνδρὶ ἁμαρτωλῷ) and becomes involved in the other's sins' (Sir. 12.13–14). There is evidence of a related allegation as Jesus is remembered for being a glutton and a drunkard in his association with tax collectors and 'sinners' (Matt. 11.19//Luke 7.34). And what if trying to get rich 'sinners' to repent did not actually work very well in practice?[42] What excuse then would there be for associating with them? Indeed, we do not get much in the way of 'sinners' actually changing their ways in the Gospel tradition and there presumably would have been plenty more stories had there been widespread successes. There are exceptions such as Zacchaeus, though even he did not give up everything (Luke 19.8) as the Markan rich man was supposed to do. And we should not rule out the possibility that this Lukan exception was created because of a lack of success. It is worth comparing the nuanced wording of Sanders here: 'no one would have objected if Jesus persuaded tax collectors to leave the ranks of the wicked: everybody else would have benefited. If he were *a successful reformer* of dishonest tax collectors, Jesus would not have drawn criticism. But in fact he was criticised *for associating with them*' (my italics).[43] Does not Sanders also emphasize the difference between *association with* tax collectors and 'sinners'/the wicked, on the one hand, and *the reforming of* 'sinners'/the wicked, on the other?

Sanders suggested that Jesus may not have imposed certain requirements on sinners and this reflects a common assumption that Jesus permitted people to bypass the Temple system.[44] Even if we put aside the point that it is likely that a call to repentance is from pre-Gospel tradition, there is not, as I have argued in detail elsewhere, sufficient evidence in the Synoptic tradition to suggest that this involved people bypassing the Temple system or 'ritual' repentance when it was required.[45] For instance, such sentiments are absent from the Synoptic tradition, as are any such criticisms, and these absences are all the more striking in light of the Synoptic tradition remembering Jesus upholding the Temple or traditional systems of retribution (Mark 1.40–5; Matt. 5.23; Luke 19.1–9). And, when we do get some discussion of what the problem was, it is because of Jesus' association with tax collectors and 'sinners', as the criticism in Mark 2.16 (and Luke 15.1–2, and the implied criticism in Matt. 11.19//Luke 7.34) makes clear: 'Why does he eat with tax collectors and sinners?'[46]

Returning to the Law

The pre-Gospel tradition, quite probably the earliest Palestinian tradition, discusses 'sinners' repenting and this would have been in the form of a return to the Law. Indeed, as Jonathan Klawans has shown, sin, particularly as understood in early Christianity, could be seen as having a defiling function for individual sinners.[47] We should therefore make some comments on what kind of understanding of the Law this would have been. As I have argued elsewhere, there is a strong tendency to present Jesus debating the specifics of the interpretation of biblical Law but never criticizing or overriding biblical Law.[48] Yet, as Klawans also points out, the emphasis on the defiling nature of 'moral' behaviour comes through in the discussions of purity, no doubt because of the related language of defilement in the relevant Gospel passages. To illustrate the kinds of 'moral' issues in the earliest Palestinian tradition (and developments) we have already seen in the case of 'sinners', we can turn to three independent purity traditions where this behaviour is constructed over against specific interpretations of purity law in Mark 7.1–23//Matt. 15.1–20 Matt. 23.25–6//Luke 11.39–41, and Luke 10.29–37. We will first cover the assumptions of early Jewish purity laws in the passages before moving on to see how the purity themes within these passages relate to the possible social contexts and how specific emphases would become redirected, ignored, or modified as inclusion of Gentiles became an issue in the Gospel tradition.

WASHING HANDS (MARK 7.1–23//MATT. 15.1–20)

Mark 7.1–23 (//Matt. 15.1–20) provides the most extensive treatment of purity in the Gospel tradition and I have discussed this in detail elsewhere.[49] The contrast between 'tradition' and biblical commandments, a contrast made or implied elsewhere (e.g. Gal. 1.13–14; *Ant.* 13. 297–8, 408–9), is strongly emphasized in Mark 7.1–13 where 'human tradition/tradition of the elders' occurs six times. Mark elaborates more precisely on the content of this 'tradition', such as washing with the hand in the shape of a fist (πυγμῇ), immersion of cups, pitchers, bronze kettles, and beds/dining couches (καὶ κλινῶν),[50] and *qorban*.[51] This context assists in the interpretation of Mark 7.15, 19. As is increasingly recognized, Mark 7.15, 19 continues the construction of biblical commandments over against the 'tradition' of hand-washing, as Matt. 15.20 stresses.[52] This becomes clearer when we turn to understandings of purity law in early Judaism. Washing hands before ordinary food (Mark 7.1–5) is discussed in rabbinic literature (e.g. *m. Hag.* 2.5; *m. Hul.* 2.5; *m. Yad.* 3.2; *t. Ber.* 4.8; 5.6; *t. Dem.* 2.11–12; *b. 'Erub.* 21b) and Mark has some precise knowledge of hand-washing practices. The inclusion of 'with the fist' (πυγμῇ) refers to a practice of using the minimal amount of water required for hand-washing whereby the hand in the shape of a fist is sufficiently relaxed to allow water to cover enough of the hand for purification (e.g. *m. Yad.* 1.1–2; 2.1–3; cf. CD 10.10–13; *y. Ber.* 8.2, 12; *b. Hul.* 106a–b).[53] Mark further explains a number of related table purity 'traditions', including Mark 7.4 and the 'tradition' of Pharisees immersing themselves on return from the market. Mark 7.4a may appear ambiguous (*ἀπ' ἀγορᾶς ἐὰν μὴ βαπτίσωνται οὐκ ἐσθίουσιν*) but the translation of self-immersion (rather than an implied immersion of food) follows the normal grammatical use (of the plural middle *βαπτίσωνται*) and well-established practices of bodily immersion (rather than immersion of food, which is otherwise unknown).[54] Moreover, as we will see, bodily immersion was discussed as a known part of table purification processes. Mark 7.4 further discusses the immersion of cups, pitchers, and bronze kettles. These 'traditions' were developments of precise laws such as Lev. 11.32–3 and Lev. 15.12, which were interpreted generally, at least by the time of the Mishnah, with reference to the relevant utensils (e.g. *m. Miqw.* 3:10; *m. Hul.* 1.6; *m. Kel.* 2.1; 5.11; 11.1; 13.6; 14.1; 15.1; 16.1–2; 17.1; 20.2; 22.1–2; 27.1). The variant reading 'and dining couches/beds' (*καὶ κλινῶν*) was also part of the interpretation of Lev. 11.32 and 15.11. These couches were immersed according to rabbinic law and the Hebrew word (מטה) is the direct equivalent of Mark's Greek word (*κλίνη*) (*m. Miqw.* 7.7; *m. Kel.* 19.1).[55] Contrary to some strands of scholarship, Mark did not polemically invent the 'traditions' of 7.1–5;[56] on the contrary, he reported these practices very precisely.

Mark 7.1–5 records these 'traditions' because they relate to discussions of the transmission of impurity.[57] In the dominant rabbinic explanation of the transmission of impurity, ordinary food is most susceptible to second degree impurity, that is, at a second remove from the scriptural source (e.g. *m. T. Yom* 4.1, 3; *m. Sotah* 5.2). Hands, assumed to be second degree impure, could not render ordinary food impure because that which is assumed to be second degree impure cannot defile something else susceptible to second degree impurity alone (e.g. *m. Yad.* 3.1). This meant that impure hands could not make ordinary food impure. This would not match with the assumed logic in Mark 7.1–23 and has led some scholars to suggest that the rabbinic system was not established in the first century.[58] However, the role of liquids suggests otherwise.[59] Liquids play an important part in the transmission of impurity. The laws surrounding liquids are precise in

Lev. 11.29–38 but were also expanded broadly in rabbinic literature and also earlier in Palestinian tradition (e.g. 4Q284a; 4Q274 3; 4Q394 8.4, 5–7; CD 12.15–17). What this meant was that hands that are assumed to be second degree impure could pass on impurity to ordinary food (e.g. *m. Parah* 8.7; *m. Zab.* 5.12; *m. Hul.* 2.5; *b. Hul.* 33a).[60] The definition of 'liquids' is clearly related to table purity: dew, water, wine, oil, blood, milk, and honey (*m. Maksh.* 6.4; cf. CD 12.15–17). At this point it is worth returning to the reference to bodily immersion in Mark 7.4 and the case of the *tebul yom* (someone who has immersed that day and is waiting for sunset to be deemed pure again; Lev. 15). A *tebul yom* can be assumed to be second degree impure (e.g. *m. Zab.* 5.3) but, crucially, a *tebul yom* cannot render liquid impure whereas impure hands can. Moreover, the hands of a *tebul yom* could be second degree impure *in distinction from* the rest of the body and are *independently* capable of defiling (e.g. *m. T. Yom* 2.2; cf. *b. Shab.* 14a; *b. Sukk.* 26b). Quite why Pharisees and rabbis were keen to prevent the transmission of impurity from hand to food to eater is less easy to establish. John Poirier has given as good an explanation as any in his interpretation of *b. Ber.* 28a and the phrase 'insides are not as their outsides'. He suggests that this phrase refers to those outside the pre-70 Pharisaic movement who did not keep their insides pure through the washing of hands.[61]

This understanding of purity law further clarifies the interpretation of Mark 7.1–23 if we place it in the context of purity law. Impurity could be contracted, for example, at the marketplace (Mark 7.4). This would require bodily immersion to remove the impurity. Nevertheless, hands were still liable to become impure and defile food and so hands would have to be washed to prevent the transmission of impurity from hand to food (via a liquid) to the insides. This background, and the Markan attention to detail in his editorial aside (Mark 7.3–4), sheds further light on the saying 'there is nothing outside a person that by going in can defile, but the things that come out are what defile' (Mark 7.15) and 'he declared all foods clean' (Mark 7.19). Mark's Jesus is critiquing the transmission of impurity from hands to the insides and, from this perspective, all foods (permitted in the Torah).

WASHING CUPS (MATT. 23.25–6//LUKE 11.3–41)

Matt. 23.25–6//Luke 11.39–41 is an example of an independent tradition which deals more precisely with the transmission of impurity and keeping the insides pure through the issue of washing cups.[62] It does not make much difference if this is a Q tradition or Luke using Matthew because there are enough similarities to understand this instance of table purity (e.g. Pharisees cleansing outsides of vessels, distinction between inside and outside, insides full of greed and self-indulgence, some kind of cleansing of the inside).[63] Matthew's reference to cleansing the inside of the cup is a potentially significant difference from Luke's giving alms. However, it is more likely that Luke is 'mistaken', as he is in the case of tithing (Luke 11.42; cf. *m. Shebi.* 9.1), as washing insides of cups in Lukan hands now refers more to human morality alone with no emphasis on the purity of vessels. Moreover, almsgiving reflects a Lukan interest and if Matthew knew of a tradition with reference to 'almsgiving', it is more difficult to appreciate why he would drop it (cf. Matt. 6.2–4). This also assumes that we are dealing with an independent tradition, though if Luke used Matthew then it is obviously more likely that Luke is the later source which in turn would mean that there are greater limitations for reconstructing the earlier tradition. We will return to the possibility of an Aramaic source underlying Matt.23.25–6//Luke 11.39–41 below.

Matt. 23.25–26//Luke 11.39–41 is to be located in the context of disputes over interpretation of purity laws. There is even a tacit endorsement of cleansing cups in 'first cleanse the inside' and this is to be expected from standard purity texts (Lev. 11.3; 15.12).[64] To understand the logic of this purity dispute we need additional discussion of the role of the transmission of impurity.[65] One of the most relevant texts for understanding Matt. 23.25–6//Luke 11.39–41 is *m. Kelim* 25, particularly as it opens with the distinction between insides and outsides of cups:[66] 'All utensils have outsides and an inside' (*m. Kelim* 25.1). Some authorities believed there were more than two parts of a utensil: 'All utensils have outer parts and an inner part, and they [further] have a part by which they are held' (*m. Kelim* 25.7a). Further nuanced debate was carried out between R. Tarfon and R. Aqiba and then R. Meir and R. Yose:

R. Tarfon says, [This distinction in the outer parts applies only] to a large wooden trough. Aqiba says, To cups. R. Meir says, To the unclean and the clean hands. Said R. Yose, They have spoken only concerning clean hands alone. How so? [If] one's hands were clean, and the outer parts of the cup were unclean, [and] one took [the cup] with its holding part, he need not worry lest his hands be made unclean on the outer parts of the cup. [If] one was drinking from a cup, the outer parts of which are unclean, one does not worry lest the liquid which is in his mouth be made unclean on the outer parts of the cup and go and render the [whole] cup unclean. A kettle [unclean on the outside] which is boiling—one does not worry lest the liquids go forth from it and touch its outer parts and go back to the inside [and make it unclean]. (*m. Kelim* 25.7–8)

Another important text for understanding the impurity of cups is *m. Ber*. 8.2: 'The House of Shammai say, "They wash the hands and then mix the cup [of wine]." But the House of Hillel say, "They mix the cup and then wash the hands."' The Tosefta explains further: 'The House of Shammai say, They wash the hands then mix the cup—lest liquids on the outer surface of the cup become impure through contact with hands and in turn render the cup impure. The House of Hillel say, The outer surface of the cup is always deemed impure' (*t. Ber*. 5.26). The traditions based on *m. Kelim* 25.7–8 and *m. Ber*. 8.2 are brought together in the Palestinian Talmud on the basis that they essentially reflect the same debate: 'R. Biban in the name of R. Yohanan, The opinion of the House of Shammai accords with the view of R. Yose, and the opinion of the House of Hillel accords with the view of R. Meir' (*y. Ber*. 8.2). The position associated with R. Yose and Shammai meant that, according to R. Yose, '[If] one's hands were clean, and the outer parts of the cup were unclean, [and] one took [the cup] with its holding part, he need not worry lest his hands be made unclean on the outer parts of the cup' (*m. Kelim* 25.8). However, this cannot apply to impure hands; as the Shammaite position has it: 'lest liquids on the outer surface of the cup become impure through contact with hands and in turn render the cup impure' (*t. Ber*. 5.26). The position associated with R. Meir and the Hillelites does not accept this. Concerning the distinction between handles and outsides, the view of R. Yose likewise applies to R. Meir if hands are pure: '[If] one's hands were clean, and the outer parts of the cup were unclean, [and] one took [the cup] with its holding part, he need not worry lest his hands be made unclean on the outer parts of the cup' (*m. Kelim* 25.8). Yet R. Meir and the Hillelites disagree with the view of R. Yose and the Shammaites that they first wash the hands 'lest liquids on the outer surface of the cup become impure through contact with hands and in turn render the cup impure'. For R. Meir and the Hillelites even impure hands could not make the whole cup impure through contact with the liquid on the outside of the cup. R. Meir appears to include a further possibility in the case of the outside being pure which goes against R. Yose and Shammai:[67] the handle of the cup can be held by impure hands and there is no concern, 'lest liquids on the outer surface of the cup become impure through contact with hands and in turn render the cup impure'.

The Shammaite position about the impurity of the outsides of cups and the discussion of the distinctions between the insides and outsides of cups would suggest that Matt. 23.25–6//Luke 11.38–41 ought to be read in light of such purity laws. However, the same sort of evidence has led to an influential counterargument and objection by Hyam Maccoby. For Maccoby, 'It is unquestionable that there was only one way of washing ritually-unclean vessels, whether wholly or partly unclean: to immerse them totally in a *Miqveh* (ritual immersion pool) ... there was no custom of washing cups on the outside only.'[68] Yet Maccoby's objection is not quite the full story. It is more likely that Matt. 23.25–6//Luke 11.39–41 refers more to a position associated with R. Aqiba, as *Kelim* mentions other outer parts of utensils (bases, rims, hangers, and handles) which require cleansing through drying or wiping:

> Bases of utensils, and their rims, and their hangers, and the handles of utensils which hold [something = which have a receptacle], on which fell [unclean] liquids—*one dries them, and they are clean* ... A utensil, the outer parts of which have been made unclean with liquids—the outer parts are unclean. Its inside, its rims, hangers, and handles are clean. [If] its inside is made unclean, the whole is unclean. (*m. Kelim* 25.6, my italics)

While not precise, in the case of the language of 'outside' (ἔξωθεν) in Matt. 23.25//Luke 11.39, we should probably envisage this as referring to the practice of drying the base, rim, hanger, and handle as distinct from the insides.[69]

Maccoby's critique was part of his larger objection to reading Matt. 23.25–6//Luke 11.38–41 in the context of purity law. Instead, Maccoby believed that hygiene is the most obvious frame of reference. He claimed that the Greek term (*καθαρίζω*) 'can be used of literal, spiritual or ritual cleansing. For the literal use, see, for example, Septuagint Proverbs 25.4, *καθαρισθήσεται*, referring to the purification of silver from dross.'[70] However, Prov. 25.4 appears to be the only 'literal' occurrence in LXX from over one hundred occurrences. Prov. 25.4 also concerns the removal of dross from silver, which is not a sufficiently close parallel to warrant such an unusual usage in the interpretation of Matt. 23.25–6//Luke 11.38–41. In contrast, the standard LXX use of the Greek term for purifying (*καθαρίζω*) is to translate some form of the precise Hebrew word (טהר) most frequently used to discuss purity and also used throughout *m. Kelim* 25 and the traditions surrounding *m. Ber.* 8.2. Collectively, this would point clearly in a similar direction for the same use of purification in Matt. 23.25–6//Luke 11.38–41. The usual usage of the Greek term for purifying (*καθαρίζω*) in New Testament texts would further undermine Maccoby's use of a rare LXX parallel. In this respect, Maccoby undermined his own argument:

> All Jews were familiar with the difference between a clean and a dirty cup, and the image of a vessel that was clean on the outside but dirty on the inside as a metaphor of hypocrisy was perfectly intelligible to them, as was the similar figure of the whitewashed tomb which is 'full of dead men's bones and all kinds of filth.'[71]

The reason this undermines Maccoby's argument is that corpse impurity was the strongest and most notorious form of impurity and the additional reference to Matt. 23.27 actually supports the reading in the context of impurity. The use of a Greek term (*ἀκαθαρσία*) which can be used in the context of moral impurity should not overlook its close relationship with 'ritual' impurity. LXX uses of the Greek term (*ἀκαθαρσία*) typically translate the precise Hebrew word (טמא) used in the context of impurity in the Hebrew Bible/Old Testament and in rabbinic literature. Once more, the collective argument strongly favours reading Matt. 23.25–6//Luke 11.38–41 in the context of purity language while Maccoby's alternative does not stand up to close scrutiny.

THE GOOD SAMARITAN (LUKE 10.29–37)

Matt. 23.25–6//Luke 11.38–41 is presented as another critique of a different emphasis on purity laws but which again works with the assumption of the general validity of the biblical purity laws. As with Mark 7.1–23, the passage also makes sense in the context of early Jewish purity discussions, although there may be more tacit acceptance of the opinions of the Pharisaic opponents. Like Mark, there is an emphasis on prioritizing 'moral' purity, as is the contrast between 'inner' and 'outer' moral purity, imagery used and implied elsewhere (e.g. Matt. 5.27–8; Matt. 6.16–18; Matt. 23.27–8). The final example—the parable of the Good Samaritan (Luke 10.29–37)—is different in that the passage most likely concerns issues surrounding corpse impurity but the overall attitude towards purity is similar to Mark 7.1–23 and Matt. 23.25–6//Luke 11.38–41.

The Lukan parable gives us a clue about the importance of corpse impurity in that the person is 'half-dead' and the characters are judged over whether they will risk touching him. In the case of the priest, the passage has been assessed in terms of a stark contrast with the priestly commandment in Lev. 21.1–3:[72]

> The Lord said to Moses: Speak to the priests, the sons of Aaron, and say to them: No one shall defile himself for a dead person among his relatives/people (בעמיו), except for his nearest kin: his mother, his father, his son, his daughter, his brother; likewise, for a virgin sister, close to him because she has had no husband, he may defile himself for her.

Yet Lev. 21.1–3 is actually an important passage in early Jewish law in Palestine for the discussion of dealing with an abandoned corpse, and Luke 10.29–37 fits in with these sorts of debates, as well as with debates over the interpretation of purity laws outside the Temple. For a start, Lev. 21.1–3 does not mention any serious punishment for transgression which stands in contrast to the rest of Lev. 21, though an impure priest would not be able to serve in the Temple (cf. Ezek. 44.25–7). There are presumably practical reasons for this lack of punishment as it is not difficult to imagine priests contracting impurity unwittingly (Lev. 5.3) and there appears to have been attempts to prevent the possibility of unwittingly contracting corpse impurity (e.g. Luke 11.44//Matt. 23.27). The case of the Nazirite

(Num. 6) provides an important analogy in that we have people who were dedicated to strict observance of purity laws yet the possibilities of contracting corpse impurity were known. The Nazirite should not contract corpse impurity even from close relatives but Num. 6 raises the possibility that a nearby person might suddenly die. If this is the case, head-shaving and offerings are required of the Nazirite (Num. 6.9–12). There is also a crucial qualification mentioned in Lev. 21.1, namely that a priest should not contract corpse impurity when 'among his relatives/people', which links to the issue of what to do with an unattended corpse in the countryside. In the case of the parable of the Good Samaritan, there is already a potential exemption for the priest as he is not among his people.[73] The reason for an abandoned corpse being problematic is found in Num. 19.16: 'Whoever in the open field touches one who has been killed by a sword or who has died, or a human bone, or a grave, will be unclean seven days.' These texts for the general legal context for the debate attributed to the late first century between R. Eliezer b. Hyrcanus and the Sages have clear similarities with the parable of the Good Samaritan (*m. Nazir* 7.1). They debate whether there should be exemptions in the case of the Nazirite and the high priest when faced with an unattended corpse:

> A high priest and a Nazir do not contract corpse uncleanness on account of [burying even] their close relatives. But they do contract corpse uncleanness on account of a neglected corpse. [If] they were going along the way and found a neglected corpse—R. Eliezer says, 'Let a high priest contract corpse uncleanness, but let a Nazir not contract corpse uncleanness.' And the Sages say, 'Let a Nazir contract corpse uncleanness, but let a high priest not contract corpse uncleanness.' (*m. Nazir* 7.1; cf. Num. 6.1–12; Lev. 21.11–12; *Spec. Leg.* 1.113–15, 250)

The passage obviously discusses the case of the high priest but clearly someone like R. Eliezer would have likely agreed with the sentiment in the parable of the Good Samaritan that the priest should have been prepared to contract corpse impurity in such circumstances.

Luke 10.29–37 provides some important further details.[74] Keeping in mind the sharp descent from Jerusalem (*War* 4.452–3),[75] the priest and the Levite are not presented as about to serve in the Temple. On the contrary: 'Now by chance a priest *was going down* (κατέβαινεν) *that road*; and when he saw him, he passed by on the other side. So likewise a Levite...' (Luke 10.31–2). Nor was the person who had been attacked en route to the Temple. They too were 'going down (κατέβαινεν) from Jerusalem to Jericho' (Luke 10.30). This means that we should not be locating the debate as an overriding of Lev. 21.1–3 because the action would then be taking place *upwards* and *towards* the Temple.[76] Rather, the debate is about the interpretation and expansion of purity law outside the Temple and is very much akin to the debate in *m. Nazir* 7.1. This also illuminates the choice of the Samaritan. This is not, as is often romantically pointed out, the 'subversive' or 'shocking' expansion of Jewish boundaries to include so-called 'despised' outsiders.[77] What works better in the context of legal disputes is the construction of Samaritans as people known to have the Pentateuch as their text and deemed to be very similar to the Sadducees in this respect (cf. *m. Sheb.* 8.10; b. *Qidd.* 75b; and *m. Nidd.* 4.2, 'The daughters of the Sadducees, if they follow the ways of their fathers, are deemed like to the women of the Samaritans').[78] With the Lukan Jesus and the scribe prioritizing the *Shema*' (Deut. 6.5) and loving the neighbour (Lev. 19.18), the presentation is once again that of 'commandments' in tension with 'tradition', as we saw more explicitly in Mark 7.1–23.

PURITY, 'HISTORICITY', AND GALILEE

The assumptions of purity laws outlined above are important for understanding the kinds of contexts in early Palestinian tradition where the details of Jewish purity laws were common enough but were less likely to be common outside the assumptions of specifically Jewish purity laws. It is clear that the general sentiment concerning purity and impurity can be located in early Palestinian tradition, or, at the very least, make best sense in first-century Palestine. Put another way, there is clear evidence that these specifically Jewish views of purity would have resonance in first-century Palestine and limited resonance among non-Jews elsewhere. One point is obvious: purity issues of the sort we find in Mark 7.1–23, Matt. 23.25–6//Luke 11.38–41, and Luke 10.29–37 are clearly the kinds of concerns associated with Palestinian Judaism (e.g. *War* 2.129–31, 150; 1QS 5.1–2, 8–9, 13, 14; *m. Ber.* 8.2; *m. Hag.* 2.5; *m. Yad.* 3.1; *t. Ber.* 5.26). We also know there are immersion pools in the region which were used for the removal of impurity (cf. Lev. 11.36; 15.13; Judith 12.6–10) and stone vessels, which were immune to impurity (*m. Kelim* 10.1–3; cf. *m. Parah* 3:2; *m. Kelim* 5.11; 6.2–4; 22.10), were also present in first-century Palestine.[79] All this reflects the concern of some for expanded purity laws and their practice outside the Temple as often as possible. Again, these were not the sort of concerns that dominated the early church.

It is also clear that we have consistent purity sentiments running across Mark 7.1–23, Matt. 23.25–6//Luke 11.39–41, and Luke 10.29–37. It is probably fair to say these passages are examples of this sentiment turning up independently, at least independent in the sense that there is no direct copying of Mark 7.1–23 in Matt. 23.25–6//Luke 11.39–41, and Luke 10.29–37, and in these two cases similar assumptions are simply made in different contexts. Individual passages give some indication that we are dealing with a pre-Gospel theme that goes back to early Palestinian tradition. In the case of Mark 7.1–23 it is certainly clear that we are dealing with Markan editing and construction. But, wherever Mark may have been written and for whatever audience(s), we are presumably dealing with a view of purity attributed to Jesus which predates the Gospel and one which, taken alone, has minimal concern for those uninterested in purity law which, as far as we know, was much of first-century Christianity, certainly outside Palestine (hence the need for the Markan explanation). It is also worth pointing out that if we could take away the editorial Mark 7.3–4, 19 we potentially have a source which assumed the complex transmission of impurity in a context where such things could be assumed. Again, this is something not associated with what we know about first-century Christianity and which would make best sense in the context of earlier Palestinian tradition with little concern for a movement engaging with non-Jews.

There might also be evidence for the possibility of Luke and Matthew sharing a common Aramaic source in the case of Matt. 23.26//Luke 11.41.[80] Wellhausen, and others working on the Aramaic substrata of the Gospels, pointed to Luke seemingly misreading the Aramaic דכו ('purify') for זכו ('give alms') so that Matthew more likely reflects the earlier pre-Gospel tradition. This view has been challenged, particularly over whether it would have been possible to confuse ד and ז, whether graphically, orally, or aurally.[81] But sometimes the debate can miss the point if, as it sometimes seems to on both sides, it works with the assumption of whether or not Luke made an 'honest mistake'. It is entirely possible, of course, that Luke made a deliberate change—an argument enhanced if Luke or his audience did not understand the sorts of practices concerning the washing of insides of cups as outlined in *m. Kelim* 25. It looks likely, for instance, that Luke 11.42, unlike Matt. 23.23, 'misunderstood' issues of tithing by adding that Pharisees tithe rue and 'all kinds of herbs' when this was not the case according to rabbinic literature (*m. Shebi.* 9.1) and may well have misread שבתא ('dill'—so Matt. 23.23) for שברא ('rue').[82] Two deliberate 'misreadings' by Luke of some very specific pieces of Jewish law in such close literary proximity must at least be a reasonable possibility. We might add that this provides further reason why an independent tradition like the Good Samaritan is important because it would suggest that Luke inherited assumptions he did not necessarily understand, that precise details were not overly important for him, and that issues of purity were not urgent for his understanding of Christianity. Nevertheless, whatever the reasoning, it remains that the two Aramaic words posited as underlying Matt. 23.25–6//Luke 11.39–41 remain strikingly similar and, at the very least, we should entertain the possibility that the two differences in Matthew and Luke can be explained with reference to an underlying Aramaic source.

Disputes and debates concerning interpretation of the Law and 'tradition' were also the sort associated with early Palestinian Judaism.[83] In the halakhic letter to opponents, 4QMMT, expositions of purity laws are included, suggesting that the following might be the best approach for the preparation for the end times: 'we have written to you some works of the Torah which we think are good for you and for your people ... Reflect on all these matters.... so that at the end of time, you may rejoice in finding that some of our words are true' (4Q399 14–17 II = 4QMMT C 25–32). Different competing interpretations of the Law were found among various individuals and different groups. Josephus describes some legal disagreements between the Pharisees and Sadducees. Jonathan the Sadducee is believed to have influenced John Hyrcanus in order that he might side with the Sadducees and abandon the Pharisees. Hyrcanus was said to have abrogated the regulations which Pharisees had established for the people, punishing those who observe them (*Ant.* 13.296). Josephus further provides a general explanation for the differences between the Sadducees and Pharisees:

the Pharisees have delivered to the people a great many observances by succession from their fathers, which are not written in the laws of Moses; and for that reason it is that the Sadducees reject them, and say that we are to esteem those observances to be obligatory which are in the written word, but are not to observe what are derived from the tradition of our forefathers. And concerning these things it is that great disputes and differences have arisen among them, while the Sadducees are able to persuade none but the rich, and have not the populace favourable to them, but the Pharisees have the multitude on their side. (*Ant.* 13.297–8)

Similarly, Paul claimed to have been 'as to the Law a Pharisee' (Phil. 3.5) who was 'far more zealous for the traditions of my ancestors' (Gal. 1.13–15; cf. Phil. 3.6). Paul's persecution of the earliest Jesus movement may have been because of legal issues, though the evidence is far from clear on the nature of the conflict.[84] We might add to all this the numerous disputes and arguments over the details of legal issues found in early rabbinic literature. Clearly, then, the purity disputes and discussions found in Mark 7.1–23, Matt. 23.25–6//Luke 11.39–41, and Luke 10.29–37 are most obviously at home in Palestinian Judaism and less obviously at home in earliest Christianity, which was more concerned about whether the Law should be observed at all.

We also have closely analogous social contexts for understanding this emphasis in the earliest tradition which tie this discussion of purity back to the discussion of tax collectors and 'sinners', not least if we were to understand texts such as Mark 2.15–17 as also involving table purity. This would make purity discussions reflect the kinds of behaviour to which they should be 'returning'. There are indications that this pre-Gospel emphasis was connected with the Galilean social upheavals that have been stressed throughout this book.[85] The example of the displacement of the population of Tiberias according to Josephus is once again important:

Tiberias . . . The new settlers were a promiscuous rabble, no small contingent being Galilean, with such as were drafted from territory subject to him [Herod Antipas] and brought forcibly to the new foundation. Some of these were magistrates. Herod accepted as participants even poor men who were brought in to join the others from any and all places of origin. It was in question whether some were even free beyond cavil. These latter he often and in large bodies liberated and benefited imposing the condition that they should not quit the city, by equipping houses at his own expense and adding new gifts of land. For he knew that this settlement was contrary to the law and tradition of the Jews because Tiberias was built on the site of tombs that had been obliterated, of which there were many there. And our law declares that such settlers are unclean for seven days. (*Ant.* 18.36–8)

The earliest Palestinian tradition would have resonated with the type of people who lived in situations where observance of certain expansions of purity traditions were either not possible or desirable and it is worth noting that Josephus indicates that these were people of differing socio-economic standing. Another closely analogous context comes from rabbinic literature and the references to 'the people of the land' ('*am ha-aretz*), even though it has often been abused as a background for understanding 'sinners'.[86] Many of these traditions come from agricultural contexts but it is not possible to generalize about socio-economic status as the 'people of the land' could include the slave-owners and landowners as well as agricultural workers (e.g. *t. Demai* 3.5; *t. Abod. Zar.* 3.9).[87] In terms of purity discussions, tax collectors could be described in ways similar to the 'people of the land' (*m. Tohor.* 7.6). This is perhaps no surprise as the 'people of the land' appear to be a group constructed and understood in terms of their observance or non-observance of rabbinic purity and tithing laws (*t. Abod. Zar.* 3.10; *b. Ber.* 43b; *b. Git.* 61a; *b. Ned.* 90b; *b. Ber.* 47b; *ARN* [A] 41), which of course had its roots in Pharisaic law (*m. Hag.* 2.7).

This analogous context is of further importance because rabbinic literature remembers the 'people of the land' being generally suspect in the transmission of impurity:

He who gives over his key to an '*am ha-aretz*—the house is clean, for he gave him only [the charge of] guarding the key. (*m. Tohorot* 7.1)

He who leaves an '*am ha-aretz* inside his house awake and found him awake, asleep and found him asleep, awake and found him asleep—the house is clean. [If he left him] sleeping and found him awake—'the house is unclean', the words of R. Meir. And the sages say, 'Unclean is only [the space] up to the place to which he stretch out and touch his hand...' (*m. Tohorot* 7.2)

R. Simeon says, 'He who gave a key to an '*am ha-aretz*—the house is unclean.' (*t. Tohorot* 8.1)

A regularly cited passage concerning the 'people of the land' is *m. Hag.* 2.7. One reason for its scholarly popularity is partly because there is a contrast between the Pharisees and the 'people of the land' and related categories which appears to be defined in terms of food:

The clothing of *'am ha-aretz* is in the status of *midras* uncleanness for Pharisees [who eat ordinary food in a state of uncleanness], the clothing of Pharisees is in the status of *midras* uncleanness for those who eat *terumah* [priests]. The clothing of those who eat heave offering is in the status of *midras* uncleanness for those who eat Holy Things [officiating priests] etc. . . . (*m. Hag.* 2.7)

The assumptions here are of some importance for passages such as Mark 7.1–23 and Matt. 23.25–6//Luke 11.38–41. The Mishnah suggests that the impurity of the clothing of the 'people of the land' is like that which has contracted impurity from one with a discharge in relation to the Pharisee. The Pharisee is assumed to eat ordinary food in a state of impurity, as shown by the immediately following discussions of impurity involved in eating priestly and Temple food. We find related sentiments in other rabbinic passages on the 'people of the land', including those which discuss 'utensils' (כלים), which includes things like cups, pitchers, and dining couches (Mark 7.1–23, Matt. 23.25–6//Luke 11.38–41), and in relation to those keen on avoiding corpse impurity like the priest and Levite in Luke 10.29–37. For example: 'He who deposits utensils with an *'am ha-aretz*—they are unclean with corpse uncleanness and unclean with *midras* uncleanness' (*m. Tohorot* 8.2). Similarly, the 'people of the land' were not said to have been reliable concerning liquids:

An *'am ha-aretz* is believed to testify, 'These pickled vegetables did I pickle in a state of uncleanness, and I did not sprinkle liquids [capable of imparting susceptibility to uncleanness] upon them.' But he is not believed to testify, 'These fish I caught in a state of cleanness, and I did not shake the net over them.' (*t. Abod. Zar.* 4.11)

The water which comes up (1) on the snares, (2) on the gins, and (3) on the nets is not under the law, *If water be put*. And if he shook [them to remove the water], it [the water which is detached] is under the law, *If water be put*. (*m. Maksh.* 5.7)

He who undertakes to be a *haber* . . . does not purchase from him wet [produce, produce which has been rendered susceptible to uncleanness . . .] (*m. Demai* 2.3)

> ... this implies that it is permitted [for the *haber* to purchase from the *'am ha-aretz*] dry [produce], since *'ammei ha-aretz* are deemed trustworthy with respect to rendering produce susceptible to impurity. (*y. Demai* 2, 22d)

As with the purity background to Mark 7.1–23 and Matt. 23.25–6// Luke 11.38–41, these laws are developments of the laws of liquids and their intensification of defilement, all based on Lev. 11.34 (cf. 4Q284a; 4Q274 3; 4Q394 8.4, 5–7; CD 12.15–17; *m. Maksh.* 6.4).

Such closely analogous contexts would suggest that the earliest Palestinian traditions included an interest in people who would not have been known for keeping themselves in a state of purity very often. As we have seen throughout, this is clearly part of a context which is not a dominant concern of the early church and certainly not reflective of a Gentile mission and Gentile inclusion. We have also hinted that this interest in analogous social contexts further suggests that the emphasis on purity in the earliest Palestinian tradition is compatible with what we have seen about 'sinners'. However, there are more significant reasons why we should link purity concerns with the discussion of 'sinners', particularly reasons that relate to the preservation and continuation of purity traditions in the Gospel tradition.

Ethics, impurity, and discontinuity

The view made popular in scholarship by Gedaliah Alon, that Gentiles had a special kind of impurity, has been overturned, particularly in the work of Jonathan Klawans and Christine Hayes.[88] As they have shown, Alon's intrinsic 'Gentile impurity' is absent in early Jewish sources, which instead focus on Gentiles as idolaters and the morally impure, which in turn meant that intermarriage was a potential problem (e.g. Lev. 18.26; Deut. 7.1–4; 1 Kgs 11.1–2; Ezra 9.1–3, 10–12; Neh. 13.26; 4Q381 frag. 69, 1–2; *Jub.* 22.16–20). Indeed, there was an established tradition of lumping Gentiles together into one stereotypical unethical mass as people who were liable to commit murder, idolatry, and sexual immorality (e.g. Exod. 34.15–16; Lev. 18.24–30; Deut. 7.2–4, 16; 20.18; *Jub.* 9.15; *Aristeas* 152; Philo, *Spec. Laws* 1.51; *Sib. Or.* 3.492, 496–500; 5.168; Tob. 14.6).[89] The idea of an intrinsic 'Gentile impurity' was, Klawans argued, a later rabbinic novelty, whereas Hayes developed this argument further by pointing out that Alon's rabbinic evidence (especially the crucial *m. Pesah.* 8.8) would not even support his case. Notably, we have rabbinic passages where Gentiles can handle priestly food and offer sacrifices (e.g. *m. Sheq.* 7.6; *m. Zev.* 4.5; *m. Men.* 5.3; 5.6; 6.1; 9.8) which would not have been possible if they had intrinsic 'Gentile impurity'. The arguments of Klawans and Hayes imply that the emphasis on the details and assumptions of specifically Jewish impurity concerns are of limited interest to a movement with a notable Gentile intake. But they are more useful still in that the concern for morality and idolatry in relation to Gentiles might tell us something about why such purity passages, which were initially concerned with people like Jewish 'sinners', continued to be of importance in the Gospel tradition.

If the views on purity we find in underlying texts such as Mark 7.1–23, Matt. 23.25–6//Luke 11.38–41, and Luke 10.29–37 were of minimal interest for non-Jews, then why are they present in the Gospel tradition, especially in Luke? One reason might be simple: it was a widespread memory in the earliest tradition. Yet there is another consistent tendency in all these purity texts which accounts for their ongoing usefulness. The kinds of misbehaviour mentioned in the Gospel purity texts are expected of both 'sinners' and Gentiles, both of which are, as we have seen, overlapping and even synonymous categories, as echoed in the Synoptic tradition (Matt. 5.46–7//Luke 6.32–3; cf. Matt. 6.32//Luke 12.30; *m. Ned.* 3.11). In Mark 7.14–23, for instance, we get details through a vice list about what comes out from a person to defile: 'For it is from within, from the human heart, that evil intentions come: fornication, theft, murder, adultery, avarice, wickedness, deceit, licentiousness, envy/evil eye, slander, pride, folly. All these things come from within, and they defile a person' (Mark 7.21–3). Vice lists were a known means of making general statements about Gentile misbehaviour in distinction from Jews (cf. *T. Dan* 5.5), as well as having a more sectarian use at Qumran (e.g. 1QS IV.10–11). A relevant example concerns idolaters in the Wisdom of Solomon: '... and all is a raging riot of blood and murder, theft and deceit, corruption, faithlessness, tumult, perjury, confusion over what is good, forgetfulness of favours, defiling of souls, sexual perversion, disorder in marriages, adultery, and debauchery' (Wisd. 14.25–6). Stereotyping of Gentile behaviour in vice lists was taken up in early Christian texts and used to describe the kinds of behaviours that must be left behind as the

Christian movement began to identify itself in, and sometimes against, the wider Greco-Roman world (e.g. Gal. 5.19–21; 1 Cor. 6.9–11; 1 Pet. 4.3–6; Rev. 9.20–1; cf. 2 Cor. 12.20–1; Rev. 21.8).

It is for these sorts of reasons that the purity texts continued to have importance in the Gospel tradition. In the case of Mark 7.1–23, we should note that the vice list in Mark 7.21–3 is a repetition and interpretation of Mark 7.15, which may well indicate its importance for Mark. Moreover, the Markan context would indicate that the 'moral' or 'inner' aspects of the understanding of purity disputes are of importance for the inclusion of Gentiles. Immediately following Mark 7.1–23 we get Jesus moving into territory remembered and constructed as non-Jewish (*Apion* 1.70; cf. *War* 2.478; 4.105; Acts 21.3–4; cf. Isa. 23; Jer. 25.17–22; 47.4; Ezek. 26–8; Joel 3.4–8; Amos 1.9–10; Zech. 9.2–4) and an engagement with the Syro-Phoenician woman.[90] Mark 7.1–23 itself is placed in the middle of a distinct section in Mark 6.30–8.21 which, in narrative terms, is 'to the Jew first and also to the Greek' (Rom. 1.16; cf. Mark 7.27–8).[91] More precisely, the section is framed in terms of the Feeding of the Five Thousand (Mark 6.30–44), which appears to be for Jews, and the Feeding of the Four Thousand (Mark 8.1–21), which appears to be for Gentiles. In the Feeding of the Five Thousand, the twelve baskets are described with a word (κοφίνων; Mark 6.43) which Juvenal uses to characterize Jewish travellers (κόφινοι; Juvenal, *Satires* 3.14; 6.542).[92] Joel Marcus further notes that the baskets in the Feeding of the Four Thousand are referred to using a different word (σπυρίδας; Mark 8.8), adding that the 'word does not have the special association with Jews that its counterpart in 6:43, *kophinos*, does'.[93] Mark 7.1–23 is further interconnected with the wider Mark 6.30–8.21, such as the links with impurity (Mark 7.25, 27–8; cf. Lev. 11.27; cf. Exod. 22.31; 1 Kgs 4.11; Matt. 7.6; *b. BQ* 83a), the theme of bread (Mark 6.38, 41, 43, 44; 7.2, 27–8; 8.4–6, 8; cf. Mark 8.16–21), and the criss-crossing of the lake.[94] After leaving the region of Tyre, the Markan Jesus takes a journey 'by way of Sidon towards the Sea of Galilee, in the region of the Decapolis' (Mark 7.31), the peculiarity of which probably emphasizes the concerns with 'Gentile territory'. The language of those coming from far away in Mark 8.3 is, as is often noted, probably reflective of the language of Gentile distance from God, hence such language could describe Gentile converts (cf. Deut. 28.49; 29.22; Josh.

9.6, 9; 1 Kgs 8.42; Ps. 148.14; Isa. 5.26; 39.3; Tob. 13.11; *Mek. Exod.* 18.15; Acts 2.39; 22.21; Eph. 2.13).[95] It is probably significant that Jesus returns to what appears to be constructed as 'Jewish territory' after the Feeding of the Four Thousand, hence the reappearance of Pharisees (Mark 8.10–11).

The other Gospel purity texts we discussed are not as explicit in their concern for Gentiles but thematically, and consciously or unconsciously, the details of 'ethical' behaviour are closely connected with the behaviour attributed to the overlapping and near-synonymous categories of 'sinners' and 'Gentiles'. Specific details on correct behaviour in relation to purity disputes are found in Matt. 23.25–6//Luke 11.38–41 and they again reflect concerns about 'sinners' and Gentiles alike though, unlike Mark, are more directly reapplied to disputes with Jewish opponents. So, for instance, 'justice' in Matt. 23.23//Luke 11.42 is neither to be expected of the 'sinners' (e.g. Sir. 11.9; 35[32].17; 4Q511 frags 63–4, col. 3.1–5; *Gen. R.* 49.6; *b. Sanh.* 109a–b) or sinful nations (cf. Ps. 9.15–16; 1QM 11.12–14; *Gen. R.* 49.6; *b. Sanh.* 109a–b). 'Greed/plunder' in Matt. 23.25/Luke 11.39 would be at home in any discussion of 'sinners' (e.g. *1 En.* 102.5–10; 103.11–15; 104.2–7; *Ps. Sol.* 17:5; *m. Qidd.* 4.14; *b. Sanh.* 109a–b) and in lists echoing stereotyped Gentile behaviour (e.g. 1 Cor. 6.9–11; Mark 7.21–3; Wisd. 14.25). We also find evidence of such sentiments in the related sayings elsewhere in Matt. 23 where the alleged behaviour of the 'sinner' is turned on the scribes and Pharisees. Matt. 23.28–9 makes claims of Pharisaic insides being 'full of the bones of the dead and of all kinds of filth'. In addition to the polemical use of corpse impurity to describe the Pharisees, we might note that *Jubilees*, for instance, claims that the nations do things like offering sacrifices to the dead and eating among graves (*Jub.* 22.16–17). Matt. 23.28–9 includes more generalizing statements which relate to behaviour deemed beyond the Law, including the explicit charge of 'hypocrisy and lawlessness' in Matt. 23.28 which could have come from a description of 'sinners' in a range of Jewish texts (e.g. Ps. 49[50].16–23; 93[94].13; 119; Ezek. 33.8, 19; 1 Macc. 2.45–8; Sir. 15.7, 9; 1 Macc. 1.34; 2.45–8, 62; *1 En.* 104.10; *Ps. Sol.* 1.1; 2.1; 4.8; 14.6; 15.5, 8). Matt. 23.28 ('So you also on the outside look righteous to others, but inside you are full of hypocrisy and lawlessness') clearly complements the saying on whitewashed tombs in Matt. 23.27. It also echoes the language we have seen associated with 'sinners', including the stark contrast with the 'righteous' (cf. Mark 2.15–17). What we also have here is a similarity with another common theme in Jewish literature on 'sinners': 'sinners' appear blessed when the opposite is the case. Finally, we might add that Matt. 23.23 includes 'faith' as being among the weightier parts of the Law and this is what people like idolaters do not practise according to Wisd. 14.25 (ἀπιστία). The reference to 'mercy' in Matt. 23.23 is precisely what 'sinners' do not have, as well as being a sign of divine favour and a model for human behaviour (cf. Hos. 6.6; Wisd. 3.9; 15.11; 1 Macc. 2.57; 13.46; 2 Macc. 6.16; 7.23; 3 Macc. 6.4; Sir. 28.4; 29.1; Matt. 5.48//Luke 6.36), and which can even be used to stand in contrast to the nations (e.g. Wisd. 4.15). It is worth noting that righteous Gentiles could be seen to be capable of mercy (e.g. 2 Macc. 4.37).

In Matthew's reapplication of these sorts of traditions in his polemics against scribes and Pharisees, he is presumably implying that their behaviour is no better than that of Gentiles. Matthew's inherited purity and legal traditions remained relevant for his presumably post-70 context and engagement with the emerging rabbinic tradition, as he was clearly engaged with Jewish interpretations of the Law. This may also partly explain why Matthew is more precisely accurate than Luke on legal issues in parallel passages (e.g. Matt. 23.23//Luke 11.42). But while Matthew does indeed focus on Jewish opponents, there is also an interest in Gentile inclusion in his Gospel, most obviously shown in Matt. 28.19–20. Elsewhere, and despite little overt concern (cf. Matt. 10.5–6), Matthew appears to be aware of Gentile inclusion and the issues it generated earlier in the Gospel, hence the revealing Matt. 5.19: 'whoever breaks one of the least of these commandments, and teaches others to do the same, will be called least in the kingdom of heaven'. Matthew does not like non-observance but presumably there were sufficient levels of it that Matthew felt could not be ignored. And note how, as in Matt. 23, Matthew cannot escape the interest in scribes and Pharisees: 'unless your righteousness exceeds that of the scribes and Pharisees, you will never enter the kingdom of heaven' (Matt. 5.20).

The context of Luke 10 can also help in understanding the transmission and survival of the parable of the Good Samaritan. Prior to the parable, we learn about the travels and successes of the seventy-odd.

While this is not a Gentile mission—Luke saves this for Acts—there is a case of foreshadowing in that Luke avoids mention of ethnocentric issues in contrast to Matthew's account, which has the Israel-centred twelve sent out and told to bring back those presumably identified similarly to Jewish 'sinners': 'Go nowhere among the Gentiles, and enter no town of the Samaritans, but go rather to the lost sheep of the house of Israel' (Matt. 10.5–6). Luke may not disagree with the idea that Jesus' interests were largely limited to Israel but it is of some significance that he does not have the same emphasis as Matthew and leaves the nature of the mission of the seventy-odd open.

The parable of the Good Samaritan itself is framed in 'ethical' terms and functions as the endorsement of the scribe's answer to gaining eternal life: 'You shall love the Lord your God with all your heart, and with all your soul, and with all your strength, and with all your mind; and your neighbour as yourself.' Luke 10.25–8 is similar to the Markan discussion of the *Shema'* (Deut. 6.5) and loving the neighbour (Lev. 19.18) but, in contrast with Mark 12.28–34, Luke keeps this sufficiently vague by not placing these commandments in order of importance and not including the prioritization of sacrifices and burnt offerings which would have been issues of limited concern for Luke. Deut. 6.5 and Lev. 19.18, as well as the conclusion of the parable (Luke 10.36–7), are texts which would suggest the kind of behaviour expected of a repentant 'sinner' in that it involved behaving as if there *were* a God and behaving without a grudge or without vengeance. Moreover, Deut. 6.5 and Lev. 19.18 were of ongoing significance beyond the earliest tradition and for issues relating to inclusion of Gentiles in both behavioural terms and in the implicit anti-idolatry. This should be clear enough from Paul who, in his letter to the Galatians, and in bitter dispute over the Law, its imposition, and Gentiles, summarizes the whole Law with reference to Lev. 19.18 (Gal. 5.14) and who, in his first letter to the Corinthians (1 Cor. 8.6), makes reference to Deut. 6.5 in the context of a discussion about idol food and idolatry.

Moving on

Distinguishing 'ritual' purity from 'moral' purity and sin is not always easy to do in early Jewish texts and is further complicated by certain ideas of the defiling nature of 'sin', as has been shown in detail by Klawans.[96] While prioritizing of morality in relation to purity (or a specific interpretation of purity) might be carried out (cf. Mark 7.15), we certainly should not be viewing purity and ethics as starkly antithetical in the earliest Palestinian tradition. According to Klawans, 'Jesus nowhere defends ritual purity as a symbol of moral purity. Prioritizing moral purity, without underscoring any connection between ritual and moral purity, leaves ritual purity without a leg to stand on.'[97] I would be reluctant to endorse this fully in terms of the earliest Palestinian tradition and in the texts we have discussed. In a context where basic purity laws are simply assumed, this would not be an issue. Yet once removed from such a context then Klawans' point becomes more significant. In terms of the development of the inclusion of Gentiles, this sort of argument holds and allows for an easier split between 'morality' and 'ritual' purity, the specifically Jewish forms of the latter having no particular relevance for non-Jewish groups in the Greco-Roman world. The dropping of 'ritual' purity among later Christians was not particularly controversial because it was not a live issue but language relating to purity could, of course, be reapplied metaphorically to new situations, as figures such as Paul probably did (e.g. 1 Cor. 6.9–20; Rom. 6.1–4).[98] Moreover, the 'moral' aspects become emphasized by Paul[99] and the behavioural aspect of the purity traditions thus became the identity marker for the earliest Christians, as Jewish law might mark out Jew from Gentile. The specific emphases on, and a concern for, purity and morality in the Palestinian tradition were partly connected with what was happening in Galilee in that the message would have worked for those unconcerned with, or unable to observe, certain expansions of purity laws (something akin to the 'people of the land'). But it is also striking that the purity traditions are also concerned with the behaviour attributed to 'sinners' who, as people perceived to be oppressive, rich, and law-breakers, were in need of returning to the Law, and who provided a bridge to interests in Gentiles, and the ongoing transmission of such material, through their behaviour being deemed near-identical. And this emphasis on wanting the rich to change their ways brings us back not only to the previous chapter and the stark warnings of eschatological reversal, but also to the chaos of the socio-economic issues of Galilee from which the earliest Palestinian traditions on purity and 'sinners' were emerging.

5

Camping with Jesus?

Gender, Revolution, and Early Palestinian Tradition

We may begin with some relatively straightforward comments on what might ordinarily in historical Jesus studies constitute a chapter or section on 'Jesus and Women'. We might follow in this scholarly tradition and argue that this chapter should try to avoid the inaccurate cliché that Jesus was especially nice to women in the sense that this was outrageous to Jews. This sort of cliché is clearly a continuation of the anti-Jewish and/or supersessionist history of understanding the Bible, and more obviously so given that the Gospels do not appear to present Jesus' association with women as shocking. Yet the idea that Jesus' association with women was apparently shocking or subversive is a view not only found in prominent works of scholarship on Jesus and women,[1] but continues to be present outside academic discourse. On the *Huffington Post* website, a number of experts in early Judaism and the New Testament (Amy-Jill Levine, Paula Fredriksen, Jonathan Klawans, Ross Kraemer, Adele Reinhartz, and Jennifer Knust) criticized a previously published piece by Frank Schaeffer which had made a number of claims about Jesus' alleged 'radicalism' in his attitudes towards women:

> Continuing his implicit comparison of Judaism with the Taliban, Mr. Schaeffer presumes that first-century Jewish women are 'nobodies' and that Jesus' association with them 'was an act of rebellion against all the things good upright self-regarding male Jews believed in'—really? Those Jews who

celebrated books like Ruth and Esther; who insisted 'Honor your mother'; who compared Wisdom to a woman? Those Pharisees who had women patrons? Those priests who welcomed women in the Temple, and those synagogues that had women in their congregations? Those rabbis who cited women as legal authorities . . . ?[2]

Not only are the superiority and differentiating aspects of the argument concerning Jesus-better-than-Jews on issues of women without support, but they work with an overly simplified notion of gender. Indeed, it is striking that such discussions in historical Jesus studies typically exclude the integration of a discussion on, or even a complementary section on, 'Jesus and Men'.[3] Instead, the discussion of gender in this chapter will follow the common academic arguments (typically located outside historical Jesus studies) that related categories (particularly constructions of feminine, masculine, male and female, as well as constructions relating to sexuality) are used in various overlapping and intersecting senses. We might also include negotiations with stereotypical and material relationships between understandings of men and women, and masculinity and femininity, which assume the superiority of men and inferiority of women, even if this was not always straightforwardly so. This might include a range of behaviours assumed to be 'masculine' or 'feminine', though, again, not straightforwardly applied to men and women and which are often contradictory. This might include societal assumptions and discourses about power and authority which are cast in terms of 'feminine' and 'masculine' language. Throughout all this, of course, we could factor in, where possible, a range of intersecting variants involving social status, marital status, economic status, age, ethnicity, sexuality, the body, cultural and philosophical affiliations, and so on. I leave it to others to provide a systematic analysis of each different 'type' of gender analysis.[4] My main goal in this chapter remains to provide some (and only some) general suggestions for a means of redirecting the ways in which scholars generally approach the study of the historical Jesus.[5]

More precisely, I want to argue that ideas about gender in the earliest Jesus tradition were somewhat chaotic, unstable, and possibly inconsistent, though the earliest traditions do not seem to have overt problems with this perceived 'inconsistency'. Nevertheless, a range of ideas about gender are present, some of which were part of the Palestinian world shaken upside down and which soon settled (if not immediately in some cases) into conventional patterns and assumptions of gender; indeed, some of the potential controversies surrounding gender effectively reinscribe conventional gender roles. However, an understanding of the importance of gender in the study of the historical Jesus and the earliest tradition does in fact lead to one important development in the emergence of Christianity which can be tied in with the earliest Palestinian tradition: the role of female patrons. Before we turn to this, we can first look at some of the ways in which gender played a role in the earliest Palestinian tradition.

Gender and the Gospel tradition

The famous Aristotelian 'one body' or 'one sex' model of a sliding gender scale—with hyper-masculinity as the ideal and hyper-femininity as its opposite—is now regularly noted in New Testament studies on gender and is said to underpin broad models of gender in the Roman world. Furthermore, some of the more significant models of performing masculinity in the Greco-Roman world are as follows: Roman imperialism constructed as particularly 'manly' and conquering the effeminate, penetrated, and feminine nations; masculinity constructed as being ideally above, or dominating, various individuals of lower social status; sexual restraint and self-control seen as betraying 'manly' qualities; and, in sexual encounters, the active and passive roles could be constructed as masculine and feminine respectively.

How such dominant discourses might have affected the historical Jesus and the earliest tradition, particularly in Galilee, is not clear. And, due to the recent studies of Dale Martin and Anthony Le Donne, we can no longer work with the once near-certain assumption that Jesus was celibate, unmarried, of unambiguous sexuality and (therefore) in some way countercultural or radical in terms of masculinity in this sense.[6] Perhaps inevitably, masculinity and gender studies can sometimes struggle in establishing local histories and, as Robert Myles points out, such studies 'tend to focus on Greek and Roman gender ideologies with little to say about the more culturally specific construction of gender in Aramaic-speaking Palestine'.[7] However, we do have one potentially gendered example where Aramaic-speaking Palestine meets Rome: Jesus' death by crucifixion. Or, put another way, this would simply have been yet another death which could easily, though certainly not *necessarily* (cf. Appian, *Civil Wars* 1.120), have been seen as another feminized victim penetrated and conquered by masculine Rome. Colleen Conway has shown that Mark in particular presents, among other things, a 'passive emasculated victim who suffers a humiliating death . . . it is as if the author cannot fully dismiss the ignominy of the crucifixion' (Mark 14–16).[8] Yet Conway further argues that this is not a common feature of the early Christian texts, with Mark also presenting a more 'manly' tradition of Jesus as strong man (Mark 1–8) and noble martyr (Mark 8–10), and with Paul already presenting a more heroic and manly figure.[9] This could suggest in the case of the humiliated Jesus that Mark might be reflecting the earliest tradition (as is implicit in Conway's argument), particularly if we use the logic that it is easier to imagine recasting a death deemed shameful and emasculating in heroic and masculine terms. But the problem remains that we do not ultimately know in what kind of narrative or narratives the earliest Palestinian traditions cast the crucifixion of Jesus. Were any emasculating features to be challenged immediately? However, what we can be more clear about is that the issue of Jesus' masculinity in relation to being crucified and penetrated with nails would have been present from the offset and that this would have been an issue known to Jesus and his followers when it became clear that he would die in such a manner. It might be argued that, with John the Baptist killed, there is a good chance that Jesus knew what would happen in Jerusalem, or, indeed, what Rome was liable to do in the event of a problematic disturbance. Difficult questions concerning masculinity were always going to be present from the beginning and would need answering.

On more familiar ground for historical Jesus studies, there are some internal and external emphases on the association of women with the Jesus movement and early Christianity, and this was something that had an impact on understandings of gender more broadly. By the end of the second century, an outsider knowledgeable of Christianity, like Celsus, could find the role of women as followers of Jesus and their inclusion in subsequent Christianity to be unfortunate, or was at least able to slur Christianity in such terms:

For such was the charm of Jesus' words, that not only were men willing to follow Him to the wilderness, but women also, forgetting the weakness of their sex and a regard for outward propriety in thus following their Teacher into desert places... By which words, acknowledging that such individuals are worthy of their God, they manifestly show that they desire and are able to gain over only the silly, and the mean, and the stupid, with women and children. (Origen, *C. Cel.* 3.10, 44; cf. 3.49)

Of course, it may be that this is little more than an ancient slur but, as we will see, a strong case has been made that women running households, women with sufficient time, and elite women played a relatively prominent role in the provision for, and implicitly the spread of, the Jesus movement in the empire.[10] There is a form of this model found in the Gospel tradition. After Jesus' crucifixion, Mark claims: 'There were also women looking on from a distance; among them were Mary Magdalene, and Mary the mother of James the younger and of Joses, and Salome. These used to follow him and provided for him when he was in Galilee; and there were many other women who had come up with him to Jerusalem' (Mark 15.40–1). Elsewhere, in what looks like an independent tradition, Luke 8.1–3 claims:

Soon afterwards he went on through cities and villages, proclaiming and bringing the good news of the kingdom of God. The twelve were with him, as well as some women who had been cured of evil spirits and infirmities: Mary, called Magdalene, from whom seven demons had gone out, and Joanna, the wife of Herod's steward Chuza, and Susanna, and many others, who provided for them out of their resources.

We will return to the importance of this passage at the end of this chapter but for now we should note that there are hints of this theme being reflective of earlier Palestinian tradition and knowledge of the Herodian court, in that the name 'Joanna' is probably a Jewish name while 'Chuza' probably reflects her husband's Nabatean background.[11] It is also notable that women are remembered as (almost) the first witnesses to the empty tomb according to Mark (Mark 16.1–8). The suggestion that the use of female witnesses is somehow proof of the historicity of the empty tomb story does not carry any weight because it simply regurgitates the old line that Jews were anti-women and would not have accepted women as witnesses (except, presumably, those Jews associated with the Christian movement). Instead, and irrespective of historicity, and leaving aside that the man dressed in white is the first witness, we should understand Mark to be reflecting a tradition which stands in line with those who did give prominent roles to women and which is reflected in stories such as Esther and Judith. Yet, as the retelling of Mark puts the emphasis on men, we can work with the evidence we have and point out that if we did want evidence of discomfort with women present at the tomb then we need look no further than the other canonical Gospels which downplay their role. This, in turn, implies that there was an earlier tradition reflected in Mark which was less uncomfortable with such gender issues and one that would not entirely go away.

We also get a different nuance in other traditions where a contrast is established between two different forms of the family in terms of gender relations:

> Then his mother and his brothers came; and standing outside, they sent to him and called him. A crowd was sitting around him; and they said to him, 'Your mother and your brothers and sisters are outside, asking for you.' And he replied, 'Who are my mother and my brothers?' And looking at those who sat around him, he said, 'Here are my mother and my brothers! Whoever does the will of God is my brother and sister and mother.' (Mark 3.31–5)

Here we get the perhaps inevitable construction of an alternative family, a theme found elsewhere in the Gospel tradition. This is a theme that, as Halvor Moxnes suggests, queers standard assumptions of households because the fictive household around Jesus is notably fatherless (at least on earth; cf. Matt. 23.9), and includes women such as a 'mother' (and, presumably, widows), as it mimics the adult Jesus' own family.[12] But what we should also note here is that we are also dealing with understandings of masculinity and the household more generally.[13] The fragmentation of households is clear enough in the Gospel tradition (e.g. Mark 3.20–2, 31–5; 10.29–30; Matt. 8.22// Luke 9.60; Matt. 10.34–6//Luke 12.51–3//*Thom.* 16; Matt. 10.37// Luke 14.26), and it is presumably significant that Jesus moves around and only returns to Nazareth once in Mark, which was remembered as a problematic return (Mark 6.1–6).[14]

Whether or not Jesus was married, unmarried, celibate, or sexually active, his alternative household shows no signs of performing certain expected roles—and how could it? It may well have been expected, of course, that, as head of the household, a man was supposed to procreate, and by doing so keep the family unit functioning socially and economically (cf. Gen. 22.17).[15] We might speculate that this may not have been possible as Jesus' group moved around Galilee. Indeed, the unusualness of a man not procreating is assumed in a well-known rabbinic story where Simeon b. Azzai got some criticism for not getting married: 'The Sages: "You preach well, but do not practise your preaching." Said Simeon ben Azzai: "My soul is in love with the Torah. The world can be kept going by others' (*b. Yeb.* 63b). This passage is, of course, much later but that the behaviour was perceived to be sufficiently unusual sheds some light on the (perhaps not-so-alien) views concerning those who would have behaved likewise. For all the surprise in this rabbinic passage, it is in line with the tradition of prioritizing commandments over family (e.g. *War* 2.119–61//*Ant.* 18.18–22; *Ant.* 3.87), which should be borne in mind when understanding the implications of the family sayings in the Gospel tradition.[16] In presenting a figure no longer in the traditional household—and who was perhaps expected to run and maintain the household—it is probably not a surprise to find that the Gospel presentation of Jesus and his alternative family can be framed in contexts of conflict.

Moxnes further suggests that there is evidence that ridicule levelled at Jesus underlay the saying on eunuchs in Matt. 19.12. Not only that, but Jesus may also have played around with such polemic in talking of 'eunuchs for the sake of the kingdom of heaven'. In terms of sexuality and gender, eunuchs were a highly ambiguous category in the ancient world, sometimes known as womanly, half-men, or effeminate, and this construction of eunuchs, in connection with travelling cultic groups in the Syria-Palestine area, may well have been known to Jesus and his opponents (cf. Lucian, *Syr. Dea* 20ff.; Apuleius, *Met.* 7.24–31; Justin, *Apol.* 1.29).[17] It is these kinds of constructions of gender that Jesus would have polemically received and reinterpreted in a symbolic sense in order to describe his socially castrated movement not living up to conventional gender roles. Moxnes uses further evidence from the Gospel tradition to strengthen his case for Jesus playing around with gender categories (cf. Mark 12.18–27; Luke 20.34–6). His suggestions concerning ridicule are intriguing and important but one problem they face is that it is difficult to establish an earlier context for the crucial eunuch saying, particularly without sustained parallel discussions in the Gospel tradition, and so this specific approach to a specific passage concerning the historical Jesus (or earliest tradition) and masculinity remains plausible but we would need more evidence from across the Synoptic tradition. And to add to the problems, would these not be exactly the sort of criticisms that would likely be ignored or even suppressed?

Gender and revolution

Yet we can make some tentative general suggestions about the early nature of these traditions to complement Moxnes' overall argument. As we have already seen with reference to Conway, and will see further below, there are gender constructions dominant in the Gospel tradition that also function as normative assumptions for the Gospel writers. Their very normativity may provide us with the kinds of gender assumptions which are in dialogue or tension with the upheaval of households and alternative households presented in the Gospel tradition. We might similarly recall that it is more likely that earlier tradition would be more problematic because, as Conway suggests, the tendency in the Gospel tradition was to present Jesus more in line with conventional understandings of gender in the Greco-Roman world. Seemingly fixed assumptions of gender and sexuality combined with potentially destabilizing notions in the context of social upheaval may also suggest a means of rethinking gender constructions (whether in rhetoric or reality) in earliest Palestinian tradition. As we saw in chapters 1 and 3, a range of reactions in the context of peasant unrest may have been possible, from a return to the status quo to millenarianism or utopianism, the latter suggestions being something that could be applied to Jesus' teaching on the kingdom.[18] Similarly, if class relations could be questioned in such contexts then the rhetoric and reality of gender relations—which are intimately tied in with class and general social structures—could be challenged too. It was presumably the case that there would have been changes in household patterns as Jesus was growing up, particularly with the building and rebuilding of Tiberias and Sepphoris. As we saw, not only would this have brought about shifts in production patterns for the surrounding villages but in the case of Tiberias we know from Josephus that there would have been dislocation and land alienation (*Ant.* 18.36–8).[19]

On the basis of these kinds of socio-economic explanations, it is possible to provide a comparative approach to the role of gender and Christian origins. Mary Ann Tétreault points out that 'If the subordination of women and other social groups is a foundation of state formation, all revolutions against state based regimes have the potential to liberate women from men as well as to liberate men from one another.'[20] The language of state is not always directly applicable in the ancient world,[21] and even less so in the context of Christian origins, but the general idea that significant shifts in deeply embedded social structures can have the potential to shake up traditional gender roles is consistent with ideas concerning social unrest. As a point of comparison, one of the classic discussions of the connection between the turmoil of mid-seventeenth-century England and understandings of gender and sexuality was provided by Christopher Hill in his chapter, 'Base Impudent Kisses'.[22] The extent to which Hill presented an accurate picture may be debated but the re-evaluation of gender and sexuality certainly was a significant feature in revolutionary England. Ann Hughes, for instance, has more recently undertaken a wide-ranging analysis of the connections, covering 'women petitioners and prophets, defiant women among royalists and parliamentarians alike... along with quarrels over the proper manliness of the king and other political leaders, discussions of family structures and gendered political metaphors... the upheavals of the 1640s provoked all kinds of "gender trouble"...'[23]

More generally, the links between social upheaval and understandings of gender are common enough, including the now traditional rethinking of the remembrance of the changing role of women. We might think of the women of the bread riots in the French Revolution, not to mention the inspiration the revolution provided for Olympe de Gouges and Mary Wollstonecraft. The Russian Revolution provided opportunities for female revolutionaries and thinkers such as Alexandra Kollontai and Nadezhada Krupskaya, whilst civil war Spain produced hierarchy-challenging armed reactions among the mixed ranks of the CNT and POUM militia before they were put back in something like their previously constructed place. Women played a notable role in the 1954–62 Franco-Algerian conflict, individually and collectively represented in Gillo Pontecorvo's film *The Battle of Algiers* (1966). We could also point to the heightened role of women in the civil rights movements in the US. More recently still, the sometimes violent social upheaval of the UK miners' strike of 1984–5 brought about an increasing awareness of sexism and the involvement of women and women's groups such as Women Against Pit Closures. These examples are, of course, far too general and so it is necessary to give evidence more relevant to a first-century Palestinian context. One roughly analogous example is found in the context of the Jewish war when Simon bar Giora is remembered by Josephus partly for his following of women, including his wife (*War* 4.538). Note the ways in which Simon and his followers were treated at Masada:

> At first they regarded him with suspicion, and permitted him and his following of women access only to the lower part of the fortress, occupying the upper quarters themselves; but afterwards, as a man of congenial disposition and apparently to be trusted, he was allowed to accompany them on their raids upon the surrounding district... (*War* 4.505–6)

Analogous with the social upheaval and millenarian utopianism we have been discussing throughout, Simon would, so the narrative goes, withdraw to the hills and surround himself with a motley crew of 'villains' (so Josephus) to proclaim liberty for the slaves (*War* 4.507–8). This provides a more precise analogy to help account for the remembrance of the role of women in the developing movement around Jesus and his own type of utopianism.

Of course, this does not just mean that the more romantic elements of social or revolutionary upheaval represent sustained changes and shifts in conventional gender relations. As well as nostalgia for the old ways, social upheaval provides new contexts to be negotiated by the more 'reactionary' (if that is always the right word) elements. We might think of conservative attitudes in support of the Church in revolutionary France or civil war Spain. Condoleezza Rice is, in her own way, a product of the civil rights movement as much as Jesse Jackson, and few in the UK forget the gender issues of a recently deceased prime minister who was, to some extent, a product of the social upheavals of the 1960s and who was, in no small part, responsible for crushing the mining industry and the miners' strike.[24] As Hughes argued concerning seventeenth-century England, 'royalist politics and ceremonial religion offered opportunities for female activism as much as parliamentarianism... the defeated royalist cause offered particular avenues for women's agency'.[25] But what we can say, of course, is that chaos can beget change and the need to negotiate change, irrespective of whether the historical actors and agents know it or like it. And, as this would already suggest, we should not get intoxicated with the idea that contexts of social unrest or revolution necessarily lead to full gender equality or anything of the sort. The basic point is that contexts of social upheaval and revolution pave the way for some kind of change—rhetorical or actual—in traditional social roles, including gender. Furthermore, we should not romanticize this process for the simple reason that we are overwhelmed with historical examples of women being utilized by men in revolutionary contexts and of the (re-)imposition of traditional gender roles in post-revolutionary contexts, and this includes the more modern socialist revolutions, from Russia to Latin America. Tétreault adds, 'because revolutions also result in the strengthening of state institutions, the continued subordination of women and other previously exploited social groups after revolutionary transformation may be structurally favoured'.[26]

Again, with language of state being put to one side or, better, modified, this is analogous with what we find in earliest Christianity. It is hardly controversial to say that the ancient world was, rhetorically and materially, androcentric and that in the long run any dominant Christian movement was never fully going to accept women taking over the leading church roles (cf. e.g. 1 Tim. 5.3–16; 2 Tim. 3.6; Rev. 2.20–3; Irenaeus, *Against Heresies* 1.25.6). Early Christianity was never *really* about revolutionizing gender roles in reality, as reflected in a number of passing comments in the early church (e.g. 1 Cor. 7.25–35; 11.2–16; 1 Cor. 14.33–6; Eph. 5.21–33). As Jorunn Økland put it in a statement which obviously has broader application in the ancient world:

> The dominant gender ideologies of our present time can be summed up in a general way in the view that women and men are different... but should have the same status, rights, possibilities and duties... I am not convinced that Paul and the first-century Corinthians shared this late-twentieth-century view of equality between the sexes that presupposes modern discourses of democracy and individual autonomy.[27]

Structurally, then, the historical context meant it was near-impossible for a potentially major movement to proceed with anything resembling gender egalitarianism, as the cultural context would keep challenges to gender (and class) relations in check, even if there was epiphenomenal change from time to time.

Using Moxnes' interpretation of Matt. 19.12, the recording of actual eunuchs can be predictably reported with a mocking tone in ancient literature (cf. Apuleius, *Met.* 7.24–31; Lucian, *Eunuch* 8–9) and so it is probably no surprise that influential ideological positions were not going to have Christianity understood in language deemed unmanly. By way of a relevant analogy, there were harsh words apparently aimed toward same-sex eroticism in scriptural texts (Lev. 18.22; 20.13) and their interpretation includes additional attacks on what might have been perceived to be non-masculine and effeminate behaviour (e.g. *Apion* 2.119; *Arist.* 152; *Sib. Or.* 3.185, 584–606, 762–6; Philo, *Spec. Leg.* 3.37–42; *Hypoth.* 7.1; *Cont.* 59–62). And, of course, Paul had his own harsh words to say on issues relating to same-sex eroticism (Rom. 1.26–8) and that which appears to be deemed non-masculine and effeminate behaviour (e.g. 1 Cor. 6.9–11; 11.14–15). And, if we are to entertain the possibility of an advocacy of celibacy in the earliest tradition,[28] there were ancient views which readily lent themselves to making anything sounding like celibacy or asceticism, or indeed the ability to abstain from sex, sound manly (cf. Philo, *Cont.* 68–69; *Hypoth.* 11.1–18).[29] If there were cases of playing around with categories of masculinity, they were not going to last all that long when Christianity was to spread far and wide.

The contextualization of Galilee and the earliest Palestinian tradition shows how it was possible that many men would have been in the position—whether they liked it or not—of not doing what was expected of them. For instance, they may no longer have been in a position to head households, which would shed some light on the traditions of household upheaval in the Gospel tradition.[30] Yet despite, or because of, the tensions with received assumptions of gendered space and behaviour, it seems clear in the Gospel tradition that, from the outset, some of these structural constraints were already implicit in the earliest tradition in that received assumptions of gender and power are reinscribed as they are mimicked. The concept of household may be queered in the Gospel tradition but the idea of a dominant male figure is hardly lost.[31] On the contrary, the fatherhood of God is a famous theme in the Gospel tradition and, as Matt. 23.9 puts it, 'call no one your father on earth, for you have one Father—the one in heaven'. We might broaden this out further still and note that, at whatever point in the history of the tradition, possibly simultaneously for all we know, there is evidence of more complexity and contradiction as a masculinizing of Jesus is likewise taking place.[32] Tat-siong Benny Liew has noted a strong tendency in Mark's Gospel to portray Jesus in 'manly' and militarized terms and some of his suggestions have direct relevance for the discussions in this chapter. For instance, Liew has pointed out that a man active outside the home, as relentlessly presented in Mark, conforms to a different Greco-Roman stereotype, with the reverse being the domestic space as the confines of women. Jesus likewise takes on traits of fatherhood in the language of fictive family in addressing others as 'sons', 'daughters', and 'children' (Mark 2.19; 5.34; 10.24), engages in conflicts of authority with opponents, and alone can take the severest of beatings on the way to the crucifixion.[33] In a related way, the story of resurrected bodies in Mark 12.18–27 may implicitly critique the dominant normality of gender roles but the whole question and answer works with the assumption of the man marrying, and indeed becoming like angels in heaven who were regularly cast in masculinized language of warriors and leaders. All of this is set against, of course, the flawed disciples who, as Myles puts it, 'appear hopelessly short of achieving their masculinity'.[34] We might make a comparison of similar kinds of reinscription from later Jewish texts. As Gwynn Kessler argues, with reference to rabbinic passages where bodies appear to blur male and female, the physiology may be somewhat incoherent but the gender is reinscribed as it remains resolutely *male*. Mordechai may be able to make the unusual move of nursing Esther, and other rabbinic passages may openly discuss men miraculously growing breasts and producing milk, but *Gen. R.* 30.8 still categorizes Mordechai as male, just as *b. Shabb.* 53b does in the case of lactating men, as well as additionally assuming that men do not typically lactate.[35]

We should also remind ourselves again of how Conway has shown how the submissive features of Jesus in Mark's Gospel do not reflect the dominant trend among the early Christian texts, as Paul is already making it clear that Jesus' death is now to be 'masculinized' in terms of, for instance, a heroic sacrifice, and that the submissive features of Mark are hardly the whole story either: 'The Markan Jesus is a divinely appointed strong man, critic of Roman "great ones," noble martyr, but also a passive, emasculated victim who suffers a humiliating death.'[36] With a readily available tradition of Maccabean martyrs, or an immediate sense of having to counter anything problematic, it is entirely possible that some of these sort of 'heroic' or 'elevated' traits go back to the earliest Palestinian tradition, alongside the problem of Jesus' crucifixion, and so the tensions about the perception of Jesus' manliness and masculinity were presumably likewise present.[37] But we can go further still and show that there is evidence not only that problematic assumptions about gender were being controlled in the earliest tradition, but also that some of the dominant stereotypes about men and women were part of the earliest tradition. And here, Mark 6.17–29 provides some of the strongest evidence of early Palestinian tradition employing or assuming conventional gender stereotypes.

Mark 6.17–29: Stabilizing gender in early Palestinian tradition

While there probably were, then, some potentially destabilizing early Palestinian traditions concerning gender, it was not simply structural problems that would prevent any significant change in assumptions of gender. On the contrary, we have what looks like an early Palestinian tradition which tries to control assumptions of gender in a more sustained way and again coping with a potentially emasculating death: Mark 6.17–29 and the decapitation of John the Baptist.[38] What we will see in this passage is that it goes out of its way to reinforce stereotypical gender constructions but it is also one which, while not being entirely alien to modern western readers, does have some striking sentiments which may help us get a general grasp on some of the features of the construction of gender present among the earliest traditions. As Robert Darnton notes, it is those aspects of a culture which might strike the reader as 'unfunny, if not downright repulsive . . . where it seems to be most opaque' which can provide some indication of our cultural distance and a useful starting point for investigation. By 'getting' the joke, proverb, riddle, ceremony, or whatever, it is possible to start grasping a 'foreign system of meaning'.[39] Mark 6.17–29 also has a number of what must surely seem odd features to many twenty-first-century Gospels scholars. After all, how many will be familiar with scenarios such as a mother using her daughter to dance alluringly in front of a king in order to secure a vow which in turn secures the decapitation of an opponent? In fact it is these very issues which provide the best point of entry in aiding our understanding of this seemingly obscure passage.

Before we turn to gender issues, some preliminary comments on historicity ought to be made to avoid confusion. This gossipy story is unlikely to be historically accurate in anything other than the general sense that Antipas had John the Baptist killed and is unusual also because of everything else we know about Antipas' attitude towards John: he was hostile and his actions ruthless. Such attitudes are not only found in the Gospel tradition, including Mark (e.g. Mark 1.14; 6.14–16; Matt. 14.5; Luke 3.19–20; 9.7–9), but also in Josephus' account where John is put to death because he had an alarming level of popular support (*Ant.* 18.116–19). Josephus does not have Antipas being respectful of a wise man or showing any remorse, and there is no indication that a mother-and-daughter team were responsible for his death. Antipas is simply presented in a way that is much more realistic: have the man killed just in case he might be a seditious threat. Only in Mark 6.17–29 is Antipas said to respect John and only here are Herodias and Salome said to be responsible for the death of John. If what Mark said really did happen, we could legitimately expect some hint somewhere else given that it runs contrary to every other explanation.[40] The other important reason against the historicity of Mark 6.17–29 is that Antipas' promise to give half his kingdom to Salome (Mark 6.22–3) would have been impossible to take seriously. Antipas' power was ultimately answerable to Rome and as such he simply would not have been able to give anything like half his kingdom away.[41]

However, this is not to say that Mark 6.17–29 is without use for our purposes, as its origins provide a heavily gendered reaction to charges of sedition and subversion, as Morton Enslin pointed out some years ago and a point to which we will return.[42] Mark (and/or his source) appears to blame women for the death of John in Mark 6.17–29.[43] Despite John telling Antipas that 'It is not lawful for you to have your brother's wife' (6.18; cf. Lev. 18.16; 20.21; Deut. 25.5–10; CD 5.8–11; *War* 2.116; *Ant.* 17.341; *b. Yeb.* 55a), it was Herodias who is said to have borne the grudge against John and wanted him imprisoned and killed. The blaming of Herodias would have potentially been received relatively positively by some with power, most notably Josephus.[44] Josephus' portrayal of her is negative and he claims she was the main reason for Antipas' eventual downfall. Josephus' Herodias is envious of the newly acquired wealth and status of her brother Agrippa I and is portrayed as effectively nagging Antipas to promote himself in Rome (*Ant.* 18.240–55). Josephus' Antipas, however, is presented as content with his lot and as one who had tried to resist but to no avail: 'The upshot was that she never flagged till she carried the day and made him her unwilling partisan, for there was no way of escape once she had cast her vote on this matter' (*Ant.* 18.246). Unfortunately for the couple, they were to be exiled to Lyons for their troubles. Josephus' presentation emphasizes that this is not expected behaviour for a wife, nor indeed a husband: 'And so God visited this punishment on Herodias for her envy of her brother and on Herod [Antipas] for listening to a woman's frivolous chatter' (*Ant.* 18.255).[45] Josephus, for one, would have accepted the idea that Herodias was deceptive and manipulative and more than capable of fooling Antipas.

In Mark's presentation, Herodias would get her way on Antipas' birthday (6.21) through her daughter, Salome (6.22). Contextualizing Salome's implied seduction of Antipas can help explain why Antipas had to go against his will and have John killed. Dancing in ancient literature does not have to be taken in a sexual sense but we should probably assume Salome's dance was meant to be taken erotically in Mark 6.17–29.[46] We might, for instance, note later Jewish stories of dancing and debauchery in wine-houses or taverns (cf. *m. Taan.* 4.8; *b. Pesah.* 49a; *b. BQ* 97a; cf. *b. Taan.* 31a).[47] The book of Esther and the rewriting of the book of Esther has had a clear influence on Mark 6.17–29, including references to women dancing (רקד) naked at the banquet and a drunken Ahasuerus wanting the same from Vashti. She refused and was slain (*Pirqe Rabbi Eliezer* 49 on Esther 1.8, 10–12, 19). According to *Megillah* 11b, commenting on Esther 1.2: 'Satan came and danced (ריקד) among them and slew Vashti.' Roger Aus has shown that this is part of the development of Esther 1 and a tradition which underpins Salome's dancing and an innocent death.[48]

Passages cited by Aus are centuries later than the Gospel passages which in itself is a problem. But while establishing whether these texts reflect first-century traditions is difficult, we do at least know that there were similar beliefs about the dangers of sexually provocative female behaviour. One example is Josephus' account of Joseph of Jerusalem and the mother of his son, Hyrcanus (*Ant.* 12.187–9). Joseph went to Alexandria to have his daughter married to someone of the right social standing. As he dined with the Egyptian king a 'dancing-girl' (ὀρχηστρίδος; cf. Mark 6.22—ὀρχησαμένης) entered with whom Joseph would fall in love. But given that she was a Gentile, she wanted to cover up the potential scandal and was saved by his creative brother Solymius who disguised his own daughter (Joseph's niece) for the romantic get-togethers. Fortunately or unfortunately, Joseph was too drunk to know what was happening, though not sufficiently inebriated to prevent him having sex. And so a loved-up Joseph was able to marry her (cf. Philo, *Embassy* 41–2). But the assumptions in the tale are clear: dancing women could be potentially dangerous.

CONTROL

We can make some interrelated points on divorce law, particularly those acts which are deemed adulterous, because they can illustrate how ambiguous dancing might have been perceived. In *m. Ketub.*7.6 a husband can divorce a wife without her marriage settlement if she transgresses Jewish 'custom' or 'law'. Jewish 'custom' or 'law' is understood to include the prohibition of going out with loosened hair and talking with men (cf. *t. Ketub.* 7.6). What this further shows is that there were related assumptions about the significance of space being controlled and gendered; perhaps most famously the case of gendered space was in the Temple. However, it was probably the most familiar place, the household, where people would regularly encounter gendered space, as Moxnes has shown in detail.[49] Compare the following construction of women's place in the household:

These are the kinds of labour which a woman performs for her husband: she grinds flour, bakes bread, does laundry, prepares meals, feeds her child, makes the bed, works in wool. If she brought with her a single slave girl, she does not grind, bake bread, or do laundry. If she brought two, she does not prepare meals and does not feed her child. If she brought three, she does not make the bed for him and does not work in wool. If she brought four, she sits on a throne. R. Eliezer says, 'Even if she brought him a hundred slave girls, he forces her to work in wool, for idleness leads to unchastity.' Rabban Simeon b. Gamaliel says, 'Also: He who prohibits a wife by a vow from performing any labour puts her away and pays off her marriage contract.' (*m. Ketub.* 5.5)

Even in what may be little more than hypothetical examples, the assumptions of a woman's idealized place are clear enough. In Mark's Gospel we get some further assumptions of what female roles in relation to male roles should entail. In Mark 1.30–1, the first thing the person identified as Simon Peter's mother-in-law does once healed is 'to serve them' and, as Loader points out, women play stereotypical roles in Jesus' parables.[50]

Yet we might also compare the behaviour of Antipas with the view attributed to Rabbi Aqiba that a man can divorce his wife if he finds a more attractive woman (*m. Gitt.* 9.10; cf. *m. Ketub.* 5.6; 7.2). Similar views are also present in the Gospel tradition. According to Matt. 19.10 the disciples are said to find it amazing that a man can only divorce a wife for sexual immorality on her part, even to the extent that they exclaim, 'If such is the case of a man with his wife, it is better not to marry.' From these perspectives, it is almost assumed that men should divorce and remarry. In these specific but relevant cases the woman is constructed as a potential seductress and male sexual activity is valorized. Salome's actions are how an idealized good wife ought not to behave, and certainly not in front of a group of men, while simultaneously providing attraction for the male gaze. This presumably underpins the expectations of how Antipas might be expected to behave and with cultural assumptions not dissimilar to those involved in the case of Joseph of Jerusalem.

Clearly, the emphasis on controlling gender partly works with the assumption that female sexuality could be deemed dangerous. The potential for gender displacement could, from this perspective, cause problems even for the most upright man. CD warns not 'to be attracted by the thoughts of a guilty inclination and lascivious eyes. For many have gone astray due to these; brave heroes stumbled on account of them, from ancient times until now' (CD 2.16–17). In first-century Palestine there was an established association between evil and seductive female sexuality.[51] This might include a woman as the personification of evil or wrongdoing. This appears to be the case in Proverbs, which has a warning against this kind of female persona: 'Do not let your hearts turn aside to her ways; do not stray into her paths; for many are those she has laid low, and numerous are her victims' (Prov. 7.25–6). 4Q184 (labelled, of course, 'The Wiles of the Wicked Woman') develops this further. The wicked woman is seductive, can entice even the elect, and lurks in the shadows:

> [Her] eyes scan hither and thither, and she raises her eyebrows impudently, to spot a just ma[n] and overtake him, and a [no]ble man, to trip him up; the upright to turn (from) the path, the righteous chosen ones from keeping the precept, to make those with a steady [mind] ridiculous with recklessness, and those who walk upright to alter the ordi[na]nce . . . and seduce the sons of men with smooth words. (4Q184 1.13–17)

The ambiguities concerning female sexuality noted above are also present in such personifications because the difference between the female personification of evil and the female personification of wisdom was not always clear.[52] Wisdom too could be personified in sexually alluring terms. The psalm of 11Q5 (cf. Sir. 51.13–19) attempts to explain this more erotically:[53]

> When I was still young, before I had gone astray, I searched for her. She came to me in her beauty, and up to the end I kept investigating her. Even when the blossom falls, when the grapes are ripening, they make the heart happy. My foot tread on a straight path, for since my youth I have known her . . . I became ablaze for her, I could not av[e]rt my face. I stirred my soul for her and on her height I was not calm. 'My hand' (ידי) opened [. . .] her nakedness I inspected. I cleansed 'my hand' (כפי) . . . (11Q5 21.11–18)

In this instance it looks as if 'hand' (and 'foot') functions euphemistically for genitals.[54] Wisdom may be construed as sexually appealing but this is also, of course, how the female personification of evil is constructed and, in Proverbs, the language to describe both is clearly overlapping and it is potentially difficult to distinguish between the two (Prov. 7.11–12; 8.1–3).[55]

The ambiguity of these personifications is also present in the stories of Esther and Salome. Esther's sexuality is constructed positively while Salome's is construed negatively. As Janice Capel Anderson comments, '"Salome" is the dark obverse of Esther—Esther's shadow sister.'[56] This is not to say that Salome in Mark 6.17–29 was understood as the personification of evil. Rather, the point is that the female personifications of evil show how female sexuality could be constructed as dangerously ambiguous.[57] And Antipas was indeed lured and in the context of the construction of dangerous ambiguity Mark 6.17–29 is relieving Antipas of some of the blame in that it was hardly his fault he was attracted to the 'young girl'.[58]

According to Mark, the 'young girl' (τῷ κορασίῳ) made Antipas 'pleased' (ἤρεσεν), a word which in relevant texts carries sexual connotations (6.22; cf. LXX Gen. 19.8; Judg. 14.1, 14.3; 14.7; Esth. 2.4, 9; Job 31.10). For instance, in the Esther tradition, the same words for 'girl' and 'pleased' can be found: 'The girl [Esther] (τὸ κοράσιον) pleased (ἤρεσεν) him [the king] and won his favour' (Esther 2.9). Throughout Esther 2 there is an emphasis on Esther pleasing the king (2.4, 9, 14, 15, 17) which is also found in the Aramaic traditions.[59] The linguistic similarities between Mark 6.22 and Esther 2.9 are further significant because the 'pleased' King Ahasuerus would promise Esther half his kingdom (Esther 5.3).[60] We might also point to the traditions concerning the attractiveness of Esther. One example is from *Esther Rabba* 6.9 on Esther 2.15, which has a discussion between R. Judah bar Ilai (second century CE) and his regular debating partner, R. Nehemiah: 'R. Judah said: She was like a statue which a thousand persons look upon and all equally admire. R. Nehemiah said: They put Median women on one side of her and Persian women on the other, and she was more beautiful than all of them.' Again, this is a later tradition but the sexual attractiveness of Esther was something discussed prior to the Gospels. For instance, the Greek 'A' version of Esther 3.14, 17–18 (MT Esther 2.16–17) claims: 'When evening came, she [Esther] would be taken to him [Ahasuerus], and in the morning she would leave. And when the king had examined all the maidens, Esther proved the most outstanding. She found favour and mercy in his sight, and set the royal crown upon her head.'[61]

With these cultural constructions understood, it should be no surprise that Salome has Antipas under her control. If Antipas was drunk, as the king was in the Esther story, then her job was no doubt assumed to be easier. As Mark put it, 'Herod said to the girl, "Ask me for whatever you wish, and I will give it." And he solemnly swore to her, "Whatever you ask me, I will give you, even half of my kingdom (ἕως ἡμίσους τῆς βασιλείας μου)"' (Mark 6.22–3). This is one of the most obvious examples of a passage which is a product of human storytelling rather than an accurate recording of words at some party for Antipas. The common explanation is that this is obviously a creative use of Esther, where the promise is likewise found (see also Esther 5.6; 9.2; 1 Targ. to Esther 5.3):

> The king said to her, 'What is it, Queen Esther? What is your request? It shall be given to you, even to the half of my kingdom (ἕως τοῦ ἡμίσους τῆς βασιλείας μου).' (Esther 5.3)
>
> On the second day, as they were drinking wine, the king again said to Esther, 'What is your petition, Queen Esther? It shall be granted to you. And what is your request? Even to the half of my kingdom (ἕως τοῦ ἡμίσους τῆς βασιλείας μου), it shall be fulfilled.' (Esther 7.2)

Note again the good/bad contrast between Esther and Salome–Herodias, as both use their culturally constructed power to please but one uses it to save life, the other(s) to kill.

Antipas' crucial mistake was that he swore (ὤμοσεν) to do what was asked of him, which of course resulted in 'the head of John the Baptizer' (6.24). An understanding of oaths and vows can also give us some insight into how Antipas might have been understood. Difficult though they may sometimes be, oaths and vows should be fulfilled (Deut. 23.21; Judg. 11.30). In the Greek 'A' version of Esther 8.7 (MT Esther 7.5) we also find a binding oath which is of obvious relevance for understanding Antipas' oath: 'But the king swore (ὤμοσεν) that she [Esther] should tell him who had behaved so arrogantly as to do this, and with an oath he undertook to do for her whatever she wished.'[62] The background of binding oaths and vows would have provided Mark 6.17–29 with further reasons to maintain Antipas' innocence and blame Salome–Herodias because Antipas, obviously, must do the honourable thing and keep his word. Indeed, the Markan passage is explicit in promoting Antipas' innocence and makes it clear that there were important witnesses: 'The king was deeply grieved; yet out of regard for his oaths and for the guests, he did not want to refuse her' (6.26). A story in Josephus shows how socially significant this would have been because it applied even to Caligula himself (*Ant.* 18.289–304). During the Caligula crisis, the emperor, somewhat relaxed by wine at a banquet, was impressed by Agrippa's ostentation and offered in return to perform 'any service that can add its weight in the scale of prosperity... with all my heart and power'. Assuming that he would ask for further territories and revenues, Caligula was instead asked by Agrippa to abandon his plan of placing his statue in the Temple. Josephus notes that this could have been a suicidal request (*Ant.* 18.298) but Caligula had to accept because he 'regarded it as unseemly to break his word *before so many witnesses*, when he had by his zealous constraint compelled Agrippa to make his request' (*Ant.* 18.298). If this applies to Caligula, how much more so Antipas! After all, as Matthew's Jesus—another figure with pretensions for global leadership of sorts (Matt. 28.18–20)—puts it in a tradition which appears to assume the existence and validity of the Jerusalem Temple (and thus is a candidate for reflecting an early Palestinian tradition):

> 'Woe to you, blind guides, who say, "Whoever swears by the sanctuary is bound by nothing, but whoever swears by the gold of the sanctuary is bound by the oath." You blind fools! For which is greater, the gold or the sanctuary that has made the gold sacred? And you say, "Whoever swears by the altar is bound by nothing, but whoever swears by the gift that is on the altar is bound by the oath."' (Matt. 23.16–18).

THE COST OF REVOLUTION

The Markan text is different from both the Esther tradition and presentations of Antipas' attitude towards John the Baptist elsewhere on the issue of the potentially seditious nature of John's movement.[63] According to Mark 6.20, 'Herod feared (ἐφοβεῖτο) John, knowing that he was a righteous and holy man, and he protected him.' Yet according to Josephus, Antipas feared John because of potential uprising and thus imprisoned him (*Ant.* 18.118). If we turn to the later interpretations of Esther, Esther 5.3 also raises issues of Jewish rebellion. Esther 5.3 reads: 'The king said to her, "What is it, Queen Esther? What is your request? It shall be given you, even to the half of my kingdom."' *1 Targ. Esther* 5.3 adds an exception concerning the rebuilding of the Temple: 'I would not permit it to be rebuilt for I am afraid (דחיל) of the Jews/Jew lest they rebel against me.'[64] Against this backdrop, the fear of uprising is conspicuous by its absence in Mark 6.20, which might raise some suspicions that anything seditious has been deliberately removed or avoided.

The decapitation of John also has potentially significant echoes in Palestinian Judaism,[65] and is particularly important as we are dealing with an interaction with the contexts of social upheaval described in Chapter 1. One obvious point of contextualization concerns decapitation as a standard treatment of perceived revolutionaries or criminals. The prophet Theudas (active under Cuspius Fadus, 44–8 CE) 'persuaded the masses' (cf. Acts 5.36) to follow him to the Jordan River where he would part the river. The reaction of Fadus was to send in soldiers to kill them, take prisoners, and cut off Theudas' head and have it brought to Jerusalem (*Ant.* 20.97–9). As with John the Baptist, it is not clear that Theudas was going to lead a physically violent attack but from the perspective of an Antipas or Fadus such niceties did not really matter. Clearly, a movement involved with someone like John the Baptist or Jesus had the potential to be perceived by the authorities as seditious, associated as they were with decapitation and crucifixion. Little wonder that certain people associated with the Baptist might want to stress that their decapitated hero is innocent and guilty of only being wise and just.

There are helpful parallels in the haggadic interpretations of Esther. In one tradition, Vashti was decapitated, and her head can even be said to be accompanied by a platter. The biblical Hebrew text provides sufficient ambiguity to generate such haggadic speculation.[66] As Esther 1.19 puts it, 'If it pleases the king, let a royal order go out from him, and let it be written among the laws of the Persians and the Medes so that it may not be altered, that Vashti is never again to come before King Ahasuerus.' *Esther Rabba* 4.9 on Esther 1.19 adds: 'He said to him: "Your majesty, say but the word and I will put her head on a platter."' *Esther Rabba* 4.11 on 1.21 confirms that 'He gave the order and they brought in her head on a platter.' While there are some traditions unsympathetic to Esther,[67] there are also traditions where the king is regretful (e.g. *2 Targ. Esther* 2.1; Midrash Abba Gorion on Esther 2.1), including one recorded by Josephus (*Ant.* 11.191–5). Josephus interprets Esther by claiming that the king casts out Vashti without having her killed. However, the king realized his love for Vashti and 'could not bear the separation' yet tragically they could not be legally reconciled and so he continued in his grieving (λυπούμενος [*Ant.* 11.195]), just as Antipas grieved for John.[68] The biblical text of Esther 2.1 may hint at this regret: 'After these things, when the anger of King Ahasuerus had abated, he remembered Vashti and what she had done and what had been decreed against her.' *Esther Rabba* 5.2 on Esther 2.1, which includes the more problematic story of Vashti's head on a platter, is more explicit: 'After he had killed her he began to feel remorse, because he realized that she acted properly.' Again, the Esther story provides a further resource for understanding John's innocence. After all, it could be understood that both Vashti (according to some traditions) and John were decapitated just as both Vashti (according to some traditions) and John were innocent. Again, this is particularly important given the allegations of rebellion aimed at John and his movement.

We might be more sceptical about some of the earliest possible contexts for the generation of Mark 6.17–25. It is difficult, for instance, to think that this propaganda piece would be persuasive while Antipas was in power. If the stories about Herodias' influence over Antipas have any value for understanding the historical Antipas, then Herodias was an influential figure at court. A story pleading for innocence might be somewhat counterproductive or even suicidal in this context. Probably the most likely earliest possible date for such a story would be when Agrippa I was growing in power in the late 30s and when Antipas was exiled in 39 CE. Josephus claims that Herodias 'begrudged her brother [Agrippa] his rise to power far above the state that her husband enjoyed' and that Agrippa's spectacular shows of grandeur 'made her especially helpless to keep this unfortunate envy to herself' (*Ant.* 18.240). And, as we saw, to keep this power in check, Josephus claimed that Herodias talked Antipas into going to Rome. Unfortunately for them Agrippa discovered their plans and ultimately gained the support of Caligula through an allegation of conspiracy levelled at Antipas, resulting in their banishment to Lyons (*Ant.* 18.240–56). Presumably there would have been no political sensitivities about writing a story such as Mark 6.17–29 in this context. On the one hand, painting the ruler in a darkly negative light could still have been perceived as seditious by any ruler. On the other, blaming someone who was perceived to be manipulative, especially towards Agrippa, would potentially be welcoming. It may be of some significance for a story pleading innocence that Agrippa was remembered as persecuting 'Christians' in Jerusalem (Acts 12).

But there are some textual clues about the origins of this story. The story was also problematic for Matthew and Luke. Luke merely notes that John was arrested (Luke 3.19–20) and beheaded (Luke 9.7–9) but lacks the actual story of how John met his death. Why Luke did this is not clear but we might suggest that Luke was influenced by what seems otherwise to be the ancient consensus: John and Herod Antipas were enemies. Luke, for instance, mentions 'all the evil things that Herod had done' (3.19–20). Matthew does include the story but abbreviates Mark and downplays the gossipy element.[69] A significant change is found in Matt. 14.5: 'Though he wanted to put him to death, he feared the crowd because they regarded him as a prophet.' The blame is now on a more sinister Antipas and this directly contradicts Mark (cf. Matt. 21.26). Certainly, Matthew's Antipas was sorry that John had to die (Matt. 14.9) but presumably this was because of fear of the reaction of the crowd. Matthew's editing reveals how one reader might view Mark 6.17–29 as being too favourable to someone who was remembered as being brutally hostile to the movement from the outset. In terms of understanding Mark (and perhaps pre-Markan tradition), Matthew emphasizes just how unusual Mark 6.17–29 could have been but it also reveals that this kind of political threat was not an immediate one for Matthew and so we get the comment about the fear of the crowd. But perhaps most significantly in terms of establishing a pre-Markan tradition, it is even possible that Mark would have agreed with Matthew's understanding of Antipas! Portraying Antipas positively is not in line with Markan tendencies (e.g. Mark 3.6; 8.15; 12.13). Strikingly, 6.17–29 is the only place in Mark's Gospel where Jesus is not the focus, which may suggest that this story comes from some kind of interaction with people closely associated with John the Baptist.[70] But why did Mark include it? Mark may have used the story to present John as forerunner to Jesus. Perhaps Mark also used the story to show how even John the Baptist was killed scandalously as a means of lessening the potentially scandalous nature of Jesus' death.[71] But what we can say more certainly is that portraying Antipas more positively is not a reason Mark included it and that going against the Markan grain is one of the stronger arguments in favour of it being a pre-Markan tradition.

There are further possibilities which might add to the argument that Mark 6.17–29 is a pre-Markan tradition and even a relatively early

Palestinian tradition.[72] A number of Semitisms in the passage would at least point to connections with an Aramaic-speaking environment.[73] Moreover, as we have seen throughout, Mark 6.17–29 has some particularly close connections with various Palestinian, Hebrew, and Aramaic haggadic traditions, as well as traditions found in Josephus. This would at least suggest that the passage emerged in a context with connections with people in or around Palestine.[74] We might add that it is even possible that this story would have been heard or relayed by those with connections to court.[75] As we have seen, Joanna, the wife of Herod's steward Chuza, became associated with Jesus according to Luke 8.3 (cf. Luke 24.10). According to Acts, among the earliest members of the Jesus movement in Antioch included 'Manaen a member of the court of Herod the tetrarch' (Acts 13.1).

Making connections

In general terms, a reading of Mark 6.17–29 in its cultural context, with its close connections with material from Josephus, the Targumim, and the Dead Sea Scrolls, gives us an indication of some (and only some) of the ways in which gender could have been understood in first-century Palestine and the kinds of gender constructions which were present in a tradition which may well have been among the earliest. Mark 6.17–29 is a particularly significant passage in that it is one of the most explicit in terms of assumptions about gender and that it negotiates some of the problems with a group associated with the social upheavals in Galilee and Palestine more widely, including the prophetic movements it generated. In this light, and contrary to some recent exegesis, it is particularly striking that any significant challenge to traditional assumptions of gender does not appear to be present in this passage. On the contrary, whoever was responsible for this passage wanted to make it clear that they too shared conventional notions of gender as they fought for their own survival.

Given this and all the above, does gender tell us very much about the emergence of the Jesus movement beyond Palestine? In one sense, the general picture is that the earliest Palestinian traditions were being adapted to the world around them, whether the suppressing or reinscribing of gender roles in the more challenging notions of gender or placing heavy emphasis on conventional gender roles in a passage such as Mark 6.17–29. However, while this adaptation may have helped the earliest Palestinian traditions—and indeed Christianity more generally—to survive, some of the earliest traditions which may have been more challenging did contribute to the development of the movement in the long run. For a start, the upheavals in Galilee were directly interconnected with assumptions of gender and, if nothing else, the shifting household patterns provide some insight into how the Jesus movement got going. But there is more still. The idea of fictive kinship, for instance, provided a precedent for justifying the movement including Gentiles without full conversion and no doubt fed into the idea of communal living (e.g. Acts 2.42–7; 4.32–7).

The role of women as followers and patrons of Jesus is probably present in the early Palestinian tradition and connected clearly with the role of women in the spread of earliest Christianity. Indeed, the structural role of women running households, women with sufficient time, and elite women remained important in the spread of Christianity, partly because of their social status. In the context where circumcision would have been some kind of an issue for converts to Christianity, it is not difficult to see how women were in a strategically significant position in that they presumably need not worry about the issues of adult circumcision.[76] Such reasoning may also underpin a still useful parallel found in Josephus, which describes events around the beginning of the war against Rome: the men of Damascus wanted to destroy the Jewish populace but, Josephus adds, 'their only fear was of their own wives who, with few exceptions, had all become converts to the Jewish religion, and so their efforts were mainly directed to keeping the secret from them' (*War* 2.560–1; cf. *Ant.* 18.81–4; 20.34–48).[77] These sorts of discussions of women in strategic positions in Josephus shed some light on Gospel stories, notably the story of Joanna, the wife of Herod's steward Chuza, who is said to have provided for him, and Susanna. As noted earlier, the name 'Joanna' is probably a Jewish name while 'Chuza' probably reflects her husband's Nabatean background.[78] It is figures such as Joanna and Susanna, along with Mary Magdalene, and Mary the mother of James the younger and of Joses, and Salome, who 'used to follow him and provided for him when he was in Galilee'. (Mark 15.40–1; cf. Luke 24:10)

The social roles of women running households, women with sufficient time, and elite women, would have placed them in a position of some significance both in the earliest Palestinian tradition and in the spread of earliest Christianity, with the connections between the two relatively straightforward and continuous.[79] In the broader Greco-Roman world, women could have found themselves with some control over matters domestic, some may have been allowed to study philosophy, and some may have inherited the household when typically older husbands died (cf. e.g. Prov. 31.10–31; Xenophon, *Econ.* 3.14–16; Musonius Rufus, frag. 3; Philostratus, *De gym.* 2.23; 272.30–1).[80] In earliest Christianity there were certainly women, for whatever reasons, in positions of social authority within households and consequently prominent positions in Christian gatherings.[81] Women, for example, may well have played a more widespread part in patronage, gatherings, and conversion to Christianity, including as heads of households (cf. e.g. Rom. 16.1–2; 1 Cor. 1.11; Col. 4.15; Acts 12.12–17; Acts 16.14–15; *C. Cel.* 3.55), than usually seen in the scope of interests recorded in ancient Christian literature.[82]

None of this is to argue that there was a Big Gender Bang in Galilee which was never to be repeated. There is enough work now done on gender and sexuality in relation to Christian origins and early Judaism to know that complexities of construction of gender and sexuality would continue to be present in various forms. However, what we can say is that a combination of crucifixion (and perhaps awareness of impending crucifixion) and the social upheavals in Galilee and Palestine generated localized questions about gender in the earliest tradition. Presumably from the earliest tradition questions were raised about Jesus' status in relation to heading the household and about his potentially emasculated status as a crucifixion victim. There are elements of an embrace, or at least awareness, of gender understood as challenging conventions but there are likewise tendencies, perhaps developing simultaneously, of reinscribing assumptions of gender and controlling gender through promoting stereotypical gender roles. It was a phallocentric world and this was not going to be changed. Indeed, the conformity to conventional understanding of gender may well have helped the earliest tradition, and the movement, survive. Yet the remembering of female patrons and followers was a significant development in the survival and continuance of the movement, particularly as women running households, women with sufficient time, and elite women would play an important role and be a point of contact as the movement spread through and beyond Palestine.

An Irrelevant Conclusion

One of the advantages of working with the general 'earliest Palestinian tradition', rather than trying more precisely to reconstruct the historical Jesus, is that it potentially allows for more evidence to assess the ways in which people were part of the complexities and chaos of historical change. To take an extreme example, i.e. one which is not directly about the historical Jesus, it allows us to use a text like Mark 6.17–29 to assess early gendered interactions with social upheaval. Or again, we can use the earliest reports of the resurrection appearances (1 Cor. 15.3–9) as part of the process of the very earliest thinking on Jesus' elevation without having to categorize strictly between 'pre-Easter' and 'post-Easter'. Besides, we do not necessarily have direct access to the words or even deeds of the historical Jesus and working more generally eases some of those more practical problems.

What we have seen throughout is how people in and around the Jesus movement interacted with the social upheavals of Galilee and Judea, as well as the Roman empire more broadly. The earliest Palestinian tradition pitted the kingdom of God against Rome, attacked wealth and privilege, supported the poorest members of society, and saw Jesus as an agent of the kingdom in both present and future. However, the earliest Palestinian tradition simultaneously mimicked power and imperialism. It looked to the kingdom of God coming in power and establishing hierarchical rule on earth with Jesus and his followers playing highly elevated roles, including one of judge. Rich and poor would be reversed but the structure of reward was not radically altered, and there is even some suggestion in the earliest Palestinian tradition of extensive reward in the present age. This imperial theology was also taken up very early, not least by Paul, and, even if it probably would have horrified some of the people responsible for the earliest Palestinian tradition, imperialist ideology is not as far removed from Constantine as is often thought.

Connected to the attempt to make the rich change their ways was the concern for 'sinners'—probably identified as wealthy and oppressive law-breakers—and their repentance. This repentance involved returning to the Law as understood in the earliest Palestinian tradition. Such observance included purity laws—but a view of purity constructed against Pharisaic purity laws and against those interested in applying non-Temple purity to everyday life. Here the earliest Palestinian tradition may be analogous to the interests of those understood as the 'people of the land' in rabbinic literature or the rewarded and/or displaced people (landowners and landless) who moved to Tiberias and who would have been uninterested in, or unwilling to keep, expanded purity laws. The emphasis on 'morality' and 'moral purity' is significant. Morality was not constructed as absolutely antithetical to purity laws but the emphasis on morality includes the exact kinds of practices that 'sinners' were said to avoid or, in the case of vice lists, practise. What is particularly significant about the 'sinners' is that they are constructed as near-synonymous with 'Gentiles'. This helps explain the survival of specifically Jewish purity material and the greater emphasis on morality as a boundary marker. Specifically Jewish purity law did not really concern Gentiles and became irrelevant, with more Gentiles involved in the earliest 'Christianity' as it spread more widely in the Greco-Roman world. The boundary-marking morality, however, was relevant as it did directly concern Gentiles. This meant that purity could be reinterpreted and used metaphorically with little connection to purity concerns in the earliest Palestinian tradition.

The socio-economic upheavals in Galilee and Judea were important for understanding gender in the earliest Palestinian tradition. The uprooting of traditional households, Jesus not heading a household, and ideas about alternative fictive families meant that there were problems for some traditional conceptions of masculinity. This upheaval may also account for the remembrance of female followers and supporters, and has a rough analogy in the female contingent identified among the followers of Simon bar Giora in the Jewish uprising against Rome. Furthermore, the crucifixion immediately presented Jesus as a potentially emasculated victim of masculine Rome. However, and again simultaneously, there were more 'reactionary' models of gender already being utilized. From early on, Jesus was probably being understood as some kind of heroic sufferer and martyr, a man outside the women's domestic place, and happy to be waited on by women. A passage such as Mark 6.17–29 further shows how the early Palestinian tradition used the most clichéd gender constructions to defend itself against charges of sedition and to control any notion of an ambiguous understanding of gender. However, the association with women running households, women with sufficient time, and even elite women would provide an important means for the spread of the movement beyond Palestine, as women with time and resources would continue as an important point of contact and conversion of households.

In many ways, the in-breaking of a more 'revolutionary' moment as seen in the earliest Palestinian tradition was always constrained by broader imperial and phallocentric structures. This brings us back to Chapter 1 and Bakunin's critique of the Marxist revolutionary and the dictatorship of the proletariat leading to the establishment of a Red Bureaucracy. Without wanting to push the analogies too far, this tension between revolution and authoritarianism has been a major cultural and political issue since the nineteenth century, especially after the rise of the Soviet Union. It has become a major theme in the arts, not least the influential work of Orwell such as *Animal Farm* (1945), *1984* (1949), and his reflections on the Spanish Civil War in *Homage to Catalonia* (1938) which played a significant role in Orwell's attitude towards Soviet-inspired Marxism. Yet this is not the full story. Orwell also saw hope in other revolutionary groups, especially the Spanish anarchists. As he wrote:

> I had dropped more or less by chance into the only community of any size in Western Europe where political consciousness and disbelief in capitalism were more normal than their opposites. Up here in Aragon one was among tens of thousands of people, mainly though not entirely of working-class origin, all living at the same level and mingling on terms of equality. In theory it was perfect equality, and even in practice it was not far from it. There is a sense in which it would be true to say that one was experiencing a foretaste of Socialism, by which I mean that the prevailing mental atmosphere was that of Socialism. Many of the normal motives of civilized life—snobbishness, money-grubbing, fear of the boss, etc.—had simply ceased to exist. The ordinary class-division of society had disappeared to an extent that is almost unthinkable in the money-tainted air of England; there was no one there except the peasants and ourselves, and no one owned anyone else as his master.

This is an idealized account of the revolution within civil war Spain which does not do justice to the complexities on the ground. Such complexities are obviously beyond what can or need to be discussed here but if we focus on a final form reading of *Homage to Catalonia* instead, it remains significant that Orwell enthusiastically picked up such radical ideas for an English-speaking audience decades before the social upheavals of the 1960s. But Orwell's fear of such revolutionary fervour being crushed lived on in memories (and was no doubt inspired by realities on the ground in civil war Spain), whether in Ken Loach's film *Land and Freedom* (1995) or the writings of Noam Chomsky. Yet hope is still apparent in both, whether passing on lessons to a new generation in the case of Loach or, in the case of Chomsky, looking for ways to challenge authority and authoritarianism and thinking about how to build a fairer society:

> ... if you take classic libertarian principles and apply them to the modern period, I think you actually come pretty close to the principles that animated revolutionary Barcelona in the late 1930s—to what's called 'anarcho-syndicalism'... I think that's about as high a level as humans have yet achieved in trying to realize these libertarian principles... I'm not saying that everything done in the revolution was right, but in its general spirit and character, in the idea of developing the kind of society that Orwell saw and described... with popular control over all the institutions of society... a lot of interesting things happened... they happened out of maybe fifty years of serious organizing, and attempts to try it, and failures, and being smashed up by the army, and trying again... there wasn't a single pattern that was followed... And that's a good example of how I think constructive change has to happen.[1]

While at this point I may seem to be indulging the genre of conclusion-writing too much, we should not for one moment think that any of this is unconnected with historical practice. One figure more familiar to social historians of Christian origins is Eric Hobsbawm, whose history writing certainly cannot be detangled from his unromanticized membership of the Communist Party and supposedly pragmatic support for Eurocommunism. For all his analysis of 'pre-political' bandits, Hobsbawm's history writing contains an ongoing narrative where history's eccentrics are said to deserve less attention. In his major history of the twentieth century, non-Communist Party radicals, including those in the Spanish Civil War, are typically dismissed as 'insignificant', 'eccentric', 'ultra-Left', etc.[2] Obviously, we need to appreciate and focus on the workings of power in order to understand historical change, but a history which ignores the possibilities raised by eccentrics, insignificants, and radicals is in danger of complying with, and imposing a narrative of, domination and power. This sort of history is effectively the academic manufacturing of consent, ignoring possibilities, no matter how small, of how we might alternatively conceive historical change, as Hobsbawm's more repentant friend E. P. Thompson knew and as Chomsky noted of Hobsbawm over forty years ago.[3] Neither the theocratic tendencies of earliest Christians nor Hobsbawm's Moscow-inspired power bloc provides the best models for the sorts of constructive changes envisaged by Chomsky. In the case of the early Christians, their historical constraints meant that they probably could not have provided a sufficient challenge to deeply embedded power structures, despite the best intentions of the 'anti-empire' tendency in contemporary biblical scholarship. But there among its eccentrics beats the heart of the heartless world and plenty of eccentric interpreters of the Bible—from William Blake through Keir Hardie and Nye Bevan to Andrea Needham, Joanna Wilson, Lotta Kronlid, and Angie Zelter—have seen this in trying to build a New Jerusalem, or at least battling Babylon, in the here and now.[4]

There may be a more modest and immediate lesson for the biblical scholar, who likewise appears to become more eccentric in the world of higher education. Stewart Lee told a story about Margaret Thatcher's visit to St Hilda's College, Oxford. When the student said she studied Norse literature, Thatcher was said to have replied, 'What a luxury.'[5] Underlying the comedic logic is the idea that academic subjects, including those which might include the study of ancient Greek, Hebrew, and Aramaic literature, need to be justified in terms of economic value.[6] One way to deal with this issue might be to follow the journalist and trained religious studies scholar Nathan Schneider, who grounded his beliefs in an epiphany at the American Academy of Religion:

The AAR was at the enormous new Washington, DC convention center. Fittingly, one of the plenary speakers was Madeleine Albright, the former secretary of state who had just written a book about why religion is so important.

What I remember her saying, which stuck with me and probably a lot of the other graduate students in the hall, were things like this: 'Our diplomats need to be trained to know the religions of the countries where they're going.' And: 'I think the Secretary of State needs to have religion advisors.' I hadn't really thought of it that way before, but it made great sense, especially with someone like Albright saying it. Religion is everywhere. It *does* matter. The ongoing sectarian violence in occupied Iraq had turned the headlines into daily reminders about the consequences of not taking religion seriously—to say nothing of politics in DC back then. Yes—sounds like a job for a religion scholar.

Here, I stand with Madeleine Albright: the world can't afford to wait for religious studies to grow up. It has come of age. It's time to be more confident about what the field has to offer. I've come to think that it imparts skills more valuable than most of those who teach and learn them even know.[7]

Schneider continues by drawing on ideas of engagement with 'the world' in the language of commerce and embraces the humanities-as-commodity rhetoric:

Traders have to know how to temporarily avoid inconvenient subjects long enough to get what they're looking for. They learn to be careful around the sensitivities of others. Scholars of religion learn to do the same thing. Both, it could be said, are *on the lookout for value*. Business tends to look for financial value, and religion scholars tend to look for social value, but it's a pretty similar task in either case. I think it's time that religious studies does more to prep its students and faculty for a more direct engagement with what I've been calling 'the world.' The field is ready for it.

However, perhaps there are still people out there who do not want their work to be so heavily corporate and government controlled (or at least not associated with the invasion of Iraq!), who do not want to provide free training for various companies, and who do not want just to prepare people for the crushing monotony of a life of work. Are not universities places which *should* be supporting the study of palaeography, Norse literature, or ancient texts?[8] Perhaps there are still people who might value prehistory, ancient history, local history, history's eccentrics, Viking material remains, translations of the Dead Sea Scrolls or Coptic texts, translators of the untranslated, new fossil remains or dinosaur bones, the workings of the universe, the Rosetta Stone, understandings of how human society got where it is, or indeed the quest for the historical Jesus, without measuring the value in *purely* economic terms. This is not, however, to embrace the idea of the well-paid aristocrat–scholar who is left alone with their genius, or indeed an educational system largely for the more privileged students. As the language of 'subversion' is so common in the study of Christian origins, perhaps scholars might be prepared to embrace the idea that their work may be mildly more subversive by embracing certain topics that do not meet market demand.[9] Perhaps something like 'social value', in a way slightly different to how it is understood by Schneider, might be an alternative whereby academics can provide more freely available scholarship, such as the wonderful resource that is Biblical Studies Online,[10] can work for widening access to higher education, and can provide more public engagement, including basic talks and seminars beyond the traditionally privileged audiences. Plenty of academics do these kinds of things and in ways that are being valued in and beyond universities. Anecdotally, I have found great enthusiasm for the quest for the historical Jesus, whether among university students or a wider public audience beyond the university. And this wider public engagement seems to me to be a different way of justifying intellectual pursuits without becoming inescapably harnessed to state or private power, which will only lead to addressing their needs. Preserving value in this way may be idealistic but it is hardly impossible.

So the lesson is clear, even for the humble historical Jesus scholar. Be idealistic! Demand the possible! Embrace irrelevancy!

Notes

INTRODUCTION

1. It will hopefully become clear throughout that this book should not be confused with the debates over the historical existence of Jesus, so-called 'mythicism'. It should be noted that questions concerning 'mythicism' are turning up closer to the mainstream of historical Jesus studies. See, for instance, R. J. Hoffmann (ed.), *Sources of the Jesus Tradition: Separating History from Myth* (Amherst, NY: Prometheus, 2010), and T. L. Thompson and T. S. Verenna (eds), *'Is This Not the Carpenter?' The Question of the Historicity of the Figure of Jesus* (Durham: Acumen, 2012). For an overview and historical contextualization of recent 'mythicist' debates in scholarship, see J. G. Crossley, *Jesus in an Age of Neoliberalism: Quests, Scholarship and Ideology* (London and Oakville: Equinox, 2012). 'Mythicism' has already provoked two prominent academic responses: B. D. Ehrman, *Did Jesus Exist? The Historical Argument for Jesus of Nazareth* (New York: HarperCollins, 2013), and M. Casey, *Jesus: Evidence and Argument or Mythicist Myths?* (London and New York: T&T Clark, 2014). The impact of 'mythicism' on mainstream scholarship has so far been minimal but it looks as if the topic of Jesus' existence will now be getting extensive (*c.*700 page) treatment and published with a mainstream biblical studies publisher: R. Carrier, *On the Historicity of Jesus: Why We Might Have Reason for Doubt* (Sheffield: Sheffield Phoenix Press, 2014 [unpublished at time of writing]).
2. D. C. Allison, *Resurrecting Jesus: The Earliest Christian Tradition and its Interpreters* (London and New York: T&T Clark, 2005), pp. 1–26.
3. For a recent overview of issues in historical Jesus studies see H. Bond, *The Historical Jesus: A Guide for the Perplexed* (London: T&T Clark, 2012).
4. P. H. Alexander, J. F. Kutsko, J. D. Ernest, S. Decker-Lucke, and D. L. Petersen (eds), *The SBL Handbook of Style for Ancient Near Eastern, Biblical, and Early Christian Studies* (Peabody, MA: Hendrickson, 1999).

CHAPTER 1

1. A. Badiou, *Saint Paul: The Foundation of Universalism* (Stanford: Stanford University Press, 2003), p. 2.

2. S. Žižek, *The Puppet and the Dwarf: The Perverse Core of Christianity* (Cambridge, MA.: MIT Press, 2003), p. 9.
3. The following summary is based on the more extensive arguments found in J. G. Crossley, *Jesus in an Age of Terror: Scholarly Projects for a New American Century* (London and Oakville: Equinox, 2008), pp. 143–94 and J. G. Crossley, *Jesus in an Age of Neoliberalism: Quests, Scholarship and Ideology* (London and Oakville: Equinox, 2012), pp. 105–32. A number of other scholarly works are also significant here (and influenced my own work); they include: R. S. Sugirtharajah, *Asian Biblical Hermeneutics and Postcolonialism: Contesting the Interpretations* (Sheffield: Sheffield Academic Press, 1998); E. S. Fiorenza, *Jesus and the Politics of Interpretation* (New York and London: Continuum, 2000); S. Kelley, *Racializing Jesus: Race, Ideology and the Formation of Modern Biblical Scholarship* (London and New York: Routledge, 2002); W. E. Arnal, *The Symbolic Jesus: Historical Scholarship, Judaism and the Construction of Contemporary Identity* (London and Oakville: Equinox, 2005); A.-J. Levine, *The Misunderstood Jew: The Church and the Scandal of the Jewish Jesus* (San Francisco: HarperCollins, 2006); F. Bermejo-Rubio, 'The Fiction of the "Three Quests": An Argument for Dismantling a Dubious Historiographical Paradigm', *JSHJ* 7 (2009), pp. 211–53. See also the special edition of *JSHJ* which includes the most up-to-date ideological critiques of the field, especially in relation to constructions of Judaism and ethnicity: J. G. Crossley, 'A "Very Jewish" Jesus: Perpetuating the Myth of Superiority', *JSHJ* 11 (2013), pp. 109–29; H. Moxnes, 'Jesus in Discourses of Dichotomies: Alternative Paradigms for the Historical Jesus', *JSHJ* 11 (2013), pp. 130–52; S. Kelley, 'Hear Then No More Parables: The Case against "Parable"', *JSHJ* 11 (2013), pp. 153–69; F. Bermejo-Rubio, 'Why is John the Baptist Used as a Foil for Jesus? Leaps of Faith and Oblique Anti-Judaism in Contemporary Scholarship', *JSHJ* 11 (2013), pp. 170–96.
4. E.g. E. P. Sanders, *Paul and Palestinian Judaism: A Comparison of Patterns of Religion* (London: SCM, 1977); E. P. Sanders, *Jesus and Judaism* (London: SCM, 1985).
5. For some (and only some) examples see Sanders, *Jesus and Judaism*, e.g. pp. 204–8, 252–5; J. D. G. Dunn, *Jesus Remembered* (Grand Rapids: Eerdmans, 2003), e.g. pp. 3–4, 62, 784 (Dunn is often more careful than most but it is still notable that the reasons for Jesus' death are discussed in terms of 'Jewish' and 'Roman' responsibility—do we *necessarily* need the ethnic tags?); N. T. Wright, *Jesus and the Victory of God* (London: SPCK, 1996), pp. xiii–662; G. Theissen and A. Merz, *The Historical Jesus: A Comprehensive Guide* (London: SCM, 1998), e.g.

pp. 366–7; D. C. Allison, *Resurrecting Jesus: The Earliest Christian Tradition and Its Interpreters* (London and New York: T&T Clark, 2005), e.g. pp. 149–97; M. Hengel and A. M. Schwemer, *Jesus und das Judentum* (Tübingen: Mohr Siebeck, 2007), e.g. pp. 21, 289; J. P. Meier, 'Did the Historical Jesus Prohibit All Oaths? Part 1' *JSHJ* 5 (2007), pp. 175–204; J. P. Meier, 'Did the Historical Jesus Prohibit All Oaths? Part 2', *JSHJ* 6 (2008), pp. 3–24. Note also the significant label for Meier's historical Jesus work: a *marginal* Jew.

6. Wright, *Victory*, p. 93.
7. J. G. Crossley, 'The Multicultural Christ: Jesus the Jew and the New Perspective on Paul in an Age of Neoliberalism', *BCT* 7 (2011), pp. 1–9.
8. For detailed discussion see Crossley, *Jesus in an Age of Neoliberalism*.
9. D. Harvey, *The Condition of Postmodernity* (Oxford: Blackwell, 1989); F. Jameson, *Postmodernism, or, The Cultural Logic of Late Capitalism* (Durham: Duke University Press, 1991).
10. Here I echo Kelley, *Racializing Jesus*.
11. Among various publications see e.g. S. Žižek, 'Multiculturalism, or, the Cultural Logic of Multinational Capitalism', *New Left Review* (1997), pp. 28–51; Žižek, *Puppet and the Dwarf*; S. Žižek *Welcome to the Desert of the Real! Five Essays on September 11 and Related Dates* (London and New York: Verso, 2002); S. Žižek, 'Liberal Multiculturalism Masks an Old Barbarism with a Human Face', *Guardian* (3 October 2010) http://www.theguardian.com/commentisfree/2010/oct/03/immigration-policy-roma-rightwing-europe; S. Žižek, *Living in the End Times* (revised edition; London and New York: Verso, 2011). For broader discussions of 'race', multiculturalism, and neoliberalism with more detailed analysis see e.g. D. T. Goldberg, *The Threat of Race: Reflections on Racial Neoliberalism* (Oxford: Wiley-Blackwell, 2009) and A. Lentin and G. Titley, *The Crises of Multiculturalism: Racism in a Neoliberal Age* (London: Zed Books, 2011).
12. It should be noted that the logic criticizing Islam (or 'religion' more generally) as being inherently or essentially violent typically shares the same assumption of compatibility with liberal democracy.
13. See e.g. R. T. McCutcheon, *Religion and the Domestication of Dissent or, How to Live in a Less Than Perfect Nation* (London and Oakville: Equinox, 2005).
14. Wright, *Victory*, pp. 399–402.
15. On which see now M. J. Sandford, *Poverty, Wealth, and Empire: Jesus and Postcolonial Criticism* (Sheffield: Sheffield Phoenix Press, 2014).
16. A.-J. Levine, *The Misunderstood Jew: The Church and the Scandal of the Jewish Jesus* (San Francisco: HarperCollins, 2006).

17. See e.g. M. Fisher, *Capitalist Realism: Is There No Alternative?* (Winchester, UK, and Washington, USA: Zero Books, 2009); C. Cremin, *Capitalism's New Clothes: Enterprise, Ethics and Enjoyment in Times of Crisis* (London: Pluto Press, 2011).
18. S. Žižek, 'Do We Still Live in a World?', http://www.lacan.com/zizrattlesnakeshake.html. For the more detailed theoretical background, see S. Žižek, *The Sublime Object of Ideology* (London and New York: Verso, 1989).
19. S. Žižek, 'Return of the Natives', *New Statesman* (4 March 2010), http://www.newstatesman.com/film/2010/03/avatar-reality-love-couple-sex.
20. E.g. M. J. Borg, *Conflict, Holiness, and Politics in the Teachings of Jesus* (orig.: Edwin Mellen: New York, 1984; Harrisburg, PA: Trinity Press International, 1998); M. J. Borg, *Jesus, a New Vision: Spirit, Culture, and the Life of Discipleship* (London: SPCK, 1993). Cf. Žižek on western forms of Buddhism: 'it enables you to fully participate in the frantic capitalist game while sustaining the exception that you are not really in it' (*First as Tragedy, Then as Farce* London and New York: Verso, 2009, p 66). Compare also Žižek's (in)famous analysis of Buddhism in Žižek, *Puppet and the Dwarf*, e.g. pp. 20–33.
21. N. Chomsky, *Understanding Power* (New York: New Press, 2002), p. 154.
22. N. T. Wright, *The Resurrection of the Son of God* (London: SPCK, 2003), p. 737.
23. Cf. Crossley, *Neoliberalism*, pp. 15–16; Wright also has form when it comes to grand claims about justice and his research. E.g. 'If what I write could help in any way towards the establishment of justice and peace there [Israel and Palestine], or indeed anywhere else, I would be deeply grateful' (Wright, *Victory*, p. xv).
24. Fisher, *Capitalist Realism*, p. 12: 'the film performs our anti-capitalism for us, allowing us to consume with impunity'.
25. Crossley, *Jesus in an Age of Terror*, pp. 59–142.
26. E.g. H. Moxnes, *The Economy of the Kingdom: Social Conflict and Economic Relations in Luke's Gospel* (Philadelphia: Fortress, 1988); K. C. Hanson and D. E. Oakman, *Palestine in the Time of Jesus: Social Structures and Social Conflicts* (Minneapolis: Augsburg Fortress, 1998); W. R. Herzog, *Prophet and Teacher: An Introduction to the Historical Jesus* (Louisville: WJK, 2005).
27. J. G. Crossley, *Why Christianity Happened: A Sociohistorical Account of Christian Origins 26–50 CE* (Louisville: WJK, 2006), pp. 3–22.
28. Crossley, *Jesus in an Age of Terror*, pp. 112–16.
29. E.g. J. P. Meier, *A Marginal Jew: Rethinking the Historical Jesus. Volume One: The Roots of the Problem and the Person* (New York: Doubleday, 1991), pp. 10–11; J. P. Meier, *A Marginal Jew: Rethinking the Historical*

Jesus. Volume Three: Companions and Competitors (New York: Doubleday, 2001), p. 67; Wright, *Victory*, pp. 52–3.

30. Wright, *Victory*, p. 52.
31. For criticism of Crossan in terms of historical anachronism, see e.g. J. H. Elliott, 'Jesus Was Not an Egalitarian: A Critique of an Anachronistic and Idealist Theory', *BTB* 32 (2002), pp. 75–91. While Elliott makes helpful points we will return to issues of gender in Chapter 5.
32. E.g. (among many, many others) E. S. Fiorenza, *In Memory of Her: A Feminist Theological Reconstruction of Christian Origins* (New York: Crossroad, 1983; second edition 1995); R. Horsley, *Jesus and the Spiral of Violence: Popular Jewish Resistance in Roman Palestine* (San Francisco: Harper & Row, 1987); Moxnes, *Economy of the Kingdom*; D. A. Fiensy, *The Social History of Palestine in the Herodian Period: The Land is Mine* (Lewiston, Queenston, and Lampeter: Edwin Mellen, 1991); Hanson and Oakman, *Palestine in the Time of Jesus*; S. Freyne, 'Herodian Economics in Galilee: Searching for a Suitable Model', in P. F. Esler (ed.), *Modelling Early Christianity: Social-Scientific Studies of the New Testament in Its Context* (London: Routledge, 1995), pp. 23–46; J. D. Crossan, *The Birth of Christianity: Discovering What Happened in the Years Immediately after the Execution of Jesus* (Edinburgh: T&T Clark, 1998); E. W. Stegemann and W. Stegemann, *The Jesus Movement: A Social History of Its First Century* (Edinburgh: T&T Clark, 1999); Herzog, *Prophet and Teacher*; Crossley, *Why Christianity Happened*; D. A. Fiensy, *Jesus the Galilean: Soundings in a First Century Life* (Piscataway: Gorgias, 2007).
33. K. Marx, *A Contribution to the Critique of Hegel's 'Philosophy of Right'* (Cambridge: Cambridge University Press, 1970), p. 131.
34. Cf. C. Martin, *Masking Hegemony: A Genealogy of Liberalism, Religion and the Private Sphere* (London and Oakville: Equinox, 2010).
35. E.g. R. Dawkins, 'Religion's Misguided Missiles', *Guardian* (15 September 2001), http://www.theguardian.com/world/2001/sep/15/september11.politicsphilosophyandsociety1; M. Amis, 'The Voice of the Lonely Crowd', *Guardian* (1 June 2002), http://www.theguardian.com/books/2002/jun/01/philosophy.society; S. Harris, *The End of Faith: Religion, Terror, and the Future of Reason* (London: Simon & Schuster, 2004); M. Amis, 'The Age of Horrorism', *Observer* (10 September 2006), http://www.theguardian.com/world/2006/sep/10/september11.politicsphilosophyandsociety; R. Dawkins, *The God Delusion* (London: Bantham, 2006). For critique and discussion (effectively of the cliché that 'religion causes all wars') see e.g. Crossley, *Jesus in an Age of Neoliberalism*, pp. 154–9; W. T. Cavanaugh, *The Myth of Religious Violence: Secular Ideology and the Roots of Modern Conflict* (Oxford: Oxford University Press, 2009).

36. For a full discussion with bibliography see Crossley, *Jesus in an Age of Terror*, pp. 58–99.
37. For convenient and succinct analyses of the political and economic contexts see e.g. D. Harvey, *A Brief History of Neoliberalism* (Oxford: Oxford University Press, 2005), pp. 171–2; N. Chomsky and G. Achcar, *Perilous Power: The Middle East and U. S. Foreign Policy* (Boulder & London: Paradigm Publishers, 2007), pp. 30–4.
38. For an earlier presentation on what follows see J. G. Crossley, 'Writing about the Historical Jesus: Historical Explanation and "the Big Why Questions", or Antiquarian Empiricism and Victorian Tomes?', *JSHJ* 7 (2009), pp. 63–90, with further thanks to Bob Webb for permissions. On the connections between dissimilarity from Judaism and the Great Man view of Jesus see G. Theissen and D. Winter, *The Quest for the Plausible Jesus: The Question of Criteria* (Louisville: WJK, 2002) and D. Winter, 'Saving the Quest for Authenticity from the Criterion of Dissimilarity: History and Plausibility', in C. Keith and A. Le Donne (eds), *Jesus, Criteria and the Demise of Authenticity* (London: T&T Clark, 2012), pp. 115–31, e.g. p. 120: 'Thus, Jesus was seen as the genius beyond compare, the great independent heroic individual who arises at a crisis time, repudiates Jewish legalism and ushers in a new historical era, before being crucified because he is dangerously new'. On this history of Jesus the Great Man in scholarship see e.g. H. Moxnes, *Jesus and the Rise of Nationalism: A New Quest for the Nineteenth Century Historical Jesus* (London and New York: I. B. Taurus, 2011) ; Crossley, *Jesus in an Age of Neoliberalism*, pp. 68–101.
39. E.g. J. G. Crossley, 'Defining History', in J. G. Crossley and C. Karner (eds), *Writing History, Constructing Religion* (Aldershot: Ashgate, 2005), pp. 9–29; J. Schröter, *Jesus von Nazaret: Jude aus Galiläa-Retter der Welt* (second edition; Leipzig: Evangelische Verlagsanstalt, 2009); A. J. M. Wedderburn, *Jesus and the Historians* (Tübingen: Mohr Siebeck, 2010); S. McKnight, *Jesus and His Death: Historiography, the Historical Jesus, and Atonement Theory* (Waco: Baylor University Press, 2005); R. L. Webb, 'The Historical Enterprise and Historical Jesus Research' in D. L. Bock and R. L. Webb (eds), *Key Events in the Life of the Historical Jesus: A Collaborative Exploration of Content and Coherence* (Tübingen: Mohr Siebeck, 2009), pp. 9–93.
40. For a wide-ranging history and analysis of the origins and development of Jesus as the great human historical actor in western bourgeois thought see D. Georgi, 'The Interest in Life of Jesus Theology as a Paradigm to the Social History of Biblical Criticism', *HTR* 85 (1992), pp. 51–83 (80–3) for the critical study of the historical Jesus). Cf. p. 76: 'The view that Jesus

had been a genius of sorts became the dominant view in the late eighteenth, nineteenth, and twentieth centuries, not only in Germany but also in western Europe and North America, among both Protestants and Catholics. The differences between conservative and liberal christology in this respect were of minor importance.' For a different kind of critique of individualism with reference to Jesus and household see H. Moxnes, *Putting Jesus in His Place: A Radical Vision of Household and Kingdom* (Louisville: WJK, 2003), pp. 22–45.

41. Sanders, *Jesus and Judaism*, p. 11; E. P. Sanders, *The Historical Figure of Jesus* (London: Penguin, 1993), pp. 10–11.
42. Sanders, *Historical Figure*, pp. 2, 4–5. It should be pointed out that Sanders' concerns as an ancient historian over against theologian have brought significant benefits to NT studies. On this see Crossley, *Why Christianity Happened*, pp. 29–32.
43. R. W. Funk, R. W. Hoover, and the Jesus Seminar, *The Five Gospels: The Search for the Authentic Words of Jesus* (New York: Schribner, 1993), p. 36.
44. B. Chilton, *Rabbi Jesus: An Intimate Biography* (New York: Doubleday, 2000), pp. 47, 104, 138, 193, 225.
45. Meier, *A Marginal Jew*, pp. 10–11.
46. Cf. H. Moxnes, 'The Historical Jesus: From Master Narrative to Cultural Context', *BTB* 28 (1999), pp. 135–49 (138–43); Herzog, *Prophet and Teacher*, pp. 1–24.
47. Sanders, *Historical Figure*, p. 183.
48. Wright, *Victory*, p. 132. The subtitle of one of Wright's popular books on Jesus also stresses biographical importance, *The Original Jesus: The Life and Vision of a Revolutionary* (Oxford: Lion, 1996).
49. Wright, *Resurrection of the Son of God*, p. 718.
50. E. H. Carr, *What is History?* (second edition; London: Penguin, 1987), p. 45.
51. Cf. Moxnes, 'Historical Jesus', pp. 143–9.
52. The discussions over agency versus structure are typically about description and interpretation of groups and/or individuals rather than ways of understanding historical change. See e.g. D. G. Horrell, 'Models and Methods in Social-Scientific Interpretation: a Response to Philip Esler', *JSNT* 22 (2000), pp. 83–105; P. F. Esler, 'Models in New Testament Interpretation: a Reply to David Horrell', *JSNT* 22 (2000), pp. 107–13; Z. A. Crook, 'Structure versus Agency in Studies of the Biblical Social World: Engaging with Louise Lawrence', *JSNT* 29 (2007), pp. 251–75; L. J. Lawrence, 'Structure, Agency and Ideology: A Response to Zeba Crook', *JSNT* 29 (2007), pp. 277–86.

53. The *theological* danger of supposedly reducing Jesus to any old charismatic leader is recognized by S. C. Barton, 'Historical Criticism and Social-Scientific Perspectives in New Testament Study', in J. B. Green (ed.), *Hearing the New Testament: Strategies for Interpretation* (Grand Rapids: Eerdmans, 1995), pp. 61–89 (76). For critical analyses of the charismatic leader in historical Jesus studies from perspectives less concerned with theological dangers see e.g. B. J. Malina, *The Social World of Jesus and the Gospels* (London: Routledge, 1996), p. 123; cf. pp. 124–42, 217–41.
54. Wright, *Victory*, pp. 156–8.
55. Allison, *Resurrecting Jesus*, pp. 22–3.
56. As ever, note the biographical relevance of the subtitles of Crossan's books on Jesus: *The Historical Jesus: The Life of a Mediterranean Jewish Peasant* (Edinburgh: T&T Clark, 1991) and *Jesus: A Revolutionary Biography* (San Francisco: HarperCollins, 1994). Cf. J. D. Crossan, *A Long Way from Tipperary* (San Francisco: HarperSanFrancisco, 2000), p. 175, for his theological concerns.
57. Cf. D. L. Denton, *Historiography and Hermeneutics in Jesus Studies: An Examination of the Work of John Dominic Crossan and Ben F. Meyer* (London and New York: T&T Clark, 2004), p. 11, 'if Crossan's Jesus portrait is an easy target, his method is not . . .'.
58. Denton, *Historiography*, p. 77.
59. Denton, *Historiography*, pp. 77–8. After analysing the methodological approaches of Crossan and Ben Meyer, Denton then proceeds to give his own, based on holistic approaches to the historical Jesus married with narrative approaches to history (*Historiography*, pp. 154–92). While I believe that Denton's narrative approach has a lot to offer, it still remains generally in the area of description and theological understanding of the individual (see below).
60. Cf. Denton, *Historiography*, pp. 57–78. As Denton observes (p. 67), 'It is to the microcosmic level that Crossan devotes most of his attention in methodological discussion, because, as he says, method stands or falls with how one handles the sources.'
61. Again, we might note that discussions of historiography in historical Jesus studies and related fields tend to direct themselves to face or embrace the challenges of postmodern historiography. See e.g. Crossley, 'Defining Religion'; Schröter, *Jesus von Nazaret*; Wedderburn, *Jesus and the Historians*; McKnight, *Death*; Webb, 'Historical Enterprise'.
62. See again Theissen and Winter, *Quest for the Plausible Jesus* and Winter, 'Saving the Quest', both of which provide important historic connections between the old criterion of dissimilarity, difference from Judaism, and the Great Man view of history. This sort of analysis also applies to the less

aggressive difference from Judaism in the 'Jewish... but not *that* Jewish' view of Jesus in contemporary scholarship.

63. Georgi, 'The Interest in Life of Jesus Theology', p. 76.
64. H. Moxnes, 'What Is It to Write a Biography of Jesus? Schleiermacher's *Life of Jesus* and Nineteenth-Century Nationalism', in H. Moxnes, W. Blanton, and J. G. Crossley (eds), *Jesus beyond Nationalism: Constructing the Historical Jesus in a Period of Cultural Complexity* (London and Oakville: Equinox, 2009), pp. 27–42; Moxnes, *Jesus and the Rise of Nationalism*.
65. Sanders, *Historical Figure*, pp. 2, 4–5.
66. Crossley, *Neoliberalism*, pp. 68–9.
67. Carr, *What Is History?*, p. 46.
68. See e.g. E. J. Hobsbawm, *Uncommon People: Resistance, Rebellion and Jazz* (London: Abacus, 1998) and *Revolutionaries* (London: Abacus, 1999), pp. 183–91. Such issues of the individual in history are also discussed, though with debatable conclusions it must be added, in Hobsbawm's autobiography, *Interesting Times: A Twentieth Century Life* (London: Abacus, 2002), e.g. pp. 265–82.
69. K. Marx, *The Eighteenth Brumaire of Louis Bonaparte* (New York: International Publishers, 1963), p. 15.
70. B. Pimlott, 'Brushstrokes,' in M. Bostridge (ed.), *Lives for Sale: Biographers' Tales* (London and New York: Continuum, 2004), pp. 165–70.
71. Pimlott, 'Brushstrokes', pp. 169–70.
72. Pimlott, 'Brushstrokes', p. 166.
73. Pimlott ('Brushstrokes', p. 166) talks of Carr's 'superficially persuasive denunciation of biography in *What Is History?*' However, as we saw with the brief look at Carr on biography, it was not a full denunciation and Pimlott's qualifications on the individual in the context of social change echo Carr's qualifications noted above.
74. T. Carlyle, *On Heroes and Hero-Worship and the Heroic in History* (Berkeley: University of California, 1993), p. 13; cf. p. 2. There was, however, more to Carlyle than this. As Carr (*What Is History?*, pp. 49–50) points out, Carlyle saw the significance of the plight of the masses over against philosophers and elites underlying the French Revolution and ultimately all revolutions. See also e.g. P. Rosenberg, 'A Whole World of Heroes', in H. Bloom (ed.), *Thomas Carlyle* (New York: Chelsea House, 1986), pp. 95–108.
75. F. Braudel, *The Mediterranean and the Mediterranean World in the Age of Philip II* (3 vols; London: Collins, 1972–3), vol. 1, p. 21. However, as Peter Burke points out, Braudel devoted several hundred pages of *Mediterranean* vol. 3 to events. Burke adds that it was Braudel's followers who tended to shift away from event-level history. See P. Burke, 'History of

Events and the Revival of the Narrative', in P. Burke (ed.), *New Perspectives on History Writing* (second edition; London: Polity, 2001), pp. 283–300 (286–7).

76. E.g. F. Engels, 'On the History of Earliest Christianity (1894)', in K. Marx and F. Engels, *Collected Works, Volume 27, Engels: 1890–95* (London: Lawrence & Wishart, 1990), pp. 447–69; K. Kautsky, *Foundations of Christianity: A Study in Christian Origins* (London: Orbach & Chambers, 1925). On the post-Engels/Kautsky Marxist tradition, see e.g. P. Kowaliński, 'The Genesis of Christianity in the Views of Contemporary Marxist Specialists of Religion', *Antonianum* 47 (1972), pp. 541–75.
77. For overviews see e.g. R. J. Evans, *In Defence of History* (second edition; London: Granta, 2000), pp. 129–90; Crossley, *Why Christianity Happened*, pp. 1–34.
78. J. D. G. Dunn, 'Mark 2.1–3.6: A Bridge between Jesus and Paul on the Question of the Law', *NTS* 30 (1984), pp. 395–415. This is updated in *Jesus, Paul and the Law: Studies in Mark and Galatians* (London: SPCK, 1991).
79. See note 32.
80. J. H. Kautsky, *The Politics of Aristocratic Empires* (Chapel Hill: University of North Carolina, 1982), e.g. pp. 278–303.
81. See e.g. R. H. Hilton, 'Peasant Society, Peasant Movements and Feudalism in Medieval Europe', in H. A. Landsberger (ed.), *Rural Protest: Peasant Movements and Social Change* (New York: Macmillan, 1973), pp. 67–94; Hobsbawm, *Uncommon People*, pp. 196–255; Crossan, *The Birth of Christianity*, pp. 154–7; Herzog, *Prophet and Teacher* (with creative discussion of Paulo Freire); Crossley, *Why Christianity Happened*, pp. 57–9.
82. See e.g. (among many and in different ways) Crossan, *The Birth of Christianity*, pp. 151–235; W. E. Arnal, *Jesus and the Village Scribes: Galilean Conflicts and the Setting of Q* (Minneapolis: Fortress, 2001); R. A. Horsley, *Jesus and Empire: The Kingdom of God and the New World Disorder* (Fortress: Minneapolis, 2003); Crossley, *Why Christianity Happened*, chapter 2.
83. M. H. Jensen, *Herod Antipas in Galilee* (Tubingen: Mohr Siebeck, 2006); M. H. Jensen, 'Herod Antipas in Galilee: Friend or Foe of the Historical Jesus?', *JSHJ* 5 (2007), pp. 7–32.
84. Hobsbawm, *Uncommon People*, p. 224.
85. C. Hill, *The World Turned Upside Down: Radical Ideas during the English Revolution* (London: Temple Smith, 1972).
86. See e.g. D. C. Allison, *Jesus of Nazareth: Millenarian Prophet* (Philadelphia: Fortress, 1998), pp. 78–94 and D. C. Allison, *Constructing Jesus:*

Memory, Imagination, and History (London: SPCK, 2010), pp. 85–8, who approaches the historical Jesus from the perspective of cross-cultural millenarian groups. Cf. C. Rowland, *Christian Origins: The Setting and Character of the Most Important Messianic Sect of Judaism* (London: SPCK, 1986), pp. 87–91, 111–17.

87. I am indebted to discussions with numerous historians of the seventeenth century at the conference 'The World Turned Upside Down—40 Years On; Revisiting Christopher Hill's Classic Work', University of Sheffield, 14 April 2012.
88. M. Braddick, *God's Fury, England's Fire: A New History of the English Civil Wars* (London: Allen Lane, 2008), p. xxv.
89. M. Foucault, 'Nietzsche, Genealogy, History', in D. F. Bouchard (ed.), *Language, Counter-Memory, Practice: Selected Essays and Interviews* (Ithaca: Cornell University Press, 1977), pp. 139–64.
90. R. Deines, 'Jesus and the Jewish Traditions of His Time', *Early Christianity* 1 (2010), pp. 344–71 (347).
91. Crossley, *Why Christianity Happened*, p. 15.
92. B. Mack, *The Christian Myth: Origins, Logic, and Legacy* (New York and London: Continuum, 2001).
93. K. L. Noll, 'Investigating Earliest Christianity without Jesus', in T. L. Thompson and T. S. Verenna (eds), *'Is This Not the Carpenter?' The Question of the Historicity of the Figure of Jesus* (Durham: Acumen, 2012), pp. 233–66.
94. Noll, 'Investigating', p. 234.
95. Noll, 'Investigating', pp. 233–4.
96. Noll, 'Investigating', p. 234.
97. Noll, 'Investigating', p. 266.
98. For example, and in addition to above: 'Paul's strain of the meme pool contained significant mutation from the Jerusalem-based original, and the doctrinal mode it constructs must be viewed as an entirely new species of religion' (p. 258); 'the creation, survival and replication of any distinctive religion' (p. 265); or 'the most interesting aspect of any religion is its continued existence' (p. 234).
99. R. T. McCutcheon, *Manufacturing Religion: The Discourse on Sui Generis Religion and the Politics of Nostalgia* (Oxford: Oxford University Press, 1997).
100. K. MacKendrick, 'From Cognitive Theory of Religion to Religious Cognition', *Religion Bulletin* (2012), http://www.equinoxpub.com/blog/2012/06/from-cognitive-theory-of-religion-to-religious-cognition/.
101. Noll, 'Investigating', p. 258.

102. Examples of the complicated nature of identity and Christian origins, and thus how difficult it is to separate specific ideas into convenient memes, are P. A. Harland, *Associations, Synagogues, and Congregations: Claiming a Place in Ancient Mediterranean Society* (Minneapolis: Fortress, 2003) and P. A. Harland, *The Dynamics of Identity in the World of the Early Christians* (London and New York: T&T Clark, 2009).
103. Noll, 'Investigating', p. 260.
104. Such issues will be discussed in Chapter 4. For now see e.g. M. Casey, *Aramaic Sources of Mark's Gospel* (Cambridge: Cambridge University Press, 1998), pp. 138–92; L. Doering, *Schabbat: Schabbathalacha und-praxis im antiken Judentum und Urchristentum* (Tübingen: Mohr Siebeck, 1999), pp. 408–76; J. G. Crossley, *The Date of Mark's Gospel: Insight from the Law in Earliest Christianity*, (London: T&T Clark, 2004), pp. 84–6, 160–72; J. H. Hellerman, *Jesus and the People of God: Reconfiguring Ethnic Identity* (Sheffield: Sheffield Academic Press, 2007), pp. 124–34; S. Moyise, *Evoking Scripture: Seeing the Old Testament in the New* (London and New York: T&T Clark, 2008), p. 27; M. Bockmuehl, 'God's Life as a Jew: Remembering the Son of God as Son of David', in B. R. Gaventa and R. B. Hays (eds), *Seeking the Identity of Jesus: A Pilgrimage* (Grand Rapids and Cambridge: Eerdmans, 2008), pp. 60–78, esp. 69–70, n. 19; R. Bauckham, 'In Response to My Respondents: *Jesus and the Eyewitnesses* in Review', *JSHJ* 6 (2008), pp. 225–53 (233–5); J. G. Crossley, 'Mark 7.1–23: Revisiting the Question of "All Foods Clean"', in M. Tait and P. Oakes (eds), *Torah in the New Testament* (London and New York: T&T Clark, 2009), pp. 8–20. Noll's argument amounts to a reference to M. J. Cook, 'Jewish Reflections on Jesus: Some Abiding Trends', in L. J. Greenspoon, D. Hamm, and B. F. LeBeau (eds), *The Historical Jesus through Catholic and Jewish Eyes* (Harrisburg: Trinity Press International, 2000), pp. 95–111, which is not really enough.
105. Žižek, *Puppet and the Dwarf*, p. 10.
106. M. Bakunin, *Selected Works* (New York: Alfred A. Knopf, 1972), pp. 283–4.
107. See further e.g. A. Hourani, *A History of the Arab Peoples with an Afterword by Malise Ruthven* (London: Faber, 2002), pp. 373–472; J. Burke, *Al-Qaeda* (London: Penguin, 2003), pp. 41–55; G. Kepel, *The Roots of Radical Islam* (London: Saqi, 2005); M. Watts, 'Revolutionary Islam', in D. Gregory and A. Pred (eds), *Violent Geographies: Fear, Terror, and Political Violence* (New York and London: Routledge, 2007), pp. 175–203.

108. M. Lilla, 'A New, Political Saint Paul?', *New York Review of Books* 55/16, (23 October 2008), pp. 1–9. Lilla aggressively critiques the potential totalitarianism in Badiou and Žižek but Paul is let off lightly as a cosy liberal figure. For Žižek on totalitarianism see e.g. S. Žižek, *Did Somebody Say Totalitarianism? Five Interventions in the (Mis)Use of a Notion* (London and New York: Verso, 2011).
109. E.g. T-s. B. Liew, 'Tyranny, Power and Might: Colonial Mimicry in Mark's Gospel', *JSNT* 73 (1999), pp. 7–31; T-s. B. Liew, *Politics of Parousia: Reading Mark Inter(con)textually* (Leiden: Brill, 1999); S. Samuel, *A Postcolonial Reading of Mark's Story of Jesus* (London and New York: T&T Clark, 2007); S. D. Moore, *Empire and Apocalypse: Postcolonialism and the New Testament* (Sheffield: Sheffield Phoenix Press, 2006).
110. Wright, *Resurrection*, p. 816.
111. Wright *Resurrection*, pp. 568–9. Other studies with a strong postcolonial influence provide a more nuanced understanding of Paul and Rome. Among others, see e.g. N. Elliott, *The Arrogance of Nations: Reading Romans in the Shadow of Empire* (Minneapolis: Fortress, 2008); D. C. Lopez, *Apostle to the Conquered: Reimagining Paul's Mission* (Minneapolis: Fortress, 2008); J. A. Marchal, *The Politics of Heaven: Women, Gender and Empire in the Study of Paul* (Minneapolis: Fortress, 2008).
112. While I share their concerns for understanding 'revolutionary' transformation in history, I hope Chapter 3 explains why I differ on issues of power, dominance, and imperialism being present from the beginning in R. A. Horsley and N. A. Silberman, *The Message and the Kingdom: How Jesus and Paul Ignited a Revolution and Transformed the Ancient World* (Minneapolis: Fortress, 2002).

CHAPTER 2

1. E.g. R. Rodriguez, 'Authenticating Criteria: The Use and Misuse of a Critical Method', *JSHJ* 7 (2009), pp. 152–67; D. C. Allison, *Constructing Jesus: Memory, Imagination, and History* (London: SPCK, 2010), pp. 1–30; D. C. Allison, 'How to Marginalize the Traditional Criteria of Authenticity', in T. Holmén and S. E. Porter (eds), *Handbook for the Study of the Historical Jesus,* vol. 1 (Leiden: Brill, 2011), pp. 3–30; J. Meggitt, 'Popular Mythology in the Early Empire and the Multiplicity of Jesus Traditions', in R. J. Hoffmann (ed.), *Sources of the Jesus Tradition: Separating History from Myth* (Amherst: Prometheus, 2010), pp. 55–80; R. Rodriguez, *Structuring Early Christian Memory: Jesus in Tradition, Performance and Text* (London: T&T Clark, 2010); C. Keith and A. Le

Donne (eds), *Jesus, Criteria and the Demise of Authenticity* (London: T&T Clark, 2012).

2. I suspect this vague scepticism about historical reconstruction is the kind of thinking that underlies much historical Jesus scholarship, even if it is not explicitly spelled out. There are examples where such vague scepticism can be spelled out in books which present a fairly precise picture of Jesus. E.g. E. P. Sanders, *Jesus and Judaism* (London: SCM, 1985), p. 13: 'a saying attributed to Jesus can seldom be proved beyond doubt to be entirely authentic or entirely non-authentic, but... each saying must be tested by appropriate criteria and assigned (tentatively) to an author—either to Jesus or to an anonymous representative of some stratum in the early church'.
3. In this respect we might compare some of the work on the slightly later constructed 'Q' community in Galilee as a product of more communal reactions to socio-economic change and conditions. See especially W. E. Arnal, *Jesus and the Village Scribes: Galilean Conflicts and the Setting of Q* (Minneapolis: Fortress, 2001).
4. So, classically, M. D. Hooker, 'Christology and Methodology', *NTS* 17 (1970–1), pp. 480–7; M. D. Hooker, 'On Using the Wrong Tool', *Theology* 75 (1972), pp. 570–81. For a powerful criticism and a critical history of dissimilarity see D. Winter, 'Saving the Quest for Authenticity from the Criterion of Dissimilarity: History and Plausibility', in Keith and Le Donne (eds), *Jesus, Criteria and the Demise of Authenticity*, pp. 115–31.
5. N. T. Wright, *Jesus and the Victory of God* (London: SPCK, 1996), p. 132.
6. See e.g. J. G. Crossley, *Jesus in an Age of Terror: Scholarly Projects for a New American Century* (London and Oakville: Equinox, 2008), pp. 143–94, and J. G. Crossley, *Jesus in an Age of Neoliberalism: Quests, Scholarship and Ideology* (London and Oakville: Equinox, 2012), pp. 105–32.
7. R. Deines, 'Jesus and the Jewish Traditions of His Time', *Early Christianity* 1 (2010), pp. 344–71 (350–1, 369–70).
8. See also the criticisms of dissimilarity in Winter, 'Saving the Quest for Authenticity', pp. 124–6.
9. P. Barnett, *Finding the Historical Christ*, After Jesus, vol. 3 (Grand Rapids: Eerdmans, 2009), pp. 223–4.
10. D. L. Bock, 'Blasphemy and the Jewish Examination of Jesus', in D. L. Bock and R. L. Webb (eds), *Key Events in the Life of the Historical Jesus: A Collaborative Exploration of Context and Coherence* (Grand Rapids and Cambridge: Eerdmans, 2009), pp. 589–667 (633, n. 104).
11. G. R. Osborne, 'Jesus' Empty Tomb and His Appearance in Jerusalem', in Bock and Webb (eds), *Key Events*, pp. 775–823 (800).

12. See further J. G. Crossley, 'Everybody's Happy Nowadays? A Critical Engagement with *Key Events* and Contemporary Quests for the Historical Jesus', *JSHJ* 11 (2013), pp. 224–41.
13. See e.g. M. Hengel, *The Charismatic Leader and His Followers* (Edinburgh: T&T Clark, 1981); Sanders, *Jesus and Judaism*, pp. 252–5; Wright, *Victory*, pp. 400–3.
14. M. Bockmuehl, *Jewish Law in Gentile Churches: Halakhah and the Beginning of Christian Public Ethics* (Edinburgh: T&T Clark, 2000), pp. 23–48.
15. See further R. Rodriguez, 'The Embarrassing Truth about Jesus: the Criterion of Embarrassment and the Failure of Historical Authenticity', in Keith and Le Donne (eds), *Jesus, Criteria and the Demise of Authenticity*, pp. 132–51.
16. Cf. M. Goodacre, 'Criticizing the Criterion of Multiple Attestation: The Historical Jesus and the Question of Sources', in Keith and Le Donne (eds), *Jesus, Criteria and the Demise of Authenticity*, pp. 152–69 (165–7).
17. G. Theissen and D. Winter, *The Quest for the Plausible Jesus: The Question of Criteria* (Louisville: WJK, 2002).
18. D. C. Allison, *Resurrecting Jesus: The Earliest Christian Tradition and Its Interpreters* (London and New York: T&T Clark, 2005), p. 150.
19. For general discussion see e.g. C. A. Evans, 'Introduction: An Aramaic Approach Thirty Years Later', in M. Black, *An Aramaic Approach to the Gospels and Acts* (Peabody: Hendrickson, 1998), pp. v–xxv; M. Casey, *Aramaic Sources of Mark's Gospel* (Cambridge: Cambridge University Press, 1998), pp. 1–110; M. Casey, *An Aramaic Approach to Q: Sources for the Gospels of Matthew and Luke* (Cambridge: Cambridge University Press, 2002), pp. 1–63; L. T. Stuckenbruck, '"Semitic Influence on Greek": An Authenticating Criterion in Jesus Research?', in Keith and Le Donne (eds), *Jesus, Criteria and the Demise of Authenticity*, pp. 73–94.
20. See Stuckenbruck, 'Semitic Influence on Greek' for a recent summary.
21. J. P. Meier, *A Marginal Jew: Rethinking the Historical Jesus*, vol. 1, *The Roots of the Problem and the Person* (New York: Doubleday, 1991), pp. 179–80.
22. Stuckenbruck, 'Semitic Influence on Greek', p. 94.
23. Stuckenbruck, 'Semitic Influence on Greek', p. 93.
24. For further discussion of the Aramaic idiom and Mark 2.23–8 see e.g. M. Casey, *The Solution to 'the Son of Man' Problem* (London and New York: T&T Clark, 2007), pp. 116–25.
25. Cf. J. P. Meier, 'The Historical Jesus and the Plucking of the Grain on the Sabbath', *CBQ* 66 (2004), pp. 561–81.
26. Indeed, Mark's editorial work in Mark 7.3–4 shows the author knew very precise details about purity laws. See J. G. Crossley, 'Halakah and Mark

7.4: "...and beds"', *JSNT* 25 (2003), pp. 433–47; J. G. Crossley, 'Halakah and Mark 7.3: "with the hand in the shape of a fist"', *NTS* 58 (2012), pp. 57–68.

27. Among many publications see e.g. R. D. Aus, *Water into Wine and the Beheading of John the Baptist: Early Jewish-Christian Interpretation of Esther 1 in John 2:1–11 and Mark 6:17–29* (Atlanta: Scholars Press, 1988); R. D. Aus, *Barabbas and Esther and Other Studies in the Judaic Illumination of Earliest Christianity* (Atlanta: Scholars Press, 1992); R. D. Aus, *Samuel, Saul, and Jesus: Three Early Palestinian Jewish Christian Gospel Haggadoth* (Atlanta: Scholars Press, 1994); R. D. Aus, *'Caught in the Act,' Walking on the Sea, and the Release of Barabbas Revisited* (Atlanta: Scholars Press, 1998); R. D. Aus, *The Death, Burial, and Resurrection of Jesus, and the Death, Burial, and Translation of Moses in Judaic Tradition* (Lanham: University Press of America, 2008); R. D. Aus, *Feeding the Five Thousand: Studies in the Judaic Background of Mark 6:30–44 par. and John 6.1–15* (Lanham: University Press of America, 2010). Aus' work has been unfairly overlooked for some time but note now that Allison mentions its significance (e.g. Allison, *Constructing Jesus*, pp. 438–9). For a comparable analysis of 'myth' in the broader context of the Roman empire see Meggitt, 'Popular Mythology'.
28. On the different interpretations of the boundaries of Israel see e.g. Bockmuehl, *Jewish Law*, pp. 61–70.
29. I remain agnostic and open-minded as to which of these two options, or indeed a combination of these two options, is the best solution to the Synoptic Problem. However, this should not have a serious impact on my arguments about reconstructing the historical Jesus as I think multiple attestation is very limited in its usefulness. Cf. Goodacre, 'Criticizing the Criterion of Multiple Attestation', pp. 153–67. On the limited nature of multiple attestation see also E. Eve, 'Meier, Miracle, and Multiple Attestation', *JSHJ* 3 (2005), pp. 23–45. We may further add that the scholarly stratification of Q would complicate matters further, though this stratification should not be read as if different themes do not cross strata, should we wish to employ such a model. For a recent discussion of much-discussed Kloppenborg-influenced use of layers or strata in Q and historical Jesus reconstruction, see the discussion in Allison, *Constructing Jesus*, pp. 118–25.
30. For standard treatments of sources see e.g. Meier, *A Marginal Jew*, pp. 41–166; J. D. G. Dunn, *Jesus Remembered* (Grand Rapids: Eerdmans, 2003), pp. 139–72; M. Casey, *Jesus of Nazareth: An Independent Historian's Account of His Life and Teaching* (London and New York: T&T Clark, 2010), pp. 61–99.

31. M. F. Bird, 'The Historical Jesus', in M. F. Bird and J. G. Crossley, *How Did Christianity Begin? A Believer and Non-Believer Examine the Evidence* (London: SPCK, 2008), p. 22: 'There are also several reasons why the miracles of Jesus have historical plausibility... such miracles are attested in every stratum of the Gospel tradition (Mark, material common to Luke and Matthew, material unique to Luke, Matthew and John).'
32. Rodriguez, 'Authenticating Criteria', e.g. pp. 159, 164–5.
33. Cf. Casey, *Jesus of Nazareth*, pp. 215, 228–34.
34. Cf. E. P. Sanders, *The Historical Figure of Jesus* (London: Penguin, 1993), pp. 179–80.
35. E.g., and in different ways, Dunn, *Jesus Remembered*; R. Bauckham, *Jesus and the Eyewitnesses: The Gospels as Eyewitness Testimony* (Grand Rapids: Eerdmans, 2006); Rodriguez, *Structuring Early Christian Memory*; A. Le Donne, 'Theological Memory Distortion in the Jesus Tradition', in S. C. Barton, L. T. Stuckenbruck, and B. G. Wold (eds), *Memory and Remembrance in the Bible and Antiquity* (Tübingen: Mohr Siebeck, 2007), pp. 163–78; A. Le Donne, *The Historiographical Jesus: Memory, Typology and the Son of David* (Baylor: Baylor University Press, 2009); A. Le Donne, *Historical Jesus: What Can We Know and How Can We Know It?* (Grand Rapids: Eerdmans, 2011); J. Schröter, 'Die Frage nach dem historischen Jesus und der Charakter historischer Erkenntnis', in A. Lindemann (ed.), *The Sayings Source Q and the Historical Jesus* (Leuven: Leuven University Press, 2001), pp. 228–33; J. Schröter, 'Von der Historizität der Evangelien: Ein Beitrag zur gegenwärtigen Diskussion um den historischen Jesus', in J. Schröter and R. Brucker (eds), *Der historische Jesus: Tendenzen und Perspektiven der gegenwärtigen Forschung* (Berlin: De Gruyter, 2002), pp. 163–212; J. Schröter, *Jesus von Nazaret: Jude aus Galiläa-Retter der Welt* (second edition; Leipzig: Evangelische Verlagsanstalt, 2009); C. S. Keener, *The Historical Jesus of the Gospels* (Grand Rapids: Eerdmans, 2009), pp. 144–53; C. Keith, 'Memory and Authenticity: Jesus Tradition and What Really Happened', *ZNW* 102 (2011), pp. 155–77; Allison, *Constructing Jesus*, pp. 1–30. Whilst the results and levels of hermeneutical suspicion may be different, this emphasis on memory and gist is not radically removed from one aspect of the methodological approach of the Jesus Seminar. After all, the voting options included: 'Jesus probably said something like this' and 'Jesus did not say this, but the ideas contained in it are close to his own' (R. W. Funk, R. W. Hoover, and the Jesus Seminar, *The Five Gospels: The Search for the Authentic Words of Jesus* [New York: Macmillan, 1993], p. 36). For recent critiques of the use of 'memory' associated with the work of Bauckham see e.g. J. C. S. Redman, 'How Accurate Are Eyewitnesses? Bauckham and

the Eyewitnesses in Light of Psychological Research', *JBL* 129 (2010), pp. 177–97; P. Foster, 'Memory, Orality, and the Fourth Gospel: Three Dead-Ends in Historical Jesus Research', *JSHJ* 10 (2012), pp. 191–227 (193–202). The study of memory and the Gospels (and biblical studies more generally) is growing rapidly and cannot be fully discussed here. See further e.g. A. Kirk, 'Memory Theory and Jesus Research', in Holmén and Porter (eds), *Handbook for the Study of the Historical Jesus*, vol. 1, pp. 809–42.

36. In this vein see the discussions in e.g. J. D. Crossan, *The Birth of Christianity: Discovering What Happened in the Years Immediately after the Execution of Jesus* (Edinburgh: T&T Clark, 1998), pp. 49–89; Meggitt, 'Popular Mythology'; Allison, *Constructing Jesus*, pp. 1–30 (who appears in the previous note); Z. A. Crook, 'Memory and the Historical Jesus', *BTB* 42 (2012), pp. 196–220; J. S. Kloppenborg, 'Memory, Performance, and the Sayings of Jesus', *JSHJ* 10 (2012), pp. 97–132. See also the discussion between Crook and Le Donne: Z. A. Crook, 'Collective Memory Distortion and the Quest for the Historical Jesus', *JSHJ* 11 (2013), pp. 53–76; A. Le Donne, 'The Problem of Selectivity in Memory Research: A Response to Zeba Crook', *JSHJ* 11 (2013), pp. 77–97; Z. A. Crook, 'Gratitude and Comments to Le Donne', *JSHJ* 11 (2013), pp. 98–105.

37. And let us not get carried away by the repeated rhetorical question which effectively functions as a criterion to help establish a host of dramatic claims about Jesus and which goes something like this: 'Why would the Romans have not crucified him if he were not making some dramatic claims for himself?' Even this seemingly trusted way of thinking is limited because, as Justin Meggitt has shown, Romans would crucify people for what might comparably be deemed the smallest of reasons. See J. J. Meggitt, 'The Madness of King Jesus: Why Was Jesus Put to Death, but His Followers Were Not?', *JSNT* 29 (2007), p. 379–413.

38. T. L. Thompson, *The Messiah Myth: The Near Eastern Roots of Jesus and David* (New York: Basic Books, 2005).

39. Classic treatments (among many others) include H. White, *The Content of the Form: Narrative Discourse and Historical Representation* (Baltimore: Johns Hopkins University Press, 1973); D. Carr, 'Narrative and the Real World: An Argument for Continuity', *History and Theory* 25 (1986), pp. 117–31; D. Carr, *Time, Narrative and History* (Bloomington, IN: Indiana University Press); S. Friedlander (ed.), *Probing the Limits of Representation: Nazism and the 'Final Solution'* (Cambridge, MA and London: Harvard University Press, 1992). There are clear connections between this intellectual tradition and the work of Le Donne, Keith,

Rodriguez, and others, which is more typically located in the intellectual traditions associated with 'social memory'.

40. Cf. the famous opening words of F. Jameson, *The Political Unconscious: Narrative as a Socially Symbolic Act* (Ithaca: Cornell University Press, 1981), p. ix: 'Always historicize!'
41. The following is based on J. G. Crossley, 'John's Gospel and the Historical Jesus: An Assessment of Recent Trends and a Defence of a Traditional View', in T. L. Thompson and T. S. Verenna (eds), *'Is This Not the Carpenter?' The Question of the Historicity of the Figure of Jesus* (Durham: Acumen, 2012), pp. 163–84. I would like to thank the editors, Thomas Thompson and Thomas Verenna, for the development of these ideas in this chapter. For further criticisms of the use of John in historical Jesus scholarship which complement mine see Foster, 'Memory, Orality, and the Fourth Gospel', pp. 212–25.
42. See e.g. P. N. Anderson, *The Fourth Gospel and the Quest for Jesus: Modern Foundations Reconsidered* (London: T&T Clark, 2006); P. N. Anderson, 'Why This Study Is Needed, and Why It Is Needed Now', in P. N. Anderson, F. Just, and T. Thatcher (eds), *John, Jesus, and History*, vol. 1*: Critical Appraisals of Critical Views* (Atlanta: SBL, 2007), pp. 13–73; P. N. Anderson, 'Das "John-, Jesus-, and History"-Projekt. Neue Beobachtungen zu Jesus und eine Bi-optische Hypothese', *ZNT* 23 (2009), pp. 12–26; P. N. Anderson, 'The John, Jesus, and History Project: New Glimpses of Jesus and a Bi-Optic Hypothesis', *Bible and Interpretation* (February 2010), http://www.bibleinterp.com/articles/john1357917.shtml; P. N. Anderson, 'A Fourth Quest for Jesus... So What, and How So?', *Bible and Interpretation* (July 2010), http://www.bibleinterp.com/opeds/fourth357921.shtml
43. Bauckham also pushes this idea. See e.g. R. Bauckham, *The Testimony of the Beloved Disciple: Narrative, History and Theology in the Gospel of John* (Grand Rapids: Baker, 2007), pp. 14, 19, ch. 4.
44. Anderson, 'Why This Study Is Needed', pp. 42–3.
45. D. A. Carson, 'The Challenge of the Balkanization of Johannine Studies', in Anderson, Just, and Thatcher (eds), *John, Jesus, and History*, vol. 1, pp. 133–59 (147); cf. M. M. Thompson, 'The Historical Jesus and the Johannine Christ', in R. A. Culpepper and C. Black (eds), *Exploring the Gospel of John: In Honor of D. Moody Smith* (Louisville: WJK, 1996), pp. 21–42; Thompson, 'The "Spiritual Gospel"'. C. S. Keener, '"We Beheld His Glory!" (John 1:14)', in P. N. Anderson, F. Just, and T. Thatcher (eds), *John, Jesus, and History*, vol. 2*: Aspects of Historicity in the Fourth Gospel* (Atlanta: SBL, 2009), pp. 15–25; C. R. Koester,

'Aspects of Historicity in John 1–4: A Response', in Anderson, Just, and Thatcher (eds), *John, Jesus, and History*, vol. 2, pp. 93–103.

46. Bauckham, *Jesus and the Eyewitnesses*; Bauckham, *Beloved Disciple.* Compare previously, e.g., J. A. T. Robinson, *The Priority of John* (London: SCM, 1985); D. A. Carson, *The Gospel According to John* (Leicester: IVP, 1991); C. L. Blomberg, *The Historical Reliability of John's Gospel* (Downers Grove, IL: IVP, 2001). Cf. also C. S. Keener, *The Gospel of John: A Commentary* (2 vols; Peabody, MA: Hendrickson, 2003).
47. Bauckham, *Eyewitnesses*, p. 411.
48. Bauckham, *Eyewitnesses*, p. 399.
49. Bauckham, *Eyewitnesses*, p. 405.
50. This is a trait in Bauckham's handling of the miraculous more generally. See Crossley, *Jesus in an Age of Neoliberalism*, pp. 145–7.
51. E.g. (each with different nuances) Schröter, *Jesus von Nazaret*; Rodriguez, 'Authenticating Criteria'; Le Donne, *Historiographical Jesus*; C. Keith, 'The Indebtedness of the Criteria Approach to Form Criticism and Recent Attempts to Rehabilitate the Search for an Authentic Jesus', in Keith and Le Donne (eds), *Jesus, Criteria and the Demise of Authenticity*, pp. 25–48; Keith, 'Memory and Authenticity'.
52. See also Crossley, *Date of Mark's Gospel*, pp. 82–124, 159–82.
53. But cf. Bauckham, *Beloved Disciple*, p. 240: 'These debates in the Gospel [of John] are often thought to reflect debates going on in the Gospel's context between Christians and non-Christian Jews who found the Christian claims for Jesus incompatible with Jewish monotheism. There may be something in this, but the passages in question are too integral to the Gospel's developing narrative and its sophisticated narrative revelation of Jesus' identity to be mere reflections of external debates.'
54. Bauckham, *Beloved Disciple*, p. 176.
55. Bauckham, *Beloved Disciple*, pp. 181–3.
56. Bauckham, *Beloved Disciple*, p. 189.
57. Ben Witherington III goes one step further in suggesting that Lazarus, after being raised from the dead, wrote the bulk of John's Gospel: 'Lazarus is the Beloved Disciple... no better solution better explains all the interesting factors in play here than the proposal that the Beloved Disciple was someone whom Jesus had raised from the dead... If our author, the Beloved Disciple, had been raised by Jesus not merely from death's door but from being well and truly dead, this was bound to change his worldview! It became quite impossible for our author to draw up a veiled-Messiah portrait of Jesus, as we find in Mark. No, our author wanted and needed to shout from the mountain tops that Jesus was "the resurrection," not merely that he performed resurrections... He had had a

personal and profound encounter of the first order with both the historical Jesus and the risen Jesus, and he knew they were one and the same. This was bound to change his worldview... Lazarus had become what he admired, and he had been made, to a lesser degree, to be like Jesus ... John of Patmos was the final editor of this Gospel after the death of Lazarus' (B. Witherington III, 'What's in a Name? Rethinking the Historical Figure of the Beloved Disciple in the Fourth Gospel', in Anderson, Just, and Thatcher (eds), *John, Jesus, and History*, vol. 2, pp. 209–12). While, presumably, it is a reasonable thing to suggest that being raised from the (well and truly) dead would dramatically change almost anyone's world-view, some historians may have a few problems with a zombie-like figure writing the bulk of John's Gospel.

58. Bauckham, *Beloved Disciple*, p. 27.
59. Bauckham, *Beloved Disciple*, pp. 137–72.
60. See further J. Frey, *Die johanneische Eschatologie III: Die eschatologische Verkündigung in den johanneischen Texten* (Mohr Siebeck: Tübingen, 2000), pp. 14–22, 260–82.
61. Bauckham, *Eyewitnesses*, pp. 339–40.
62. Cf. D. Catchpole, 'On Proving Too Much: Critical Hesitations about Richard Bauckham's Jesus and the Eyewitnesses', *JSHJ* 6 (2008), pp. 169–81.
63. For a helpful critique of memory and John's Gospel see J. Painter, 'Memory Holds the Key: The Transformation of Memory in the Interface of History and Theology in John', in Anderson, Just, and Thatcher (eds), *John, Jesus, and History*, vol. 1, pp. 229–45. Painter also suggests a parallel in Plato providing a first-hand account of Socrates for a similar reflexive and interpretative account of a historical figure. Painter does not discuss Bauckham's work but the critique applies nonetheless.
64. Anderson, 'Why This Study Is Needed', p. 23.
65. Anderson, 'Why This Study Is Needed', p. 36.
66. Anderson, 'Why This Study Is Needed', pp. 63–5.
67. Anderson, 'Why This Study Is Needed', p. 63.
68. Anderson, 'Why This Study Is Needed', p. 65.
69. Anderson, 'Why This Study Is Needed', pp. 69–70.
70. Casey, *Aramaic Approach to Q*, pp. 105–45. See also Andrew Lincoln's careful qualifications concerning Jesus and baptizing in A. T. Lincoln, '"We Know That His Testimony is True": Johannine Truth Claims and Historicity', in Anderson, Just, and Thatcher (eds), *John, Jesus, and History*, vol. 1, pp. 179–97(187–91).

71. See e.g. J. F. McGrath, '"Destroy This Temple": Issues of Historicity in John 2.13–22', in Anderson, Just, and Thatcher (eds), *John, Jesus, and History*, vol. 2, pp. 35–43.
72. Cf. D. Moody Smith, 'John: A Source for Jesus Research?', in Anderson, Just, and Thatcher (eds), *John, Jesus, and History*, vol. 1, pp. 165–78. See also p. 178: 'the Jesus who talks the Christology is not the Jesus of Nazareth. Despite all the historical difficulties they may present, as well as their narrative and christological bias, the Synoptics nevertheless more faithfully represent the historical figure of Jesus as he was.'
73. Cf. Marianne Meye Thompson's summary of the historical Jesus by E. P. Sanders. Sanders claims: 'Jesus' case—briefly put, that he was God's spokesman, knew what his next major action in Israel's history would be, and could specify who would be in the kingdom—put him equally obviously against any reasonable interpretation of the scripture. If we give full weight to Jesus' extraordinary statements about the kingdom and about the role of his disciples—and thus, by implication, about himself—we have no trouble seeing that his claims were truly offensive . . . [E]xegesis indicates that there were specific issues at stake between Jesus and the Jewish hierarchy, and that the specific issues revolved around a *basic question*: who spoke for God?' (E. P. Sanders, *Jesus and Judaism* [London: SCM, 1985, pp. 280–81]). Thompson adds, 'I have often thought that no better summary could be given of the Gospel of John than this one' (M. M. Thompson, 'The "Spiritual Gospel": How John the Theologian Writes History', in Anderson, Just, and Thatcher (eds), *John, Jesus, and History*, vol. 1, pp. 103–7 [107]). This only works at the very general level with some very general statements (e.g. God's spokesman, truly offensive, exegetical differences) but if for the moment we assumed Sanders' portrait of Jesus in only a little more detail it starts to break down. Sanders' Jesus preaches the imminent kingdom of God; John's does not. John's Jesus makes comments deemed offensive on the issue of being equal with God; Sanders' Jesus does not. Both may have claimed to have spoken for God, but are their messages really the same? Note also the reference to 'kingdom' in Sanders' summary, the very term so downplayed and reapplied in John's Gospel.
74. See H. Bond, 'At the Court of the High Priest: History and Theology in John 18:13–24', in Anderson, Just, and Thatcher (eds), *John, Jesus, and History*, vol. 2, pp. 313–24 (318–21).
75. Anderson, 'Why This Study Is Needed', p. 40.
76. Similar points apply to John's portrayal of Jesus associating with Samaritans (cf. John 4) because Jesus would have had to travel through Samaria

to get to and from Jerusalem (cf. *Ant.* 20.118; *Life* 269). All this shows, of course, is that John knew his geography.

77. See the points made by Painter, 'Memory Holds the Key', pp. 233–4.
78. See e.g. M. Appld, 'Jesus' Bethsaida Disciples: A Study in Johannine Origins', in Anderson, Just, and Thatcher (eds), *John, Jesus, and History*, vol. 2, pp. 27–34, but with the response by Koester, 'Aspects of Historicity in John 1–4', pp. 95–7.
79. Susan Miller makes some general points of comparison between Jesus' message and Samaritan theology and suggests reasons why Samaritans might have been attracted to Jesus' message. See S. Miller, 'The Woman at the Well: John's Portrayal of the Samaritan Woman', in Anderson, Just, and Thatcher (eds), *John, Jesus, and History*, vol. 2, pp. 73–81. General similarity, however, cannot function as a strong argument in favour of the historical Jesus attracting and interacting with Samaritans because more precise arguments in favour of historicity, and how to deal with the problem of Matt. 10.5–6, are required. See also the points raised by Koester, 'Aspects of Historicity in John 1–4', pp. 100–1.
80. The idea of working with a level of generality and emphasizing the significance of Palestinian tradition has some (and only some) echoes of Schröter's narrative-historical approach and focus on Jesus' location and traces of the figure/location in the Gospels (Schröter, *Jesus von Nazaret*). The analysis in A. J. M. Wedderburn, *Jesus and the Historians* (Tübingen: Mohr Siebeck, 2010), pp. 13–32, is helpful, including the argument, that this does not mean we abandon entirely the idea of 'getting behind' the text to earlier tradition. My approach is implicitly attempting to bridge more traditional concerns with, for instance, Le Donne's idea of the 'earliest mnemonic refractions of a memory-story' (Le Donne, *Historiographical Jesus*, p. 87) and Allison's generalizing and impressionistic handling of the Gospel tradition (Allison, *Constructing Jesus*).
81. G. Vermes, *The Religion of Jesus the Jew* (London: SCM, 1993), p. 7. Vermes also reacted sharply to Meier's response and concern for more rules. See G. Vermes, *Providential Accidents: An Autobiography* (London: SCM, 1998), p. 219.

CHAPTER 3

1. For the connections between Jesus as apocalyptic prophet and millenarianism, see D. C. Allison, *Jesus of Nazareth: Millenarian Prophet* (Philadelphia: Fortress, 1998), pp. 78–94, and D. C. Allison, *Constructing Jesus: Memory, Imagination and History* (London: SPCK, 2010), pp. 85–97.
2. For this chapter I am grateful for the feedback from Deane Galbraith.

3. See further J. Frey, 'Die Apokalyptik als Herausforderung der neutestamentlichen Wissenschaft. Zum Problem: Jesus und die Apokalyptik', in M. Becker and M. Öhler (eds), *Apokalyptik als Herausforderung neutestamentlicher Theologie* (Tübingen: Mohr Siebeck, 2006), pp. 23–94.
4. B. Ehrman, *Jesus: Apocalyptic Prophet of the New Millennium* (Oxford: Oxford University Press, 1999); E. Adams, *The Stars Will Fall from Heaven: Cosmic Catastrophe in the New Testament and Its World* (London: T&T Clark, 2007); M. Casey, *Jesus of Nazareth: An Independent Historian's Account of His Life and Teaching* (London: T&T Clark, 2010), pp. 212–26; Allison, *Constructing Jesus*, pp. 31–220. I have added some more modest arguments in J. G. Crossley, *The Date of Mark's Gospel: Insight from the Law in Earliest Christianity* (London: T&T Clark, 2004), pp. 19–43.
5. See further e.g. Frey, 'Jesus und die Apokalyptik', pp. 76–8, alongside Ehrman, *Jesus*, pp. 176–81; Casey, *Jesus of Nazareth*, pp. 212–15, 223–4. See also the discussion in Allison, *Constructing Jesus*, pp. 98–116, where he concludes 'If Jesus sometimes, as so many are convinced, proclaimed the presence of God's kingdom, this is insufficient reason to urge that he did not also proclaim its future, apocalyptic revelation' (116).
6. S. J. Patterson, 'An Unanswered Question: Apocalyptic Expectation and Jesus' *Basileia* Proclamation', *JSHJ* 8 (2010), pp. 67–79.
7. Allison, *Constructing Jesus*, p. 164.
8. See further e.g. (among many) E. P. Sanders, *The Historical Figure of Jesus* (London: Penguin, 1993), pp. 169–88; M. Casey, *Is John's Gospel True?* (London and New York: Routledge, 1996), pp. 80–3, 163; P. Fredriksen, *Jesus of Nazareth, King of the Jews: A Jewish Life and the Emergence of Christianity* (New York: Alfred A. Knopf, 2000), pp. 78–89; J. Frey, *Die johanneische Eschatologie*, vol. 3: *Die eschatologische Verkündigung in den johanneischen Texten* (Mohr Siebeck: Tübingen, 2000), pp. 14–22, 260–82; Allison, *Constructing Jesus*, pp. 33–55.
9. Despite eschatology being a central feature of Wright's historical Jesus work, including a sustained attempt to argue that Jesus was not mistaken and that eschatological language should not be taken so literally, it is somewhat surprising to find that 2 Peter 3 is relegated to the status of a lowly footnote, N. T. Wright, *The New Testament and the People of God* (London: SPCK, 1992), p. 463, n. 83, with the explanation that this is 'an exception' which is 'perhaps dealing with a non-Jewish misunderstanding of Jewish apocalyptic language'. This is not the most convincing attempt to deal with the obvious. Similarly, 2 Peter 3 (v.3) turns up once in the index in N. T. Wright, *Jesus and the Victory of God* (London: SPCK, 1996), with reference to n. 83 on p. 219: 'It is true that, because they

believed that this new phase was the final Act in the drama, they spoke sometimes of living in "the last days"... But, equally importantly, they were conscious of living in the first days of this *new* Act.' John 21.20–3 does not appear at all.

10. One of the most explicit examples in recent Jesus scholarship is R. A. Horsley, *Jesus and Empire: The Kingdom of God and the New World Disorder* (Minneapolis: Fortress, 2003).
11. Cf. Casey, *Jesus of Nazareth*, p. 215: 'If this was reapplied to the time of Jesus.... .it was bound to mean that the Romans would be driven out of Israel and made subject to the Jewish people.' We will turn to the imperial aspect of the kingdom in 'The imperial kingdom'.
12. J. G. Crossley, 'The Damned Rich (Mark 10.17–31)', *ExpT* 116 (2005), pp. 397–401.
13. On reward in the here and now for observing commandments see e.g. Deut. 28.1–14; Job 1.10; 42.10; Isa. 3.10; Prov. 10.22; Tob. 12.9; Sir. 3.1, 6; 25.7–11; 35.13; 44.10–15; 51.27–30; Bar. 4.1.
14. See especially R. J. Bauckham, 'Rich Man and Lazarus: The Parable and the Parallels', *NTS* 37 (1991), pp. 225–46.
15. M. Hengel, *The Charismatic Leader and his Followers* (Edinburgh: T&T Clark, 1981), pp. 3–15. But see also the qualifications in M. Bockmuehl, 'Let the Dead Bury Their Dead (Matt. 8.22/Luke 9.60): Jesus and the Halakah', *JTS* 49 (1998), pp. 553–81.
16. See further Bauckham, 'The Rich Man and Lazarus', pp. 228, 232–3, 235–6. Against J. B. Green, *Gospel of Luke* (Grand Rapids: Eerdmans, 1997), pp. 604–5, n. 326, there is no indication that 'the rich man is condemned for not taking seriously his scriptural responsibility to use his wealth on behalf of the needy'. Even 16.29 does not indicate that rich people should be using wealth 'responsibly' and the only reasoning is given in Luke 16.25 and it is explicitly related to stark economic difference.
17. Of course, it might be the case that there is not a great distinction between Lukan redaction/memory and earlier tradition/memory. Luke may have been most impressed with this tradition and so included it, possibly with little alteration. On the preservation of earlier 'radicalism' in Luke see e.g. G. Theissen, *Social Reality and the Early Christians* (Edinburgh: T&T Clark, 1993), p. 58. Cf. J. D. G. Dunn, *Jesus Remembered* (Grand Rapids: Eerdmans, 2003), pp. 524–5.
18. J. A. Fitzmyer, *Luke X–XXIV* (New York: Doubleday, 1985), pp. 1125, 1127.
19. E.g. R. W. Funk, R. W. Hoover, and the Jesus Seminar, *The Five Gospels: The Search for the Authentic Words of Jesus* (San Francisco: HarperCollins, 1993), p. 36.

20. Bauckham, 'The Rich Man and Lazarus', p. 243, who further suggests the argument that there may be extended support in the notable variant of απελθη instead of ἀναστῇ in 16.31. In 16.30–31 εγερθη is found in P[75] as an alternative, which may likewise be an attempt to bring the text in line with more 'Christianized' thinking about physical resurrection.
21. J. G. Crossley, 'The Semitic Background to Repentance in the Teaching of John the Baptist and Jesus', *JSHJ* 2 (2004), pp. 139–58.
22. Casey, *Jesus of Nazareth*, p. 215.
23. Allison, *Constructing Jesus*, pp. 180–1. On Jesus and territory see K. J. Wenell, *Jesus and Land: Sacred and Social Space in Second Temple Judaism* (London: T&T Clark, 2007).
24. Allison, *Constructing Jesus*, pp. 184–6.
25. See further C. A. Evans, 'Daniel in the New Testament: Visions of God's Kingdom', in J. J. Collins and P. W. Flint (eds), *The Book of Daniel: Composition and Reception* (Leiden: Brill, 2001), pp. 490–527.
26. C. Rowland, 'Review of J. G. Crossley, *Why Christianity Happened*', *JTS* 59 (2008), pp. 765–7. C. Rowland, *Christian Origins: The Setting and Character of the Most Important Messianic Sect of Judaism* (London: SPCK, 1986), pp. 111–13.
27. Allison, *Constructing Jesus*, pp. 85–6, based on Allison, *Jesus of Nazareth*, 78–94.
28. Allison, *Constructing Jesus*, pp. 221–304; see pp. 253–63 for cross-cultural comparisons.
29. For a selection of views see e.g. M. Casey, *From Jewish Prophet to Gentile God: The Origins and Development of New Testament Christology* (Louisville: WJK, 1991); L. W. Hurtado, *Lord Jesus Christ: Devotion to Jesus in Earliest Christianity* (Grand Rapids: Eerdmans, 2003); L. T. Stuckenbruck and W. E. S. North (eds), *Early Jewish and Christian Monotheism* (London and New York: T&T Clark, 2004); R. Bauckham, *Jesus and the God of Israel: God Crucified and Other Studies on the New Testament's Christology of Divine Identity* (Milton Keynes: Paternoster, 2008); J. F. McGrath, *The Only True God: Early Christian Monotheism in Its Jewish Context* (Champaign, IL: University of Illinois Press, 2012).
30. It seems to me that Allison, *Constructing Jesus*, p. 247, needs more overt evidence of Jesus claiming that 'God's kingdom was his kingdom' (247) from the earliest material because this may not have been the automatic assumption of those hearing the language of the kingdom of God and a lack of sustained discussion of God as king may instead imply that it was assumed.
31. On what follows, I summarize Crossley, *Date*, pp. 19–27.
32. I would cautiously support the suggestion that Mark 13.14 (and indeed much of Mark 13, and possibly even intensification of parousia sayings) emerges out of the Caligula crisis. On this see e.g. C. C. Torrey,

Documents of the Primitive Church (London and New York: Harper & Brothers, 1941), pp. 1–40; G. Zuntz, 'Wann wurde das Evangelium Marci geschrieben?', in H. Cancik (ed.), *Markus-Philologie* (Tübingen: Mohr Siebeck, 1984), pp. 47–71; G. Theissen, *The Gospels in Context: Social and Political History in the Synoptic Tradition* (Edinburgh: T&T Clark, 1992), pp. 125–65; N. H. Taylor, 'Palestinian Christianity and the Caligula Crisis. Part II: The Markan Eschatological Discourse', *JSNT* 62 (1996), pp. 13–41; Crossley, *Date*, pp. 27–37.

33. For such developments see e.g. L. W. Hurtado, 'Resurrection-Faith and the "Historical" Jesus', *JSHJ* 11 (2011), pp. 35–52.

34. See Casey, *Jesus of Nazareth*, pp. 470–3; Allison, *Constructing Jesus*, pp. 249–51, for discussion of the nuances of exaltation and enthronement.

35. M. D. Hooker, *The Gospel According to St Mark* (A&C Black: London, 1991), p. 249. See also M. D. Hooker, *Jesus and the Servant: The Influence of the Servant Concept of Deutero-Isaiah in the New Testament* (London: SPCK, 1959); C. K. Barrett, 'The Background of Mark 10.45', in A. J. B. Higgins (ed.), *New Testament Essays: Studies in Memory of T. W. Manson* (Manchester: Manchester University Press, 1959), pp. 1–18; C. K. Barrett 'Mark 10.45: A Ransom for Many', *New Testament Essays* (London: SPCK, 1972), pp. 20–6; J. Downing, 'Jesus and Martyrdom', *JTS* NS 14 (1963), pp. 279–93; M. de Jonge, 'Jesus' Death for Others and the Death of the Maccabean Martyrs', in *Jewish Eschatology, Early Christian Christology, and the Testaments of the Twelve Patriarchs: Collected Essays of Marinus de Jonge* (Leiden: Brill, 1991), pp. 125–34. On Mark 10.35–45 in relation to martyr theology and the 'son of man' saying see M. Casey, *Aramaic Sources of Mark's Gospel* (Cambridge: Cambridge University Press, 1998), pp. 193–218, and Casey, *Jesus of Nazareth*, pp. 404–7.

36. Cf. Allison, *Constructing Jesus*, p. 245: 'Jesus and his hearers had no access to a royal court, so that, unlike weddings and fathers, lilies and the birds of the air, their firsthand knowledge of kings was nil.'

37. G. E. Lenski, *Power and Privilege: A Theory of Social Stratification* (New York: McGraw-Hill, 1966), pp. 263–5; cf. R. H. Hilton, 'Peasant Society, Peasant Movements and Feudalism in Medieval Europe', in H. A. Landsberger (ed.), *Rural Protest: Peasant Movements and Social Change* (New York: Macmillan, 1973), pp. 67–94 (89–90); D. A. Fiensy, *The Social History of Palestine in the Herodian Period: The Land is Mine* (Lewiston, Queenston, and Lampeter: Edwin Mellen, 1991), pp. 155–76; J. D. Crossan, *The Birth of Christianity: Discovering What Happened in the Years Immediately after the Execution of Jesus* (New York: HarperCollins, 1998), pp. 154–7.

38. For recent discussion see e.g. P. F. Craffert, *The Life of a Galilean Shaman: Jesus of Nazareth in Anthropological-Historical Perspective* (Cambridge: James Clarke & Co., 2008), pp. 245–308; Casey, *Jesus of Nazareth*, pp. 237–79.
39. G. Vermes, *Jesus the Jew: A Historian's Reading of the Gospel* (London: SCM, 1973), pp. 58–82. Cf. Sanders, *Historical Figure of Jesus*, pp. 138–43, 149–53.
40. Casey, *Jesus of Nazareth*, pp. 212–13.
41. There are clear similarities here with A. Le Donne, *The Historiographical Jesus: Memory, Typology and the Son of David* (Baylor: Baylor University Press, 2009) and his argument concerning the refracted memories of earlier interpretations surrounding Jesus, 'Davidic'/'Solomonic' themes, and related ideas. For further discussion see the summary of the arguments and evidence in M. F. Bird, *Are You the One Who Is to Come? The Historical Jesus and the Messianic Question* (Grand Rapids: Baker Academic, 2009); Allison, *Constructing Jesus*, pp. 279–93; Casey, *Jesus of Nazareth*, pp. 392–8.
42. Summarized and developed in Allison, *Constructing Jesus*, pp. 233–40.
43. This point would still complement Justin Meggitt's argument that Jesus was executed and his followers not because he was deemed mad. See J. J. Meggitt, 'The Madness of King Jesus: Why Was Jesus Put to Death, but His Followers Not?', *JSNT* 29 (2007), pp. 379–413.
44. J. D. Crossan, *The Historical Jesus: The Life of a Mediterranean Jewish Peasant* (Edinburgh: T& T Clark, 1991), pp. 225–302.
45. Ehrman, *Jesus*, p. 181.
46. Note that Ehrman, *Jesus*, p. 123, earlier states: 'In preparation for his coming [the Son of Man who would set up God's Kingdom], the people of Israel needed to turn to God, trusting him as a kindly parent and loving one another as his special children. Those who refused to accept this message would be liable to the judgment of God, soon to arrive with the coming of the Son of Man.'
47. E.g. R. A. Horsley and N. A. Silberman, *The Message and the Kingdom: How Jesus and Paul Ignited a Revolution and Transformed the Ancient World* (Minneapolis: Fortress, 2002).
48. S. D. Moore, *Empire and Apocalypse: Postcolonialism and the New Testament* (Sheffield: Sheffield Phoenix Press, 2006), pp. 45–74.
49. E.g. T. Thatcher, *Greater than Caesar: Christology and Empire in the Fourth Gospel* (Minneapolis: Fortress, 2009), which engages with the reading of John in Moore, *Empire and Apocalypse*.
50. Thatcher, *Greater than Caesar*, p. 138.
51. Thatcher, *Greater than Caesar*, p. 15.

52. M. Huie-Jolly, 'Maori "Jews" and a Resistant Reading of John 5.10–47', in M. W. Dube and J. L. Staley (eds), *John and Postcolonialism: Travel, Space and Power* (London: T&T Clark, 2002), pp. 94–110.
53. Huie-Jolly, 'Maori "Jews"', pp. 95–6.
54. I use 'monotheizing' in a deliberately vague sense here, whilst appreciating that other terms would do the job equally well and equally problematically. When I write about 'monotheizing' I include the idea of a supreme god being the overall ruler or divine principle with various angels, elevated figures, emanations, and/or lesser gods as part of the divine court and world. We could look at this differently, as Paula Fredriksen has done in one of her two 'egregious generalizations' which makes essentially the same point: '*In antiquity, all monotheists were polytheists*' (orig. italics); see P. Fredriksen, 'Compassion Is to Purity as Fish Is to Bicycle: Thoughts on the Construction of "Judaism" in Current Research on the Historical Jesus', in J. S. Kloppenborg with J. W. Marshall (eds), *Apocalypticism, Anti-Semitism, and the Historical Jesus* (London: T & T Clark, 2005), pp. 55–68 (56). On definitions and broader tendencies in the ancient world, see e.g. P. Athanassiadi and M. Frede (eds), *Pagan Monotheism in Late Antiquity* (Oxford: Oxford University Press, 1999) and S. Mitchell and P. van Nufflen (eds), *Pagan Monotheism in the Roman Empire* (Cambridge: Cambridge University Press, 2010). On the nature and nuances of what might or might not have constituted ancient 'monotheism' in relation to elevated figures see e.g. L. W. Hurtado, *One Lord, One God: Early Christian Devotion and Ancient Jewish Monotheism* (Philadelphia: Fortress, 1988), pp. 17–69; Casey, *From Jewish Prophet to Gentile God*, pp. 78–96; J. J. Collins, *The Scepter and the Star: The Messiahs of the Dead Sea Scrolls and Other Ancient Literature* (New York: Doubleday, 1995), pp. 136–94; Fredriksen, 'Compassion Is to Purity as Fish Is to Bicycle', pp. 56–60; N. MacDonald, *Deuteronomy and the Meaning of 'Monotheism'* (Tübingen: Mohr Siebeck, 2003); J. G. Crossley, 'Moses and Pagan Monotheism', in T. Römer (ed.), *La Construction de la figure de Moïse* (Paris: Gabalda, 2007), pp. 319–39; McGrath, *The Only True God*, pp. 23–37. On the controversial arguments concerning monotheism and Egypt see e.g. D. B. Redford, *Egypt, Canaan, and Israel in Ancient Times* (Princeton: Princeton University Press, 1992), 209–10, 380; J. Assmann, *Moses the Egyptian: The Memory of Egypt in Western Monotheism* (Cambridge, MA.: Harvard University Press, 1997); J. Assmann, *Of God and Gods: Egypt, Israel, and the Rise of Monotheism* (Madison: University of Wisconsin Press, 2008); J. Assmann, *The Price of Monotheism* (Stanford: Stanford University Press, 2010).

55. P. Nolan and G. Lenski, *Human Societies: An Introduction to Macrosociology* (ninth edition; Boulder and London: Paradigm, 2004), pp. 169–72. See further R. Stark, *One True God: Historical Consequences of Monotheism* (Princeton and Oxford: Princeton University Press, 2001).
56. Earlier forms of such political divinity, from which more 'monotheistic' views could develop, are found in the ancient Near East, such as taking away statues of a defeated god as spoils of war (cf. e.g. *ANET* 286, 287, 293, 299, 302, 304), ideas about the god of all gods (e.g. Ashur, Marduk, Sin) in Neo-Assyrian and Neo-Babylonian empires, demotion of conquered gods, and the assumption of a head role for the 'king of gods' (cf. e.g. *ANET* 307, 310, 311, 312).
57. Cf. Origen, *C. Cels.* 8.35: 'The satrap of a Persian or Roman monarch, or ruler or general or governor, yea, even those who fill lower offices of trust or service in the state, would be able to do great injury to those who despised them; and will the satraps and ministers of earth and air be insulted with impunity?'
58. For an overview of ancient Persian religion see P. Briant, *From Cyrus to Alexander: A History of the Persian Empire* (Winona Lake: Eisenbrauns, 2002), pp. 240–54.
59. It may well be, as has often been pointed out, that the vague and general 'the God of Heaven' in the Old Testament/Hebrew Bible (cf. Gen. 24.3; Jer. 10.11; Jon. 1.19; Ezra 1.2; Neh. 1.5; 2.4; 2 Chron. 36.22–3; Isa. 54.5) pragmatically uses the language of Persian imperial theology. Note, for instance, the decree from Cyrus in 2 Chron. 36.22–3 and Ezra 1.1–4 (cf. Ezra 7.12–26) where his authority comes from 'the Lord, the God of heaven' who has given Cyrus 'all the kingdoms of the earth'.
60. B. Lincoln, *Religion, Empire and Torture: The Case of Achaemenian Persia, with a Postscript on Abu Ghraib* (Chicago and London: University of Chicago Press, 2007), p. 16.
61. M. Frede, 'Monotheism and Pagan Philosophy in Later Antiquity', in P. Athanassiadi and M. Frede (eds), *Pagan Monotheism in Late Antiquity* (Oxford: Oxford University Press, 1999), pp. 41–67.
62. W. Burkert, *Greek Religion* (Oxford: Blackwell, 1985), p. 306.
63. G. Theissen, *A Theory of Primitive Christian Religion* (London: SCM, 1999), pp. 53–4.
64. See also Frede, 'Monotheism and Pagan Philosophy', pp. 58–9.
65. The following is based on Crossley, 'Moses and Pagan Monotheism'. For a more general discussion of Julian's thought see P. Athanassiadi-Fowden, *Julian and Hellenism* (Oxford: Oxford University Press, 1981); R. Smith, *Julian's Gods: Religion and Philosophy in the Thought and Action of Julian the Apostate* (London: Routledge, 1995). For further

discussion of the key texts of Julian on Moses and monotheism see e.g. J. G. Gager, *Moses in Greco-Roman Paganism* (Nashville: Abingdon Press, 1973), pp. 108–11; J. G. Cook, *The Interpretation of the Old Testament in Greco-Roman Paganism* (Tübingen: Mohr Siebeck, 2004), pp. 248–344.

66. R. Boer, 'Apocalyptic and Apocalypticism in the Poetry of E. P. Thompson', *Spaces of Utopia* 7 (2009), pp. 34–53 (45, 50).
67. See J. G. Crossley, *Harnessing Chaos: The Bible in English Political Discourse since 1968* (London: T&T Clark, 2014); The Archbishop of Canterbury's Commission on Urban Priority Areas, *Faith in the City: A Call for Action by Church and Nation* (London: Church House Publishing, 1985).

CHAPTER 4

1. For a non-exhaustive range of literature on Jesus and the 'sinners' see e.g. J. Jeremias, 'Zöllner und Sünder' *ZNW* 30 (1931), pp. 293–300; J. Jeremias, *New Testament Theology*, pt 1: *The Proclamation of Jesus* (London: SCM, 1971), e.g. pp. 108–13; E. P. Sanders, 'Jesus and the Sinners', *JSNT* 19 (1983), pp. 5–36; E. P. Sanders, *Jesus and Judaism* (London: SCM, 1985), pp. 174–211; E. P. Sanders, *The Historical Figure of Jesus* (London: Penguin, 1993), pp. 226–37; R. Horsley, *Jesus and the Spiral of Violence: Popular Jewish Resistance in Roman Palestine* (San Francisco: Harper & Row, 1987), pp. 217–21; J. D. G. Dunn, 'Pharisees, Sinners and Jesus', in P. Borgen, J. Neusner, E. S. Frerichs, and R. Horsley (eds), *The Social World of Formative Christianity and Judaism: Essays in Tribute to Howard Clarke Kee* (Philadelphia: Fortress, 1988), pp. 264–89; J. D. G. Dunn, *Jesus, Paul and the Law: Studies in Mark and Galatians* (London: SPCK, 1990), pp. 61–88; J. D. G. Dunn, 'Jesus, Table-Fellowship, and Qumran', in J. H. Charlesworth (ed.), *Jesus and the Dead Sea Scrolls* (New York: Doubleday, 1992), pp. 254–72; J. D. G. Dunn, *Jesus Remembered* (Grand Rapids and Cambridge: Eerdmans, 2003), pp. 526–33; N. T. Wright, *Jesus and the Victory of God* (London: SPCK, 1996), pp. 264–8; C. L. Blomberg, *Contagious Holiness: Jesus' Meals with Sinners* (Leicester and Downers Grove: IVP, 2005), pp. 19–31; C. L. Blomberg, 'The Authenticity and Significance of Jesus' Table Fellowship with Sinners', in D. L. Bock and R. L. Webb (eds), *Key Events in the Life of the Historical Jesus: A Collaborative Exploration of Context and Coherence* (Grand Rapids and Cambridge: Eerdmans, 2009), pp. 215–50; J. G. Crossley, *Why Christianity Happened: A Sociohistorical Account of Christian Origins, 26–50 CE* (Louisville: WJK,

2006), pp. 75–96; G. Carey, *Sinners: Jesus and His Earliest Followers* (Waco: Baylor University Press, 2009).

2. Blomberg, 'Jesus' Table Fellowship with Sinners', pp. 219, 232, 237, 242–4. For a more nuanced discussion of sex workers and biblical texts see e.g. R. Charles, 'Rahab: A Righteous Whore in James', *Neot.* 45 (2011), pp. 207–21. A crucial publication on sex workers and the reception of biblical texts is A. Ipsen, *Sex Working and the Bible* (London and Oakville: Equinox, 2009).
3. Blomberg, 'Jesus' Table Fellowship with Sinners', pp. 243–4.
4. For a more detailed presentation of the early sources see Crossley, *Why Christianity Happened*, pp. 76–87.
5. D. A. Neale, *None but the Sinners: Religious Categories in the Gospel of Luke* (Sheffield: JSOT, 1991), pp. 75–81.
6. See e.g. Pss. 7.9; 31[32].10; 33[34].21; 57[58].10; 67[68].2; 74[75].8; 96[97].10; 111[112].10; 140[141].5; 145[146].9; Prov. 11.31; cf. Dan. 12.10.
7. See also Pss. 36[37].10, 14, 17, 20; 57[58].10; 90[91].8; 91[92].7; 100[101].8; 105[106].18; 144[145].20; 145[146].9; 146[147].6; Prov. 11.31; 24.19; Isa. 14.5; Ezek. 33.8). On judgement of sinners in the LXX Psalms see also Neale, *None but the Sinners*, pp. 82–3.
8. E.g. Dunn, *Jesus, Paul and the Law*, pp. 73–7; Dunn, 'Table-Fellowship', p. 259.
9. Cf. Wisd. 4.10; Sir. 2.12; 3.27; 5.9; 8.10; 15.12; 16.6; 21.6; 23.8; 41.5; *1 En.* 1.9; 5.6; 22.10–13; 98.6; *T. Abr.* [A]11.11; 12.10; 14.11; *Ps. Sol.* 12.6; 17.23, 25, 36.
10. E.g. Wisd. 4.10; Sir. 13.17; 19.22; 36[33].14; *T. Abr.* [A] 13.3, 9; 17.8; *T. Abr.* [B—MS 'E'] 13.20; *Pss. Sol.* 3.9; 4.8; 14.6; 15.7–8.
11. E.g. Sir. 5.6; 7.16; 12.6; 16.13–14; 25.19; 40.8; 41.5; 1 Macc. 2.62; *1 En.* 1.9; 22.10, 12, 13; 97.7; 100.2–3, 9; 102.3, 5–6; *T. Abr.* [A] 11.11; 12.10; 13.3, 9, 12; 14.11; 17:8; *T. Abr.* [B—MS 'E'] 13.20; *T. Jud.* 25.5; *Pss. Sol.* 2.34–5; 3.11–12; 4.2, 8, 23; 12.6; 13.2, 5–8, 11; 14.6; 16.5; 17.23, 25, 36. Compare also Horsley, *Spiral*, pp. 218–19; Neale, *None but the Sinners*, pp. 83–5.
12. E.g. 1QM 11.12–14; 1Q27 1.1, 11; 4Q169 frag. 3, 4.1, 5; 4Q171 2.18; 4Q544 2.3; 11Q10 3.6; 7.4; 11.3; 25.6; 34.8; cf. 1QS 10.19; CD 6.15; 19.17; 4Q204 frag. 5, 2.25–8; 4Q510 1.7; 4Q511 10.3; 35.1, 9; 11Q10 2.7.
13. E.g. 1QpHab 5.5; 13.4; 1QM 4.4; 1QS 8.7; 1Q28b 5.25; 1Q34 frag. 3, 1.5, 2.5; CD 1.19; 4.7; 7.9; 19.6; 20.26; 4Q171 3.12; 4Q212 4.16; 4Q398 11–13.5; 4Q511 63, 3.4; 11Q10 3.6; 7.4; 11.3; 34.8; cf. 1QM 14.7; 15.2; 1Q28a 1.3.

14. E.g. 1Q34 frag. 3, 2.5; 4Q510 2.1; 11Q5 24.6; 11Q10 7.4; 24.1; cf. 1QapGen 1.2; 4Q511 18, 2.6; 4Q506 131–132.14.
15. E.g. 1Q27 1, 1.5–6; 1Q34 frag. 3, 1.2, 5; CD 1.19; 20.21; 4Q171 2.9–16; 4Q212 4.16; 4Q 185 frags 1–2, 2.9; 4Q508 1.1; 11Q5 18.12–15; 11Q10 3.6; 7.4; 11Q13 1, 2.11.
16. E.g. 1QpHab 5.5; 1QM 1.2; 1Q27 1.1, 5–6; CD 1.19; 2.3; 11.21; 4Q171 3.12; 4Q174 1, 1.14; 4Q511 63, 3.4; 11Q5 18.12–15; 4Q504 1–2 2.10; 4Q504 1–2 5.19. Cf. M. Casey, *An Aramaic Approach to Q* (Cambridge: Cambridge University Press, 2002), p. 139.
17. E.g. 1QpHab 13.4; 1QM 1.2; 11.14; CD 8.8–12; 4Q169 frag. 3 1.1–2; cf. 1QM 14.7; 15.2.
18. Sanders, *Historical Figure*, p. 227, with reference to רשעים, is partly right but it omits some important other Aramaic words: 'I shall refer to them as the "wicked", since that is almost certainly is the word that was used by Jesus and his critics. (They spoke Aramaic rather than Hebrew, but the word is the same.)' See also Sanders, *Jesus and Judaism*, p. 177.
19. B. D. Chilton, 'Jesus and the Repentance of E. P. Sanders', *TynBul* 39 (1988), pp. 1–18 (9).
20. Crossley, *Why Christianity Happened*, pp. 84–6.
21. E.g. Pesh. Pss. 7.9; 9.17; 9.23–5 [10.2–4]; 33[34].21[22]; 36[37].10, 14, 17, 20, 21; 57[58].10[11]; 67[68].2[3]; 72[73].3; 74[75].8[9]; 81[82].2, 4; 90[91].8; 91[92].7; 93[94].3, 13; 96[97].10; 100[101].8; 111[112].10).
22. E.g. Pesh. Pss. 105[106].18; 119.61, 95, 155; 144[145].20; 145[146].9; 146[147].6.
23. E.g. Pesh. Pss. 9.36 [10.15]; 49[50].16; 119.53, 110.
24. Chilton, 'Repentance', pp. 9–10.
25. M. Black, *An Aramaic Approach to the Gospels and Acts* (third edition; Oxford: Oxford University Press, 1967), p. 140; Chilton, 'Repentance', pp. 10–12; M. Casey, *Aramaic Sources of Mark's Gospel* (Cambridge: Cambridge University Press, 1998), pp. 60, 85; Casey, *Aramaic Approach*, p. 139.
26. Cf. Sanders, *Historical Figure*, pp. 227–9.
27. Cf. Dunn, 'Table-Fellowship', pp. 257–60.
28. For further discussion of 'repentance' and the numerous texts see e.g. J. G. Crossley, 'The Semitic Background to Repentance in the Teaching of John the Baptist and Jesus', *JSHJ* 2 (2004), pp. 138–57.
29. Cf. Neale, *None but the Righteous*, pp. 90–5.
30. Chilton, 'Repentance', p. 10.
31. E.g. compare the qualifications in R. H. Bell, 'Teshubah: The Idea of Repentance in Ancient Judaism', *Journal of Progressive Judaism* 5 (1995), pp. 22–52 (24) with E. Würthwein, 'μετανοέω, etc.: B. Repentance and Conversion in the Old Testament', *TDNT*, pp. 980–9 (989).

32. Crossley, 'Repentance', p. 145.
33. Crossley, 'Repentance', p. 147.
34. See also J. G. Crossley, *The Date of Mark: Insight from the Law in Earliest Christianity* (2004), pp. 82–124, 159–205.
35. There are, of course, differences between Matt. 18.12–14 and the parallel in Luke 15.3–7, as Sanders, *Historical Figure*, pp. 233–4, noted. Of most relevance is that Matthew has the shepherd pursuing the lost sheep while Luke has the lost sheep returning. For Sanders, the Matthean emphasis is most likely to reflect Jesus. However, repentance understood in terms of *teshubah* can include both the sinner returning and seeking out a sinner so it is not so easy to choose which might reflect an earlier tradition (cf. Ezek. 33.7–9, 11, 19; 4Q393 1–2 ii, 4–7; *T. Abr.* 10.14 [A]; Tob. 13.6). See further Crossley, 'Repentance', p. 141, n. 8.
36. Sanders, *Jesus and Judaism*, pp. 106–13; Sanders, *Historical Figure*, pp. 230–5.
37. See further e.g. D. C. Allison, 'Jesus and the Covenant', *JSNT* 29 (1987), pp. 57–78 (70–1); Chilton, 'Repentance'; N. T. Wright, *Jesus and the Victory of God* (London: SPCK), pp. 246–58.
38. Cf. E. P. Sanders, *Paul and Palestinian Judaism: A Comparison of Patterns of Religion* (London: SCM, 1977), pp. 176–9.
39. Sanders, *Historical Figure*, p. 236.
40. See e.g. Dunn, *Jesus, Paul and the Law*, pp. 61–86; M. Hengel, and R. Deines, 'E. P. Sanders' "Common Judaism", Jesus, and the Pharisees', *JTS* 46 (1995), pp. 1–70; Crossley, *Date*, pp. 131–3; Casey, *Jesus of Nazareth*, pp. 313–52.
41. Cf. Dunn, 'Table-Fellowship', pp. 254–5, 259–68.
42. Cf. the much later *b. Sanh.* 25b: 'A usurer: this includes both lender and borrower. And when are they judged to have repented? When they tear up their bills and undergo a complete reformation, that they will not lend [on interest] even to a gentile.'
43. Sanders, *Historical Figure*, p. 236.
44. Sanders, *Jesus and Judaism*, p. 206.
45. A more recent variant of this argument is T. Hägerland, 'Jesus and the Rites of Repentance', *NTS* 52 (2006), pp. 166–87. For criticisms of Jesus supposedly remembered as bypassing Temple and 'ritual' acts of repentance see Crossley, *Date*, pp. 62–76, 83–4, 87–98, 107–10, 115–23. Another common suggestion is that John the Baptist also accepted the bypassing of the Temple. But again, there is little evidence to support this. John is not remembered as being critical of the Law but is remembered for stressing certain pieties and commandments (Mark 6.17–20; Luke

3.10–14; *Ant.* 18.116–19). Sir. 5.5–8 is also comparable to John's teaching but would not be seen as overriding the Temple system.

46. See further Dunn, *Jesus, Paul and the Law*, pp. 19–20.
47. J. Klawans, *Impurity and Sin in Ancient Judaism* (Oxford: Oxford University Press, 2000), pp. 136–57 (cf. p. 157: 'John, Jesus and Paul were... interested, rather, in the effects these sins might have on individual sinners').
48. Crossley, *Date*, pp. 82–124, 159–205. For a recent proponent of such a view in relation to the historical Jesus, see Casey, *Jesus of Nazareth*, pp. 281–312.
49. E.g., among others, Crossley, *Date*, pp. 183–203.
50. On 'and beds/dining couches' in Mark 7:4 as the earliest reading see J. G. Crossley, 'Halakah and Mark 7.4: "... and beds"', *JSNT* 25 (2003), pp. 433–47.
51. For detailed discussion of these 'traditions' see Crossley, *Date*, pp. 183–93.
52. On this reading see e.g. Crossley, *Date*, pp. 191–204; S. Moyise, *Evoking Scripture: Seeing the Old Testament in the New* (London and New York: T&T Clark, 2008), p. 27; M. Bockmuehl, 'God's Life as a Jew: Remembering the Son of God as Son of David', in B. R. Gaventa and R. B. Hays (eds), *Seeking the Identity of Jesus: A Pilgrimage* (Grand Rapids and Cambridge: Eerdmans, 2008), pp. 60–78, esp. pp. 69–70, n. 19; R. Bauckham, 'In Response to My Respondents: *Jesus and the Eyewitnesses* in Review', *JSHJ* 6 (2008), pp. 225–53 (233–5); J. G. Crossley, 'Mark 7.1–23: Revisiting the Question of "All Foods Clean"', in M. Tait and P. Oakes (eds), *Torah in the New Testament* (London and New York: T&T Clark, 2009), pp. 8–20; D. Boyarin, *The Jewish Gospels: The Story of the Jewish Christ* (New York: New Books, 2012), ch. 3. Cf. the discussions in D. Catchpole, *Jesus People: The Historical Jesus and the Beginnings of Community* (London: Darton, Longman and Todd; Grand Rapids: Baker, 2006), pp. 196–201; D. A. Fiensy, *Jesus the Galilean: Soundings in a First Century Life* (Piscataway: Gorgias Press, 2007), pp. 147–86; Y. Furstenberg, 'Defilement Penetrating the Body: A New Understanding of Contamination in Mark 7.15', *NTS* 54 (2008), pp. 176–200; T. Kazen, *Issues of Impurity in Early Judaism* (Winona Lake: Eisenbrauns, 2010), pp. 113–35.
53. For full discussion see J. G. Crossley, 'Halakah and Mark 7.3: "with the hand in the shape of a fist"', *NTS* 58 (2012), pp. 57–68.
54. R. P. Booth, *Contrasts: Gospel Evidence and Christian Belief* (Bognor Regis: Paget Press, 1990), pp. 206–7.
55. Crossley, 'Halakah and Mark 7.4'.

56. The classic work representing this view is K. Niederwimmer, 'Johannes Markus und die Frage nach dem Verfasser des zweiten Evangeliums', *ZNW* 58 (1967), pp. 172–88, esp. 178–85.
57. For wide-ranging contextualization of Jesus and early Jewish purity law see T. Kazen, *Jesus and Purity Halakhah: Was Jesus Indifferent to Impurity?* (Stockholm: Almqvist & Wiksell International, 2002); Crossley, *Date*, pp. 183–205. Booth, *Jesus and the Laws of Purity* is still an excellent resource for understanding purity and the Gospel tradition. I became aware of T. Kazen, *Scripture, Interpretation or Authority? Motives and Argument in Jesus' Halakic Conflicts* (Tübingen: Mohr Siebeck, 2013), pp. 113–94, too late. Such works also provide some correction to E. P. Sanders' more sceptical views on Mark's knowledge of hand-washing in e.g. E. P. Sanders, *Jewish Law from the Bible to the Mishnah* (London: SCM, 1990), pp. 39–40, 230. For critical interaction with Sanders on hand-washing and purity in the first century see e.g. Dunn, *Jesus, Paul and the Law*, pp. 61–88; H. K. Harrington, 'Did Pharisees Eat Ordinary Food in a State of Ritual Purity?', *JSJ* 26 (1995), pp. 42–54; J. C. Poirier, 'Why did the Pharisees Wash their Hands?', *JJS* 47 (1996), pp. 217–33; E. Regev, 'Pure Individualism: The Idea of Non-Priestly Purity in Ancient Judaism', *JSJ* 31 (2000), pp. 176–202; J. C. Poirier, 'Purity beyond the Temple in the Second Temple Era', *JBL* 122 (2003), pp. 247–65; Kazen, *Issues of Impurity*. The Sanders-influenced J. P. Meier, *A Marginal Jew: Rethinking the Historical Jesus. Law and Love* (New York: Doubleday, 2009) lacks interaction with some of the more detailed recent criticisms of the position Meier favours for understanding Mark 7.1–23. For criticisms of Meier on Jesus and purity, including his (uncharacteristic) lack of interaction with certain scholarly sources, see e.g. M. Casey, *Jesus of Nazareth: An Independent Historian's Account of his Life and Teachings* (London and New York: T&T Clark, 2010), p. 57; Kazen, *Issues of Impurity*, p. 161.
58. E.g. H. Hübner, *Das Gesetz in der synoptischen Tradition* (Witten: Luther-Verlag, 1973), pp. 163–4.
59. See esp. R. P. Booth, *Jesus and the Laws of Purity* (Sheffield: JSOT, 1986), pp. 183–4.
60. See G. Alon, *Jews, Judaism and the Classical World: Studies in Jewish History in the Times of the Second Temple and Talmud* (Jerusalem: Magnes, 1977), p. 210.
61. Poirier, 'Pharisees'. *B. T.* typically retains the dominant assumptions of the transmission of impurity which was stable over centuries and has to explain the assumptions.

62. For a full discussion see Crossley, *Why Christianity Happened*, pp. 104–12; J. G. Crossley, *Jewish Law and the New Testament: A Guide for the Perplexed* (London and New York: Continuum, 2010), pp. 58–62.
63. For attempts at reconstructions of an earlier (Q) tradition see e.g. S. Schultz, *Q:— Die Spruchquelle der Evangelisten* (Zürich: TVZ, 1971), pp. 96–7; J. S. Kloppenborg, 'Nomos and Ethos in Q', in J. E. Goehring, J. T. Sanders, and C. W. Hedrick (eds), *Gospel Origins and Christian Beginnings: In Honor of James M. Robinson* (Sonoma: Polebridge, 1990), pp. 35–48 (38, n. 16); D. R. Catchpole, *The Quest for Q* (Edinburgh: T&T Clark, 1993), pp. 266–8; J. M. Robinson, P. Hoffmann, and J. S. Kloppenborg (eds), *The Critical Edition of Q: Synopsis, Including the Gospels of Matthew and Luke, Mark and Thomas, with English, German and French Translations of Q and Thomas* (Leuven: Peeters, 2000), pp. 268–73; Casey, *Aramaic Approach*, pp. 78–83.
64. See e.g. J. Neusner, '"First Cleanse the Inside": The "Halakhic" Background of a Controversy Saying', *NTS* 22 (1976), pp. 486–95; Schulz, *Spruchquelle*, pp. 97–9; C. M. Tuckett, *Q and the History of Early Christianity: Studies on Q* (Edinburgh: T&T Clark, 1996), pp. 412–13; Casey, *Aramaic Approach*, pp. 77–83. Kloppenborg has, however, argued that this passage 'betrays knowledge of the Shammaite distinctions, but no sympathy with them. By subverting the boundaries between inside and outside and by diverting attention to ethical issues, Q is actually undermining the entire system of purity that depends for its existence on a well defined taxonomy of the cosmos' (Kloppenborg, 'Nomos and Ethos', p. 40). However, 'criticizing distinctions of inside and outside does not necessarily go as far as undermining the entire system of purity and this passage is in line with typical Synoptic polemic aimed at Pharisees and specific interpretations of biblical law, and echoes prioritization of purity and sacrifice (e.g. Isa. 1.10–17; Jer. 6.20; 7.21–8; Hos. 6.6; Amos 5.21–7; Ps. 51.15–19; *Aristeas* 170–1, 234).
65. See e.g. J. Neusner, 'First Cleanse the Inside'; Poirier, 'Pharisees'; H. Maccoby, 'The Law about Liquids: A Rejoinder', *JSNT* 67 (1997), pp. 115–22; H. Maccoby, *Ritual and Morality: The Ritual Purity System and Its Place in Judaism* (Cambridge: Cambridge University Press, 1999); Crossley, *Why Christianity Happened*, pp. 107–8.
66. Neusner, 'First Cleanse the Inside', pp. 488–91.
67. Cf. Neusner, 'First Cleanse the Inside', p. 490.
68. H. Maccoby, 'The Washing of Cups', *JSNT* 14 (1982), pp. 3–15 (5), followed by Kloppenborg, 'Nomos and Ethos', p. 39 and L. E. Vaage,

Galilean Upstarts: Jesus' First Followers According to Q (Valley Forge: Trinity, 1994), pp. 66–86.

69. For more precise linguistic discussion of the language of 'outside' in Matt. 23.25//Luke 11.39, see Crossley, *Why Christianity Happened*, pp. 109–11.
70. Maccoby, 'Washing', p. 13, n. 5.
71. Maccoby, 'Washing', p. 7.
72. E.g. E. P. Sanders and M. Davies, *Studying the Synoptic Gospels* (London: SCM, 1989), pp. 181–2; Wright, *Victory*, p. 307.
73. So Bockmuehl, 'Bury', p. 561.
74. Crossley, *Date*, pp. 117–20; Casey, *Jesus of Nazareth*, pp. 301–5.
75. See further, J. A. Fitzmyer, *Luke X–XXIV* (New York: Doubleday, 1985), p. 886; J. L. Nolland, *Luke 9:21–18:34* (Dallas: Word, 1993), p. 593.
76. Against R. J. Bauckham, 'The Scrupulous Priest and the Good Samaritan: Jesus' Parabolic Interpretation of the Law of Moses', *NTS* 44 (1998), pp. 475–89. Despite Bauckham providing much important analysis of the parable, I would contest his argument that the love commandment is prioritized over purity laws in instances of conflicting scenarios. Again, if this were the case, it would also be more likely that the priest was *going up to* the Temple in order to establish an unambiguous contrast between two commandments.
77. Bauckham, 'The Scrupulous Priest and the Good Samaritan', deals with this view effectively.
78. On Samaritans and the Pentateuch, including Aqiba's relatively positive view on Samaritans, see e.g. G. Sellin, 'Lukas als Gleichniserzähler: Die Erzählung vom Barmherzingen Samariter (Lk. 10:25–37)', *ZNW* 66 (1975), pp. 19–60 (42–3). On the Lukan Samaritan representing the Torah, see e.g. Bauckham, 'The Scrupulous Priest and the Good Samaritan'; Casey, *Jesus of Nazareth*, pp. 303–4. Bauckham, however, adds that the Samaritan may have been perceived as not particularly observant. However, while this may have been possible, it is not necessarily if certain rabbinic passages are anything to go by (e.g. *m. Nid.* 4.2; *m. Sheb.* 8.10; *b. Qidd.* 75b).
79. Cf. Regev, 'Purity', pp. 181–4; R. Deines, *Jüdische Steingefäße und pharisäische Frömmigkeit: Eine archäologisch-historischer Beitrag zum Verständnis von Joh 2,6 und der jüdischen Reinheitshalacha zur Zeit Jesu* (Tübingen: Mohr Siebeck, 1993).
80. J. Wellhausen, *Einleitung in die drei ersten Evangelien* (second edition; Berlin: G. Reimer, 1911), p. 27; Black, *Aramaic Approach to the Gospels and Acts*, p. 2; Casey, *Aramaic Approach*, pp. 22–4, 82.
81. P. M. Head and P. J. Williams, 'Q Review', *Tyn. Bul.* 54 (2003), pp. 119–44 (133).

82. See e.g. E. Nestle, '"Anise" and "Rue"', *Exp.T.* 15 (1904), p. 528; Black, *Aramaic Approach to the Gospels and Acts*, p. 194; Casey, *Aramaic Approach*, pp. 73–4.
83. See e.g. Dunn, *Jesus, Paul and the Law*, pp. 61–86; Hengel and Deines, 'E. P. Sanders' "Common Judaism", Jesus, and the Pharisees'; Crossley, *Date*, pp. 131–3; Casey, *Jesus of Nazareth*, pp. 313–52.
84. Crossley, *Date*, pp. 131–41.
85. In this respect, see C. Keith, *Jesus against the Scribal Elite: The Origins of the Conflict* (Ada, MI: Baker, 2014) and its discussion of perceptions of authoritative status and literacy, which may further complement the arguments on socio-economic context.
86. The 'people of the land' have been identified as poor people oppressed by Pharisees. On which see the critique in Sanders, *Jesus and Judaism*, pp. 174–211. For an overview of the various issues and their relevance for the Gospel tradition see Neale, *None but the Sinners*, pp. 40–67. Neale also shows with some justification that the 'people of the land' were more of a 'religious' category than a label for a social underclass.
87. See further A. Oppenheimer, *The 'Am Ha-aretz: A Study in the Social History of the Jewish People in the Hellenistic-Roman Period* (Leiden: Brill, 1977), pp. 18–22.
88. J. Klawans, 'Notions of Gentile Impurity in Ancient Judaism', *Association for Jewish Studies Review* 20 (1995), pp. 285–312; J. Klawans, *Impurity and Sin in Ancient Judaism* (Oxford: Oxford University Press, 2000), pp. 43–60, 134–5; C. E. Hayes, *Gentile Impurities and Jewish Identities: Intermarriage and Conversion from the Bible to the Talmud* (Oxford: Oxford University Press, 2002), pp. 107–44, 199–221. Cf. G. Alon, 'The Levitical Uncleanness of Gentiles', in *Jews, Judaism and the Classical World: Studies in Jewish History in the Times of the Second Temple and Talmud* (Jerusalem: Magnes, 1977), pp. 146–89.
89. Hayes, *Gentile Impurities*, e.g. pp. 22–34, 53–9, 145–92.
90. See Crossley, *Why Christianity Happened*, ch. 4.
91. For a detailed discussion of the various issues see J. Marcus, *Mark 1–8: A New Translation with Introduction and Commentary* (New York: Doubleday, 2000), pp. 404–515.
92. Marcus, *Mark 1–8*, p. 411. Cf. e.g. R. A. Guelich, *Mark 1–8:26* (Dallas: Word, 1989), p. 343; W. D. Davies and D. C. Allison, *A Critical and Exegetical Commentary on the Gospel According to Saint Matthew VIII–XVIII* (Edinburgh: T&T Clark, 1991), p. 492.
93. Marcus, *Mark 1–8*, p. 489.
94. Cf. esp. J. Svartvik, *Mark and Mission: Mark 7.1–23 in its Narrative and Historical Contexts* (Stockholm: Almqvist & Wiksell, 2000).

95. See e.g. F. W. Danker, 'Mark 8:3', *JBL* 82 (1963), pp. 215–16; B. W. F. van Iersel, 'Die wunderbare Speisung und das Abendmahl in der synoptischen Tradition (Mk VI.35–44 par VIII.1–20 par)', *NovT* 7 (1964), pp. 167–94; Guelich, *Mark 1–8:26*, p. 404; Marcus, *Mark 1–8*, p. 487. Against this see e.g. R. H. Gundry, *Mark: A Commentary on His Apology for the Cross* (Grand Rapids and Cambridge: Eerdmans, 1993), p. 396.
96. Klawans, *Impurity and Sin.*
97. J. Klawans, 'The Impurity of Immorality in Ancient Judaism', *JJS* 48 (1997), pp. 1–16 (15).
98. See further M. Newton, *The Concept of Purity at Qumran and in the Letters of Paul* (Cambridge: Cambridge University Press, 2005).
99. See Klawans, *Impurity and Sin*, pp. 150–7.

CHAPTER 5

1. See the comments in M. Casey, *Jesus of Nazareth: An Independent Historian's Account of His Life and Teaching* (London: T&T Clark, 2010), p. 196, criticizing the exaggerated claims of B. Witherington, *Women in the Ministry of Jesus: A Study of Jesus' Attitude to Women and Their Roles as Reflected in His Earthly Life* (Cambridge: Cambridge University Press, 1984), p. 117.
2. A.-J. Levine et al., 'Getting Judaism, and Jesus, Wrong', *Huffington Post* (17 January 2014), http://www.huffingtonpost.com/amyjill-levine/getting-judaism-and-jesus_b_4617731.html, with reference to F. Schaeffer, 'Jesus Hated Women – Right?', *Huffington Post* (15 January 2014), http://www.huffingtonpost.com/frank-schaeffer/jesus-hated-women-right_b_4598039.html
3. There may be something of the masculine unconscious here in light of the critique in S. D. Moore, *God's Beauty Parlor and Other Queer Spaces in and around the Bible* (Stanford: Stanford University Press, 2001), ch. 2.
4. There is, of course, a huge amount of secondary literature on the topic of gender in Gospel studies. For an overview of issues in gender studies and biblical studies, see e.g. S. D. Moore, '"O Man, Who Art Thou . . . ?": Masculinity Studies and New Testament Studies', in S. D. Moore and J. C. Anderson (eds), *New Testament Masculinities* (Atlanta, GA: SBL, 2003), pp. 1–22; V. Burrus, 'Mapping as Metamorphosis: Initial Reflections on Gender and Ancient Religious Discourses', in T. Penner and C. vander Stichele (eds), *Mapping Gender in Ancient Religious Discourses* (Boston: Brill, 2007), pp. 1–10; J. Økland and R. Boer, 'Towards Marxist Feminist Biblical Criticism', in R. Boer and J. Økland (eds), *Marxist*

Feminist Criticism of the Bible (Sheffield: Sheffield Phoenix Press, 2008), pp. 1–25.

5. More wide-ranging work on gender and the historical Jesus has, of course, been carried out in different ways by e.g. E. S. Fiorenza, *In Memory of Her: A Feminist Theological Reconstruction of Christian Origins* (second edition; London: SCM, 1995), H. Moxnes, *Putting Jesus in His Place: A Radical Vision of Household and Kingdom* (Louisville: WJK, 2003), and W. Loader, *Sexuality and the Jesus Tradition* (Grand Rapids: Eerdmans, 2005). The present chapter differs from Loader, *Sexuality and the Jesus Tradition*, whose book has a more conventional exegetical emphasis on the study of the Gospel tradition (e.g. locating Jesus' teaching on divorce in the context of early Jewish law, establishing the precise meaning of Jesus' saying on adultery). This, it should be stated clearly, is not a criticism but a notice that Loader's book is not quite as relevant for the sort of study represented in this chapter as might be implied by the title of his book.
6. D. B. Martin, *Sex and the Single Savior: Gender and Sexuality in Biblical Interpretation* (Louisville: WJK, 2006), pp. 94–8; A. Le Donne, *The Wife of Jesus: Ancient Texts and Modern Scandals* (New York: Oneworld, 2013), though Le Donne does investigate concepts of masculinity in relation to celibacy.
7. R. J. Myles, 'Dandy Discipleship: A Queering of Mark's Male Disciples', *Journal of Men, Masculinities, and Spirituality* 4 (2010), pp. 66–81 (66), with reference to M. W. Gleason, 'By Whose Gender Standards (If Anybody's) was Jesus a Real Man?', in S. D. Moore and J. C. Anderson (eds), *New Testament Masculinities* (Atlanta, GA: SBL, 2003), pp. 325–7 (327), who calls for more discussion of the social construction of gender in Aramaic-speaking Palestine. Daniel Boyarin has developed work on gender and Judaism, including in the context of imperial engagements. See e.g. D. Boyarin, 'Homotopia: The Feminized Jewish Man and the Lives of Women in Late Antiquity', *differences* 7 (1995), pp. 42–80; D. Boyarin, *Carnal Israel: Reading Sex in Talmudic Culture* (Berkeley: University of California Press, 1995); D. Boyarin, *Unheroic Conduct: The Rise of Heterosexuality and the Invention of the Jewish Man* (Berkeley: University of California Press, 1997), pp. 81–125; D. Boyarin, *Dying for God: Martyrdom and the Making of Christianity and Judaism* (Stanford: Stanford University Press, 1999), pp. 67–92.
8. C. M. Conway, *Behold the Man: Jesus and Greco-Roman Masculinity* (Oxford: Oxford University Press, 2008), pp. 89, 100.
9. Conway, *Behold the Man*, e.g. p. 73: 'when Jesus is portrayed as one who willingly dies for the good of others, his death becomes a noble,

courageous, and thereby manly act...the noble, manly death and the emasculating crucifixion are not ideas that are easily held together in the gendered ideology of the first century'.

10. For critical qualifications on the role of women in earliest Christianity, including Celsus' famous polemic, see e.g. E. A. Castelli, 'Gender, Theory, and the Rise of Christianity: A Response to Rodney Stark', *Journal of Early Christian Studies* 6 (1998), pp. 227–57; J. Lieu, 'The "Attraction of Women" in/to Early Judaism and Christianity: Gender and the Politics of Conversion', *JSNT* 72 (1998), pp. 5–22; C. Osiek and M. Y. MacDonald with J. H. Tulloch, *A Woman's Place: House Churches in Earliest Christianity* (Minneapolis: Fortress, 2006), pp. 221–43.
11. Bauckham, *Gospel Women*, pp. 135–61; Casey, *Jesus of Nazareth*, pp. 193–4.
12. See esp. Moxnes, *Jesus in His Place*, pp. 101, 105.
13. Le Donne, *Wife of Jesus*, pp. 118–29, brings cultural assumptions involving household, economics, and masculinity (among other things) under the label 'civic masculinity' to which Jesus, he argues, posed an alternative.
14. T-s.B. Liew, 'Re-Mark-able Masculinities: Jesus, the Son of Man, and the (Sad) Sum of Manhood?', in S. D. Moore and J. C. Anderson (eds), *New Testament Masculinities* (Atlanta, GA: Society of Biblical Literature, 2003), pp. 93–135 (98). It is not clear that there is enough support for Loader's claim that Mark 3.20–2, 31–5, and 6.1–6 are not only 'a new family, a new system of belonging' but that in this 'new system women are no longer defined as mother or spouse. They are people' (Loader, *Sexuality and the Jesus Tradition*, p. 58). The gendered labels may be fictionalized but they seem to remain.
15. Cf. Martin, *Sex and the Single Savior*, p. 106.
16. S. C. Barton, *Discipleship and Family Ties in Mark and Matthew* (Cambridge: Cambridge University Press, 1995).
17. Moxnes, *Jesus in His Place*, pp. 78–80.
18. The comments of Dale C. Allison, *Constructing Jesus: Memory, Imagination and History* (London: SPCK, 2010), p. 135, are also relevant here: 'Concern for the disaffected, egalitarianism, the breaking of hallowed customs, the replacing of familiar bonds with fictive kin, the mediation of the sacred through new channels, the demand for intense commitment and unconditional loyalty, and focus on a charismatic leader are, for example, characteristic not only of the Jesus tradition but also of millenarian movements.'
19. On the intersection of economics, structure, and agency in homelessness and the Gospel tradition, see R. Myles, *Jesus the Homeless in the Gospel of Matthew* (Sheffield: Sheffield Phoenix Press, 2014).

20. M. A. Tétreault, 'Women and Revolution: A Framework for Analysis', in M. A. Tétreault (ed.), *Women and Revolution in Africa, Asia, and the New World* (Columbia: University of South Carolina Press, 1994), pp. 3–30 (19).
21. Cf. E. J. Hobsbawm, *Nations and Nationalism Since 1780: Programme, Myth, Reality* (second edition; Cambridge: Cambridge University Press/ Canto, 1992); K. W. Whitelam, *The Invention of Ancient Israel: The Silencing of Palestinian History* (London: Routledge, 1996).
22. C. Hill, *The World Turned Upside Down: Radical Ideas during the English Revolution* (London: Temple Smith, 1972), pp. 306–23.
23. A. Hughes, *Gender and the English Revolution* (London: Routledge, 2012), pp. 2, 29.
24. See J. G. Crossley, *Harnessing Chaos: The Bible in English Political Discourse since 1968* (London: T&T Clark, 2014). On constructing gender and the persona of Thatcher see H. Nunn, *Thatcher, Politics and Fantasy: The Political Culture of Gender and Nation* (London: Lawrence and Wishart, 2002).
25. Hughes, *Gender and the English Revolution*, p. 7.
26. Tétreault, 'Women and Revolution', p. 19.
27. J. Økland, *Women in Their Place: Paul and the Corinthian Discourse of Gender and Sanctuary Space* (London and New York: T&T Clark, 2004), p. 40. Cf. Osiek and MacDonald with Tulloch, *A Woman's Place*, pp. 140–1.
28. On celibacy and the early tradition, see Loader, *Sexuality and the Jesus Tradition*, pp. 121–82.
29. Moxnes, *Jesus in His Place*, pp. 76–84.
30. Moxnes, *Jesus in His Place*, pp. 46–107.
31. On absence of 'father' and a reinstatement of patriarchy, see A. H. Cadwallader, 'The Markan/Marxist Struggle for the Household: Juliet Mitchell and the Challenge to Patriarchal/Familial Ideology', in R. Boer and J. Økland (eds), *Marxist Feminist Criticism of the Bible* (Sheffield: Sheffield Phoenix Press, 2008), pp. 151–81 (177–8).
32. Myles, 'Dandy Discipleship', pp. 74–6.
33. Liew, 'Re-Mark-able Masculinities', pp. 99–100, 105, 111. See also E. Thurman, 'Looking for a Few Good Men: Mark and Masculinity', in S. D. Moore and J. C. Anderson (eds), *New Testament Masculinities* (Atlanta, GA: Society of Biblical Literature, 2003), pp. 137–61.
34. Myles, 'Dandy Discipleship', p. 67.
35. G. Kessler, 'Bodies in Motion: Preliminary Notes on Queer Theory and Rabbinic Literature', in T. Penner and C. vander Stichele (eds), *Mapping*

Gender in Ancient Religious Discourses (Leiden: Brill, 2007), pp. 389–409 (394–6).

36. Conway, *Behold the Man*, p. 89. Though not technically on the 'historical Jesus' and covering a broader time frame, complementary points are raised about the 'myth of Christ' in T. Prosic, 'Schizoid Christ: Christ and the Feminine', in R. Boer and J. Økland (eds), *Marxist Feminist Criticism of the Bible* (Sheffield: Sheffield Phoenix Press, 2008), pp. 47–69. On Jesus as 'strong man', the exorcism stories, which may well reflect earliest Palestinian tradition, have Jesus dominant and in control over the spiritual world, and indeed over strong men.
37. While working on slightly different contexts, still relevant here are: S. D. Moore and J. C. Anderson, 'Taking It Like a Man: Masculinity in 4 Maccabees', *JBL* 117 (1998), pp. 249–73; Boyarin, *Dying for God*; E. A. Castelli, *Martyrdom and Memory: Early Christian Culture Making* (New York: Columbia University Press, 2007).
38. For an earlier presentation of what follows see J. G. Crossley, 'History from the Margins: The Death of John the Baptist', in J. G. Crossley and C. Karner (eds), *Writing History, Constructing Religion* (Aldershot: Ashgate, 2005), pp. 147–61.
39. R. Darnton, 'Workers Revolt: The Great Cat Massacre of the Rue Saint-Séverin', in *The Great Cat Massacre and Other Episodes in French Cultural History* (London: Allen Lane, 1984), pp. 75–104 (77–8).
40. These points make it very difficult to accept Hoehner's attempt at harmonizing the Gospels and Josephus. See H. W. Hoehner, *Herod Antipas* (Cambridge: Cambridge University Press, 1972), pp. 158–64.
41. It has been argued that to give away half a kingdom/half of your possessions was proverbial, e.g. A. E. J. Rawlinson, *St Mark* (London: Methuen, 1925), pp. 81–2; Hoehner, *Herod Antipas*, pp. 150–1; J. R. Edwards, *The Gospel According to Mark* (Grand Rapids and Cambridge: Eerdmans, 2002), p. 188. Yet there is little evidence to suggest such a proverb was firmly established. Hoehner notes 1 Kings 13.8 and Luke 19.8 but even if these were good parallels they still would not provide strong enough evidence of an established proverb. As with Esther, 1 Kings is set in a situation where the king theoretically has the power to redistribute land whereas Antipas did not. Moreover, in 1 Kings the context is explicitly hyperbolic. Luke 19.8 (which, of course, makes no mention of 'kingdom') refers to a man giving half his possessions to the poor and is not necessarily proverbial given what we have seen in the Synoptic tradition. As will be discussed in more detail, it should be accepted that Mark 6.22–3 is a direct reference to Esther (5.3; 5.6; 7.2), not least due to precise linguistic correspondence and the strong links with the Esther traditions

throughout Mark 6.17–29 as established by R. D. Aus, *Water into Wine and the Beheading of John the Baptist: Early Jewish-Christian Interpretation of Esther 1 in John 2:1–11 and Mark 6:17–29* (Atlanta: Scholars Press, 1988).

42. M. S. Enslin, 'John and Jesus', *ZNW* 66 (1975), pp. 1–18 (13–14).
43. Jennifer Glancy suggests that the role of the women in the death of John the Baptist has been exaggerated in interpretations of Mark 6:17–29 and more should be placed on Herod Antipas as he holds the real power (J. A. Glancy, 'Unveiling Masculinity: The Construction of Gender in Mark 6:17–29', *Bib. Int.* 2 (1994), pp. 34–50. While Glancy has countered certain unfounded assumptions (e.g. her argument that there is no evidence for Herodias being sexually depraved is surely correct), it might also be because of Antipas holding the power that the story has to find a way of laying the blame elsewhere. It might therefore be suggested that the emphasis on the women being responsible begins with this story where at least some of the first-century readers would accept the validity of Antipas' actions.
44. Cf. J. E. Taylor, *The Immerser: John the Baptist within Second Temple Judaism* (Grand Rapids and Cambridge: Eerdmans, 1997), p. 247.
45. It should be stressed that this is Josephus' opinion because this judgement has too often influenced modern historical scholarship (cf. Glancy, 'Unveiling Masculinity', p. 46).
46. Gerd Theissen claims that women at men's banquets can only be taken in a sexual sense. See e.g. G. Theissen, *The Gospels in Context: Social and Political History in the Synoptic Tradition* (Edinburgh: T&T Clark, 1992), pp. 91–3.
47. In *b. BQ* 97a and *b. Pesach.* 49a מרקיד (from רקד) is used and this is one of the words translated by ὀρχέομαι (used in Mark 6.22) in the LXX: see Isa. 13.21; 1 Chron. 15.29; Eccles. 3.4.
48. Aus, *Beheading of John the Baptist*, pp. 52–3.
49. Moxnes, *Jesus in His Place*.
50. Loader, *Sexuality and the Jesus Tradition*, p. 57.
51. See e.g. J. M. Baumgarten, 'On the Nature of the Seductress in 4Q184', *Revue de Qumrân* 15 (1991), pp. 133–43.
52. Baumgarten, 'On the Nature of the Seductress', p. 143; cf. Y. Zur, 'Parallels between Acts of Thomas 6–7 and 4Q184', *Revue de Qumrân* 16 (1993), pp. 103–7.
53. See e.g. J. A. Sanders, *The Psalms Scroll of Qumrân Cave 11* (Oxford: Clarendon, 1965), pp. 79–85; T. Muraoka, 'Sir. 51:13–30: An Erotic Hymn to Wisdom?', *JSJ* 10 (1979), pp. 168–78; A. S. van der Woude, 'Wisdom at Qumran', in J. Day, R. P. Gordon, and H. G. M. Williamson

(eds), *Wisdom in Ancient Israel: Essays in Honour of J. A. Emerton* (Cambridge: Cambridge University Press), pp. 244–56 (253–4).

54. On יד and genitals see e.g. 1QS VII.13 (cf. e.g. Song 5.4); on כף and genitals see e.g. *t. Nid.* 6.4; *y. Yeb.* 1, 2d; and *y. Sanh.* 8, 26a. See further M. Delcor, 'Two Special Meanings of the Word *yad* in Biblical Hebrew: Notes on Hebrew Lexicography', *Journal of Semitic Studies* 12 (1967), pp. 230–40.
55. Cf. C. V. Camp, 'Woman Wisdom and the Strange Woman: Where is Power to be Found?', in T. M. Beal and D. M. Gunn (eds), *Reading Bibles, Writing Bodies: Identity and the Book* (London and New York: Routledge, 1996), pp. 85–112 (92–4, 96–7).
56. J. C. Anderson, 'Feminist Criticism: The Dancing Daughter', in J. C. Anderson and S. D. Moore (eds), *Mark and Method: New Approaches in Biblical Studies* (Minneapolis: Fortress Press, 1992), pp. 103–34 (128).
57. Cf. M. Broshi, 'Beware the Wiles of the Wicked Woman: Dead Sea Scroll Fragment (4Q184) Reflects Essene Fear of, and Contempt for, Women', *Biblical Archaeology Review* 9 (1983), pp. 54–6.
58. Compare also Judith 16:6, 9, where the beautiful Judith uses her charms to cut off the head of Holofernes and save the day for the Jews.
59. Aus, *Beheading of John the Baptist*, pp. 53–5.
60. Aus, *Beheading of John the Baptist*, pp. 53–5; J. Marcus *Mark 1–8: A New Translation with Introduction and Commentary* (New York: Doubleday, 2000), p. 396.
61. See D. J. A. Clines, *The Esther Scroll: The Story of a Story* (Sheffield: JSOT Press, 1984), pp. 222–3.
62. See Clines, *Esther Scroll: The Story of a Story*, pp. 238–9.
63. On 'fearing' John the Baptist, see Aus, *Beheading of John the Baptist*, pp. 56–8, including n. 101.
64. For what it is worth, φοβέω and derivatives, used in Mark 6.20, translates the Aramaic דחל (Dan. 5.19; 6.26[27]; 2.31; 7.7, 19; cf. 4.2).
65. On the general Hellenistic background see e.g. Marcus, *Mark 1–8*, p. 402.
66. Aus, *Beheading of John the Baptist*, pp. 62–3.
67. Aus, *Beheading of John the Baptist*, p. 65, including n. 151.
68. Aus, *Beheading of John the Baptist*, p. 65. Note that Josephus' λυπούμενος is from the same root (λυπ-) used when Mark 6.26 describes Antipas' grieving (περίλυπος).
69. On Luke omitting tricky details see e.g. Crossley, *Date of Mark's Gospel*, pp. 181, 202. On different reasons for Luke's omission of Mark 6:17–29 see Hoehner, *Herod Antipas*, pp. 112–13.
70. Theissen notes that the characteristics of John's preaching are missing, as are more developed details concerning John himself (Theissen, *Gospels in*

Context, pp. 84–5). From this Theissen believes that it does not come from Baptist circles. However, if the theory is correct, as will be suggested below, that the story was written to defend against persecution then these criticisms lose weight. The writers/speakers were concerned with other issues. This does not prove that it does come from Baptist circles but it does show that the possibility certainly remains.

71. See e.g. W. D. Davies and D. C. Allison, *A Critical and Exegetical Commentary on the Gospel According to Saint Matthew VIII–XVIII* (Edinburgh: T&T Clark, 1991), pp. 474–6; W. Wink, *John the Baptist in the Gospel Tradition* (Cambridge: Cambridge University Press, 1968), pp. 8–13.
72. For further indications of a pre-Markan tradition see e.g. Marcus, *Mark 1–8*, pp. 397–8.
73. Summarized in Hoehner, *Herod Antipas*, p. 118, n. 3. See also the suggestions in Aus, *Beheading of John the Baptist*, pp. 60–2.
74. Cf. Davies and Allison, *Matthew VIII–XVIII*, p. 465; Theissen, *Gospels in Context*, pp. 81–9, 96.
75. Cf. C. H. H. Scobie, *John the Baptist* (London: SCM Press, 1964), p. 180.
76. For further discussion see Crossley, *Why Christianity Happened*, ch. 5. For further discussion on female converts to Judaism see T. Ilan, *Jewish Women in Greco-Roman Palestine: An Inquiry into Image and Status* (Tübingen: Mohr Siebeck, 1995), pp. 211–14. On the famous conversion story of Izates and the House of Adiabene, see e.g. J. Neusner, 'The Conversion of Adiabene to Judaism: A New Perspective', *JBL* 83 (1964), pp. 60–6; L. H. Schiffman, 'The Conversion of the Royal House of Adiabene in Josephus and Rabbinic Sources', in L. H. Feldman and G. Hata (eds), *Josephus, Judaism, and Christianity* (Detroit: Wayne State University Press, 1987), pp. 293–312; D. Schwartz, 'God, Gentiles, and Jewish Law: On Acts 15 and Josephus' Adiabene Narrative', in H. Cancik, H. Lichtenberger, and P. Schäfer (eds), *Geschichte—Tradition—Reflection: Festschrift für Martin Hengel*, vol. 1: *Judentum* (Tübingen: Mohr Siebeck, 1996), pp. 263–82. Indeed, the retelling of the story of Izates further emphasizes how problematic circumcision could be for conversion. Compare *Gen. R.* 46.10: 'Once Monabaz and Izates, the sons of King Ptolemy, were sitting and reading the book of Genesis. When they came to the verse, "And you shall be circumcised" [Gen. 17.11] one turned his face towards the wall and commenced to weep, and the other turned his face to the wall and commenced to weep. Then each went and had himself circumcised.'

77. See Osiek and MacDonald with Tulloch, *A Woman's Place*, pp. 144–63, 194–243.
78. Bauckham, *Gospel Women*, pp. 135–61; Casey, *Jesus of Nazareth*, pp. 193–4.
79. See further Bauckham, *Gospel Women*, pp. 121–61.
80. See Osiek and MacDonald with Tulloch, *A Woman's Place*, pp. 144–63, 194–243.
81. For further discussion see e.g. Fiorenza, *In Memory of Her*; R. Stark, *The Rise of Christianity: A Sociologist Reconsiders History* (Princeton: Princeton University Press, 1996), pp. 95–128; Castelli, 'Gender, Theory, and the Rise of Christianity'; Lieu, 'The "Attraction of Women"', pp. 5–22; Osiek and MacDonald with Tulloch, *A Woman's Place*.
82. Osiek and MacDonald with Tulloch, *A Woman's Place*, pp. 221–43.

CONCLUSION

1. N. Chomsky, *Understanding Power* (New York: New Press, 2002), pp. 222–3.
2. E. Hobsbawm, *The Age of Extremes: The Short Twentieth Century, 1914–1991* (London: Abacus, 1994), e.g. pp. 74, 142–77, 188. For criticisms see D. Evans, 'Spain and the World: Aspects of the Spanish Revolution and Civil War (7)', *Radical History Network* (31 August 2011), http://radicalhistorynetwork.blogspot.co.uk/2011/08/spain-and-world-aspects-of-spanish.html.
3. E. P. Thompson, *The Making of the English Working Class* (Harmondsworth: Pelican Books, 1963); N. Chomsky, *American Power and the New Mandarins* (New York: Pantheon Books, 1969), pp. 76–7.
4. J. G. Crossley, *Harnessing Chaos: The Bible in English Political Discourse since 1968* (London: T&T Clark, 2014), chs 1 and 9.
5. S. Lee. 'Will Cameron's Recipe for "Successful" Films Result in a Glut of Silent Comedies?', *Observer* (22 January 2012), http://www.guardian.co.uk/commentisfree/2012/jan/22/stewart-lee-david-cameron-pinewood-film.
6. See e.g. S. Collini, *What Are Universities For?* (London: Penguin, 2004).
7. N. Schneider, 'Why the World Needs Religious Studies', *Religion Dispatches* (20 November 2011), http://www.religiondispatches.org/archive/culture/4636/why_the_world_needs_religious_studies_/
8. J. Crace, 'Writing off the UK's Last Palaeographer', *Guardian* (9 February 2010), http://www.theguardian.com/education/2010/feb/09/writing-off-last-palaeographer-university. If cost is everything, one way of saving money for more academic study might be to cut or cap the salaries of extremely well-paid senior academics and managers, or even encourage

job sharing to create more positions and more free time. Here I would agree with Roland Boer's 'University of Utopia' which 'does not overpay its staff in return for overwork' but provides a comfortable but not excessive salary with the savings going towards 'paying adequate administrative staff, more teaching positions, multiple PhD scholarships, and a world-class library'. R. Boer, 'University of Utopia', *Stalin's Moustache* (25 September 2009), http://stalinsmoustache.wordpress.com/2009/09/25/the-university-of-utopia/. On managerial culture and universities see now B. Ginsberg, *The Fall of the Faculty: The Rise of the All Administrative University and Why It Matters* (Oxford: Oxford University Press, 2011).

9. T. Eagleton, *After Theory* (New York: Basic Books, 2003), pp. 39–40; E. Repphun, 'Dysenchanted Worlds: Rationalisation, Dystopia, and Therapy Culture in Ninni Holmqvist's The Unit', *Dunedin School* (25 September 2009), http://dunedinschool.wordpress.com/2009/09/25/dysenchanted-worlds-rationalisation-dystopia-and-therapy-culture-in-ninni-holmqvist's-the-unit/; S. Žižek, *Living in the End Times* (revised edition; London and New York: Verso, 2011), pp. 411–12.
10. www.biblicalstudiesonline.wordpress.com.

Bibliography

Adams, E., *The Stars Will Fall from Heaven: Cosmic Catastrophe in the New Testament and Its World* (London: T&T Clark, 2007)

Alexander, P. H., et al. (eds), *The SBL Handbook of Style for Ancient Near Eastern, Biblical, and Early Christian Studies* (Peabody, MA: Hendrickson, 1999)

Allison, D. C., 'Jesus and the Covenant', *JSNT* 29 (1987), pp. 57–78

Allison, D. C., *Jesus of Nazareth: Millenarian Prophet* (Philadelphia: Fortress, 1998)

Allison, D. C., *Resurrecting Jesus: The Earliest Christian Tradition and its Interpreters* (London and New York: T&T Clark, 2005)

Allison, D. C., *Constructing Jesus: Memory, Imagination, and History* (London: SPCK, 2010)

Allison, D. C., 'How to Marginalize the Traditional Criteria of Authenticity', in T. Holmén and S. E. Porter (eds), *The Handbook for the Study of the Historical Jesus*, vol. 1 (Leiden: Brill, 2011), pp. 3–30

Alon, G., *Jews, Judaism and the Classical World: Studies in Jewish History in the Times of the Second Temple and Talmud* (Jerusalem: Magnes, 1977)

Amis, M., 'The Voice of the Lonely Crowd', *Guardian* (1 June 2002), <http://www.theguardian.com/books/2002/jun/01/philosophy.society>

Amis, M., 'The Age of Horrorism', *Observer* (10 September 2006), <http://www.theguardian.com/world/2006/sep/10/september11.politicsphilosophyandsociety>

Anderson, J. C., 'Feminist Criticism: The Dancing Daughter', in J. C. Anderson and S. D. Moore (eds), *Mark and Method: New Approaches in Biblical Studies* (Minneapolis: Fortress Press, 1992), pp. 103–34

Anderson, P. N., *The Fourth Gospel and the Quest for Jesus: Modern Foundations Reconsidered* (London: T&T Clark, 2006)

Anderson, P. N., 'Why This Study Is Needed, and Why It Is Needed Now', in P. N. Anderson, F. Just, and T. Thatcher (eds), *John, Jesus, and History*, vol. 1: *Critical Appraisals of Critical Views* (Atlanta: SBL, 2007), pp. 13–73

Anderson, P. N., 'Das "John-, Jesus-, and History"-Projekt Neue Beobachtungen zu Jesus und eine Bi-optische Hypothese', *ZNT* 23 (2009), pp. 12–26

Anderson, P. N., 'The John, Jesus, and History Project: New Glimpses of Jesus and a Bi-Optic Hypothesis', *Bible and Interpretation* (February 2010), <http://www.bibleinterp.com/articles/john1357917.shtml>

Anderson, P. N., 'A Fourth Quest for Jesus . . . So What, and How So?', *Bible and Interpretation* (July 2010), <http://www.bibleinterp.com/opeds/fourth357921.shtml>

Appld, M., 'Jesus' Bethsaida Disciples: A Study in Johannine Origins', in P. N. Anderson, F. Just, and T. Thatcher (eds), *John, Jesus, and History*, vol. 2: *Aspects of Historicity in the Fourth Gospel* (Atlanta: SBL, 2009), pp. 27–34

Arnal, W. E., *Jesus and the Village Scribes: Galilean Conflicts and the Setting of Q* (Minneapolis: Fortress, 2001)

Arnal, W. E., *The Symbolic Jesus: Historical Scholarship, Judaism and the Construction of Contemporary Identity* (London and Oakville: Equinox, 2005)

Assmann, J., *Moses the Egyptian: The Memory of Egypt in Western Monotheism* (Cambridge, MA: Harvard University Press, 1997)

Assmann, J., *Of God and Gods: Egypt, Israel, and the Rise of Monotheism* (Madison: University of Wisconsin Press, 2008)

Assmann, J., *The Price of Monotheism* (Stanford: Stanford University Press, 2010)

Athanassiadi, P., and M. Frede (eds), *Pagan Monotheism in Late Antiquity* (Oxford: Oxford University Press, 1999)

Athanassiadi-Fowden, P., *Julian and Hellenism* (Oxford: Oxford University Press, 1981)

Aus, R. D., *Water into Wine and the Beheading of John the Baptist: Early Jewish-Christian Interpretation of Esther 1 in John 2:1–11 and Mark 6:17–29* (Atlanta: Scholars Press, 1988)

Aus, R. D., *Barabbas and Esther and Other Studies in the Judaic Illumination of Earliest Christianity* (Atlanta: Scholars Press, 1992)

Aus, R. D., *Samuel, Saul, and Jesus: Three Early Palestinian Jewish Christian Gospel Haggadoth*, Atlanta: Scholars Press, 1994)

Aus, R. D., *'Caught in the Act,' Walking on the Sea, and the Release of Barabbas Revisited* (Atlanta: Scholars Press, 1998)

Aus, R. D., *The Death, Burial, and Resurrection of Jesus, and the Death, Burial, and Translation of Moses in Judaic Tradition* (Lanham: University Press of America, 2008)

Aus, R. D., *Feeding the Five Thousand: Studies in the Judaic Background of Mark 6:30–44 par. and John 6.1–15* (Lanham: University Press of America, 2010)

Badiou, A., *Saint Paul: The Foundation of Universalism* (Stanford: Stanford University Press, 2003)

Bakunin, M., *Selected Works* (New York: Alfred A. Knopf, 1972)

Barnett, P., *Finding the Historical Christ*, After Jesus, vol. 3 (Grand Rapids: Eerdmans, 2009)

Barrett, C. K., 'The Background of Mark 10.45', in A. J. B. Higgins (ed.), *New Testament Essays: Studies in Memory of T. W. Manson* (Manchester: Manchester University Press, 1959), pp. 1–18

Barrett, C. K., *New Testament Essays* (London: SPCK, 1972)
Barton, S. C., *Discipleship and Family Ties in Mark and Matthew* (Cambridge: Cambridge University Press, 1995)
Barton, S. C., 'Historical Criticism and Social-Scientific Perspectives in New Testament Study', in J. B. Green (ed.), *Hearing the New Testament: Strategies for Interpretation* (Grand Rapids: Eerdmans, 1995), pp. 61–89
Bauckham, R. J., 'Rich Man and Lazarus: The Parable and the Parallels', *NTS* 37 (1991), pp. 225–46
Bauckham, R. J., 'The Scrupulous Priest and the Good Samaritan: Jesus' Parabolic Interpretation of the Law of Moses', *NTS* 44 (1998), pp. 475–89
Bauckham, R. J., *Jesus and the Eyewitnesses: The Gospels as Eyewitness Testimony* (Grand Rapids: Eerdmans, 2006)
Bauckham, R. J., *The Testimony of the Beloved Disciple: Narrative, History and Theology in the Gospel of John* (Grand Rapids: Baker, 2007)
Bauckham, R. J., 'In Response to My Respondents: *Jesus and the Eyewitnesses* in Review', *JSHJ* 6 (2008), pp. 225–53
Bauckham, R. J., *Jesus and the God of Israel: God Crucified and Other Studies on the New Testament's Christology of Divine Identity* (Milton Keynes: Paternoster, 2008)
Baumgarten, J. M., 'On the Nature of the Seductress in 4Q184', *Revue de Qumrân* 15 (1991), pp. 133–43
Bell, R. H., 'Teshubah: The Idea of Repentance in Ancient Judaism', *Journal of Progressive Judaism* 5 (1995), pp. 22–52
Bermejo-Rubio, F., 'The Fiction of the "Three Quests": An Argument for Dismantling a Dubious Historiographical Paradigm', *JSHJ* 7 (2009), pp. 211–53
Bermejo-Rubio, F., 'Why is John the Baptist Used as a Foil for Jesus? Leaps of Faith and Oblique Anti-Judaism in Contemporary Scholarship', *JSHJ* 11 (2013), pp. 170–96
Bird, M. F., *Are You the One Who Is to Come? The Historical Jesus and the Messianic Question* (Grand Rapids: Baker Academic, 2009)
Bird, M. F., and J. G. Crossley, *How Did Christianity Begin? A Believer and Non-Believer Examine the Evidence* (London: SPCK, 2008)
Black, M., *An Aramaic Approach to the Gospels and Acts* (third edition; Oxford: Oxford University Press, 1967)
Blomberg, C. L., *The Historical Reliability of John's Gospel* (Downers Grove, IL: IVP, 2001)
Blomberg, C. L., *Contagious Holiness: Jesus' Meals with Sinners* (Leicester and Downers Grove: IVP, 2005)
Blomberg, C. L., 'The Authenticity and Significance of Jesus' Table Fellowship with Sinners', in D. L. Bock and R. L. Webb (eds), *Key Events in the Life of*

the Historical Jesus: A Collaborative Exploration of Context and Coherence (Grand Rapids and Cambridge: Eerdmans, 2009), pp. 215–50

Bock, D. L., 'Blasphemy and the Jewish Examination of Jesus', in D. L. Bock and R. L. Webb (eds), *Key Events in the Life of the Historical Jesus: A Collaborative Exploration of Context and Coherence* (Grand Rapids and Cambridge: Eerdmans, 2009), pp. 589–667

Bockmuehl, M., 'Let the Dead Bury their Dead (Matt. 8.22/Luke 9.60): Jesus and the Halakah', *JTS* 49 (1998), pp. 553–81

Bockmuehl, M., *Jewish Law in Gentile Churches: Halakhah and the Beginning of Christian Public Ethics* (Edinburgh: T&T Clark, 2000)

Bockmuehl, M., 'God's Life as a Jew: Remembering the Son of God as Son of David', in B. R. Gaventa and R. B. Hays (eds), *Seeking the Identity of Jesus: A Pilgrimage* (Grand Rapids and Cambridge: Eerdmans, 2008), pp. 60–78

Boer, R., 'Apocalyptic and Apocalypticism in the Poetry of E. P. Thompson', *Spaces of Utopia* 7 (2009), pp. 34–53

Boer, R., 'University of Utopia', *Stalin's Moustache* (25 September 2009), <http://stalinsmoustache.wordpress.com/2009/09/25/the-university-of-utopia/>

Bond, H., 'At the Court of the High Priest: History and Theology in John 18:13–24', in P. N. Anderson, F. Just, and T. Thatcher (eds), *John, Jesus, and History*, vol. 2: *Aspects of Historicity in the Fourth Gospel* (Atlanta: SBL, 2009), pp. 313–24

Bond, H., *The Historical Jesus: A Guide for the Perplexed* (London: T&T Clark, 2012)

Booth, R. P., *Jesus and the Laws of Purity: Tradition and Legal History in Mark 7* (Sheffield: JSOT Press, 1986)

Booth, R. P., *Contrasts: Gospel Evidence and Christian Belief* (Bognor Regis: Paget Press, 1990)

Borg, M. J., *Jesus, a New Vision: Spirit, Culture, and the Life of Discipleship* (London: SPCK, 1993)

Borg, M. J., *Conflict, Holiness, and Politics in the Teachings of Jesus* (orig.: New York: Edwin Mellen, 1984; Harrisburg, PA: Trinity Press International, 1998)

Boyarin, D., *Carnal Israel: Reading Sex in Talmudic Culture* (Berkeley: University of California Press, 1995)

Boyarin, D., 'Homotopia: The Feminized Jewish Man and the Lives of Women in Late Antiquity', *differences* 7 (1995), pp. 42–80

Boyarin, D., *Unheroic Conduct: The Rise of Heterosexuality and the Invention of the Jewish Man* (Berkeley: University of California Press, 1997)

Boyarin, D., *Dying for God: Martyrdom and the Making of Christianity and Judaism* (Stanford: Stanford University Press, 1999)

Boyarin, D., *The Jewish Gospels: The Story of the Jewish Christ* (New York: New Books, 2012)

Braddick, M., *God's Fury, England's Fire: A New History of the English Civil Wars* (London: Allen Lane, 2008)

Braudel, F., *The Mediterranean and the Mediterranean World in the Age of Philip II* (3 vols; London: Collins, 1972–3)

Briant, P., *From Cyrus to Alexander: A History of the Persian Empire* (Winona Lake: Eisenbrauns, 2002)

Broshi, M., 'Beware the Wiles of the Wicked Woman: Dead Sea Scroll Fragment (4Q184) Reflects Essene Fear of, and Contempt for, Women', *Biblical Archaeology Review* 9 (1983), pp. 54–6

Burke, J., *Al-Qaeda* (London: Penguin, 2003)

Burke, P., 'History of Events and the Revival of the Narrative', in P. Burke (ed.), *New Perspectives on History Writing* (second edition; London: Polity, 2001), pp. 283–300

Burkert, W., *Greek Religion* (Oxford: Blackwell, 1985)

Burrus, V., 'Mapping as Metamorphosis: Initial Reflections on Gender and Ancient Religious Discourses', in T. Penner and C. vander Stichele (eds), *Mapping Gender in Ancient Religious Discourses* (Boston: Brill, 2007), pp. 1–10

Cadwallader, A. H., 'The Markan/Marxist Struggle for the Household: Juliet Mitchell and the Challenge to Patriarchal/Familial Ideology', in R. Boer and J. Økland (eds), *Marxist Feminist Criticism of the Bible* (Sheffield: Sheffield Phoenix Press, 2008), pp. 151–81

Camp, C. V., 'Woman Wisdom and the Strange Woman: Where is Power to be Found?', in T. M. Beal and D. M. Gunn (eds), *Reading Bibles, Writing Bodies: Identity and the Book* (London and New York: Routledge, 1996), pp. 85–112

Carey, G., *Sinners: Jesus and His Earliest Followers* (Waco: Baylor University Press, 2009)

Carlyle, T., *On Heroes and Hero-Worship and the Heroic in History* (Berkeley: University of California, 1993)

Carr, D., 'Narrative and the Real World: An Argument for Continuity', *History and Theory* 25 (1986), pp. 117–31

Carr, D., *Time, Narrative and History* (Bloomington, IN: Indiana University Press, 1991)

Carr, E. H., *What is History?* (second edition; London: Penguin, 1987)

Carrier, R., *On the Historicity of Jesus: Why We Might Have Reason for Doubt* (Sheffield: Sheffield Phoenix Press, 2014)

Carson, D. A., *The Gospel According to John* (Leicester: IVP, 1991)

Carson, D. A., 'The Challenge of the Balkanization of Johannine Studies', in P. N. Anderson, F. Just, and T. Thatcher (eds), *John, Jesus, and History*, vol. 1: *Critical Appraisals of Critical Views* (Atlanta: SBL, 2007), pp. 133–59

Casey, M., *From Jewish Prophet to Gentile God: The Origins and Development of New Testament Christology* (Louisville: WJK, 1991)

Casey, M., *Is John's Gospel True?* (London and New York: Routledge, 1996)

Casey, M., *Aramaic Sources of Mark's Gospel* (Cambridge: Cambridge University Press, 1998)

Casey, M., *An Aramaic Approach to Q: Sources for the Gospels of Matthew and Luke* (Cambridge: Cambridge University Press, 2002)

Casey, M., *The Solution to 'the Son of Man' Problem* (London and New York: T&T Clark, 2007)

Casey, M., *Jesus of Nazareth: An Independent Historian's Account of His Life and Teaching* (London and New York: T&T Clark, 2010)

Casey, M., *Jesus: Evidence and Argument or Mythicist Myths?* (London and New York: T&T Clark, 2014)

Castelli, E. A., 'Gender, Theory, and the Rise of Christianity: A Response to Rodney Stark', *Journal of Early Christian Studies* 6 (1998), pp. 227–57

Castelli, E. A., *Martyrdom and Memory: Early Christian Culture Making* (New York: Columbia University Press, 2007)

Catchpole, D. R., *The Quest for Q* (Edinburgh: T&T Clark, 1993)

Catchpole, D. R., *Jesus People: The Historical Jesus and the Beginnings of Community* (London: Darton, Longman and Todd; Grand Rapids: Baker, 2006)

Catchpole, D. R., 'On Proving Too Much: Critical Hesitations about Richard Bauckham's Jesus and the Eyewitnesses', *JSHJ* 6 (2008), pp. 169–81

Cavanaugh, W. T., *The Myth of Religious Violence: Secular Ideology and the Roots of Modern Conflict* (Oxford: Oxford University Press, 2009)

Charles, R., 'Rahab: A Righteous Whore in James', *Neot.* 45 (2011), pp. 207–21

Chilton, B. D., 'Jesus and the Repentance of E. P. Sanders', *TynBul* 39 (1988), pp. 1–18

Chilton, B. D., *Rabbi Jesus: An Intimate Biography* (New York: Doubleday, 2000)

Chomsky, N., *American Power and the New Mandarins* (New York: Pantheon Books, 1969)

Chomsky, N., *Understanding Power* (New York: New Press, 2002)

Chomsky, N., and G. Achcar, *Perilous Power: The Middle East and U.S. Foreign Policy* (Boulder and London: Paradigm Publishers, 2007), pp. 30–4

Clines, D. J. A., *The Esther Scroll: The Story of a Story* (Sheffield: JSOT Press, 1984)

Collini, S., *What Are Universities For?* (London: Penguin, 2004)

Collins, J. J., *The Scepter and the Star: The Messiahs of the Dead Sea Scrolls and Other Ancient Literature* (New York: Doubleday, 1995)

Conway, C. M., *Behold the Man: Jesus and Greco-Roman Masculinity* (Oxford: Oxford University Press, 2008)

Cook, J. G., *The Interpretation of the Old Testament in Greco-Roman Paganism* (Tübingen: Mohr Siebeck, 2004)

Cook, M. J., 'Jewish Reflections on Jesus: Some Abiding Trends', in L. J. Greenspoon, D. Hamm, and B. F. LeBeau (eds), *The Historical Jesus through Catholic and Jewish Eyes* (Harrisburg: Trinity Press International, 2000), pp. 95–111

Crace, J., 'Writing off the UK's Last Palaeographer', *Guardian* (9 February 2010), <http://www.theguardian.com/education/2010/feb/09/writing-off-last-palaeographer-university>

Craffert, P. F., *The Life of a Galilean Shaman: Jesus of Nazareth in Anthropological-Historical Perspective* (Cambridge: James Clarke & Co., 2008)

Cremin, C. *Capitalism's New Clothes: Enterprise, Ethics and Enjoyment in Times of Crisis* (London: Pluto Press, 2011)

Crook, Z. A., 'Structure versus Agency in Studies of the Biblical Social World: Engaging with Louise Lawrence', *JSNT* 29 (2007), pp. 251–75

Crook, Z. A., 'Memory and the Historical Jesus', *BTB* 42 (2012), pp. 196–220

Crook, Z. A., 'Collective Memory Distortion and the Quest for the Historical Jesus', *JSHJ* 11 (2013), pp. 53–76

Crook, Z. A., 'Gratitude and Comments to Le Donne', *JSHJ* 11 (2013), pp. 98–105

Crossan, J. D., *The Historical Jesus: The Life of a Mediterranean Jewish Peasant* (Edinburgh: T&T Clark, 1991)

Crossan, J. D., *Jesus: A Revolutionary Biography* (San Francisco: HarperCollins, 1994)

Crossan, J. D., *The Birth of Christianity: Discovering What Happened in the Years Immediately after the Execution of Jesus* (Edinburgh: T&T Clark, 1998)

Crossan, J. D., *A Long Way from Tipperary* (San Francisco: HarperSanFrancisco, 2000)

Crossley, J. G., 'Halakah and Mark 7.4: "...and beds"', *JSNT* 25 (2003), pp. 433–47

Crossley, J. G., *The Date of Mark's Gospel: Insight from the Law in Earliest Christianity* (London: T&T Clark, 2004)

Crossley, J. G., 'The Semitic Background to Repentance in the Teaching of John the Baptist and Jesus', *JSHJ* 2 (2004), pp. 138–57

Crossley, J. G., 'The Damned Rich (Mark 10.17–31)', *ExpT* 116 (2005), pp. 397–401

Crossley, J. G., 'Defining History', in J. G. Crossley and C. Karner (eds), *Writing History, Constructing Religion* (Aldershot: Ashgate, 2005), pp. 9–29

Crossley, J. G., 'History from the Margins: The Death of John the Baptist', in J. G. Crossley and C. Karner (eds), *Writing History, Constructing Religion* (Aldershot: Ashgate, 2005), pp. 147–61

Crossley, J. G., *Why Christianity Happened: A Sociohistorical Account of Christian Origins, 26–50 CE* (Louisville: WJK, 2006)

Crossley, J. G., 'Moses and Pagan Monotheism', in T. Römer (ed.), *La Construction de la figure de Moïse* (Paris: Gabalda, 2007), pp. 319–39

Crossley, J. G., *Jesus in an Age of Terror: Scholarly Projects for a New American Century* (London and Oakville: Equinox, 2008)

Crossley, J. G., 'Mark 7.1–23: Revisiting the Question of "All Foods Clean"', in M. Tait and P. Oakes (eds), *Torah in the New Testament* (London and New York: Continuum and T&T Clark, 2009), pp. 8–20

Crossley, J. G., 'Writing about the Historical Jesus: Historical Explanation and "the Big Why Questions", or Antiquarian Empiricism and Victorian Tomes?', *JSHJ* 7 (2009), pp. 63–90

Crossley, J. G., *Jewish Law and the New Testament: A Guide for the Perplexed* (London and New York: Continuum, 2010)

Crossley, J. G., 'The Multicultural Christ: Jesus the Jew and the New Perspective on Paul in an Age of Neoliberalism', *BCT* 7 (2011), pp. 1–9

Crossley, J. G., 'Halakah and Mark 7.3: "with the hand in the shape of a fist"', *NTS* 58 (2012), pp. 57–68

Crossley, J. G., *Jesus in an Age of Neoliberalism: Quests, Scholarship and Ideology* (London and Oakville: Equinox, 2012)

Crossley, J. G., 'John's Gospel and the Historical Jesus: An Assessment of Recent Trends and a Defence of a Traditional View', in T. L. Thompson and T. S. Verenna (eds), *'Is This Not the Carpenter?' The Question of the Historicity of the Figure of Jesus* (Durham: Acumen, 2012), pp. 163–84

Crossley, J. G., 'Everybody's Happy Nowadays? A Critical Engagement with *Key Events* and Contemporary Quests for the Historical Jesus', *JSHJ* 11 (2013), pp. 224–41

Crossley, J. G., 'A "Very Jewish" Jesus: Perpetuating the Myth of Superiority', *JSHJ* 11 (2013), pp. 109–29

Crossley, J. G., *Harnessing Chaos: The Bible in English Political Discourse since 1968* (London: T&T Clark, 2014)

Danker, F. W., 'Mark 8:3', *JBL* 82 (1963), pp. 215–16

Darnton, R., 'Workers Revolt: The Great Cat Massacre of the Rue Saint-Séverin', in *The Great Cat Massacre and Other Episodes in French Cultural History* (London: Allen Lane, 1984), pp. 75–104

Davies, W. D., and D. C. Allison, *A Critical and Exegetical Commentary on the Gospel According to Saint Matthew VIII–XVIII* (Edinburgh: T&T Clark, 1991)

Dawkins, R., 'Religion's Misguided Missiles', *Guardian* (15 September 2001), <http://www.theguardian.com/world/2001/sep/15/september11.politics philosophyandsociety1>

Dawkins, R., *The God Delusion* (London: Bantham, 2006)

Deines, R., *Jüdische Steingefäße und pharisäische Frömmigkeit: Eine archäologisch-historischer Beitrag zum Verständnis von Joh 2,6 und der jüdischen Reinheitshalacha zur Zeit Jesu* (Tübingen: Mohr Siebeck, 1993)

Deines, R., 'Jesus and the Jewish Traditions of His Time', *Early Christianity* 1 (2010), pp. 344–71

de Jonge, M., *Jewish Eschatology, Early Christian Christology, and the Testaments of the Twelve Patriarchs: Collected Essays of Marinus de Jonge* (Leiden: Brill, 1991)

Delcor, M., 'Two Special Meanings of the Word *yad* in Biblical Hebrew: Notes on Hebrew Lexicography', *Journal of Semitic Studies* 12 (1967), pp. 230–40

Denton, D. L., *Historiography and Hermeneutics in Jesus Studies: An Examination of the Work of John Dominic Crossan and Ben F. Meyer* (London and New York: T&T Clark, 2004)

Doering, L., *Schabbat: Schabbathalacha und-praxis im antiken Judentum und Urchristentum* (Tübingen: Mohr Siebeck, 1999)

Downing, J., 'Jesus and Martyrdom', *JTS* NS 14 (1963), pp. 279–93

Dunn, J. D. G., 'Mark 2.1–3.6: A Bridge between Jesus and Paul on the Question of the Law', *NTS* 30 (1984), pp. 395–415

Dunn, J. D. G., 'Pharisees, Sinners and Jesus', in P. Borgen, J. Neusner, E. S. Frerichs, and R. Horsley (eds), *The Social World of Formative Christianity and Judaism: Essays in Tribute to Howard Clarke Kee* (Philadelphia: Fortress, 1988), pp. 264–89

Dunn, J. D. G., *Jesus, Paul and the Law: Studies in Mark and Galatians* (London: SPCK, 1991)

Dunn, J. D. G., 'Jesus, Table-Fellowship, and Qumran', in J. H. Charlesworth (ed.), *Jesus and the Dead Sea Scrolls* (New York: Doubleday, 1992), pp. 254–72

Dunn, J. D. G., *Jesus Remembered* (Grand Rapids: Eerdmans, 2003)

Eagleton, T., *After Theory* (New York: Basic Books, 2003)

Edwards, J. R., *The Gospel According to Mark* (Grand Rapids and Cambridge: Eerdmans, 2002)

Ehrman, B. D., *Jesus: Apocalyptic Prophet of the New Millennium* (Oxford: Oxford University Press, 1999)

Ehrman, B. D., *Did Jesus Exist? The Historical Argument for Jesus of Nazareth* (New York: HarperCollins, 2013)

Elliott, J. H., 'Jesus Was Not an Egalitarian: A Critique of an Anachronistic and Idealist Theory', *BTB* 32 (2002), pp. 75–91

Elliott, N., *The Arrogance of Nations: Reading Romans in the Shadow of Empire* (Minneapolis: Fortress, 2008)

Engels, F., 'On the History of Earliest Christianity (1894)', in K. Marx and F. Engels, *Collected Works*, vol. 27, *Engels: 1890–95* (London: Lawrence & Wishart, 1990), pp. 447–69

Enslin, M. S., 'John and Jesus', *ZNW* 66 (1975), pp. 1–18

Esler, P. F., 'Models in New Testament Interpretation: A Reply to David Horrell', *JSNT* 22 (2000), pp. 107–13

Evans, C. A., 'Introduction: An Aramaic Approach Thirty Years Later', in M. Black, *An Aramaic Approach to the Gospels and Acts* (Peabody: Hendrickson, 1998), pp. v–xxv

Evans, C. A., 'Daniel in the New Testament: Visions of God's Kingdom', in J. J. Collins and P. W. Flint (eds), *The Book of Daniel: Composition and Reception* (Leiden: Brill, 2001), pp. 490–527

Evans, D., 'Spain and the World: Aspects of the Spanish Revolution and Civil War (7)', *Radical History Network* (31 August 2011), <http://radicalhistorynetwork.blogspot.co.uk/2011/08/spain-and-world-aspects-of-spanish.html>

Evans, R. J., *In Defence of History* (second edition; London: Granta, 2000)

Eve, E., 'Meier, Miracle, and Multiple Attestation', *JSHJ* 3 (2005), pp. 23–45

Fiensy, D. A., *The Social History of Palestine in the Herodian Period: The Land is Mine* (Lewiston, Queenston, and Lampeter: Edwin Mellen, 1991)

Fiensy, D. A., *Jesus the Galilean: Soundings in a First Century Life* (Piscataway: Gorgias, 2007)

Fiorenza, E. S., *In Memory of Her: A Feminist Theological Reconstruction of Christian Origins* (New York: Crossroad, 1983; second edition 1995)

Fiorenza, E. S., *Jesus and the Politics of Interpretation* (New York and London: Continuum, 2000)

Fisher, M., *Capitalist Realism: Is There No Alternative?* (Winchester, UK, and Washington, USA: Zero Books, 2009)

Fitzmyer, J. A., *Luke X–XXIV* (New York: Doubleday, 1985)

Foster, P., 'Memory, Orality, and the Fourth Gospel: Three Dead-Ends in Historical Jesus Research', *JSHJ* 10 (2012), pp. 191–227

Foucault, F., 'Nietzsche, Genealogy, History', in D. F. Bouchard (ed.), *Language, Counter-Memory, Practice: Selected Essays and Interviews* (Ithaca: Cornell University Press, 1977), pp. 139–64

Frede, M., 'Monotheism and Pagan Philosophy in Later Antiquity', in P. Athanassiadi and M. Frede (eds), *Pagan Monotheism in Late Antiquity* (Oxford: Oxford University Press, 1999), pp. 41–67

Fredriksen, P., *Jesus of Nazareth, King of the Jews: A Jewish Life and the Emergence of Christianity* (New York: Alfred A. Knopf, 2000)

Fredriksen, P., 'Compassion Is to Purity as Fish Is to Bicycle: Thoughts on the Construction of "Judaism" in Current Research on the Historical Jesus', in J. S. Kloppenborg with J. W. Marshall (eds), *Apocalypticism, Anti-Semitism, and the Historical Jesus* (London: T & T Clark, 2005), pp. 55–68

Frey, J., *Die johanneische Eschatologie*, vol. 3: *Die eschatologische Verkündigung in den johanneischen Texten* (Mohr Siebeck: Tübingen, 2000)

Frey, J., 'Die Apokalyptik als Herausforderung der neutestamentlichen Wissenschaft. Zum Problem: Jesus und die Apokalyptik', in M. Becker and M. Öhler (eds), *Apokalyptik als Herausforderung neutestamentlicher Theologie* (Tübingen: Mohr Siebeck, 2006), pp. 23–94

Freyne, S., 'Herodian Economics in Galilee: Searching for a Suitable Model', in P. F. Esler (ed.), *Modelling Early Christianity: Social-Scientific Studies of the New Testament in Its Context* (London: Routledge, 1995), pp. 23–46

Friedlander, S. (ed.), *Probing the Limits of Representation: Nazism and the 'Final Solution'* (Cambridge, MA and London: Harvard University Press, 1992)

Funk, R. W., R. W. Hoover, and the Jesus Seminar, *The Five Gospels: The Search for the Authentic Words of Jesus* (New York: Schribner, 1993)

Furstenberg, Y., 'Defilement Penetrating the Body: A New Understanding of Contamination in Mark 7.15', *NTS* 54 (2008), pp. 176–200

Gager, J. G., *Moses in Greco-Roman Paganism* (Abingdon Press: Nashville, 1973)

Georgi, D., 'The Interest in Life of Jesus Theology as a Paradigm to the Social History of Biblical Criticism', *HTR* 85 (1992), pp. 51–83

Ginsberg, B., *The Fall of the Faculty: The Rise of the All Administrative University and Why It Matters* (Oxford: Oxford University Press, 2011)

Glancy, J. A., 'Unveiling Masculinity: The Construction of Gender in Mark 6:17–29', *Bib. Int.* 2 (1994), pp. 34–50

Gleason, M. W., 'By Whose Gender Standards (If Anybody's) was Jesus a Real Man?' , in S. D. Moore and J. C. Anderson (eds), *New Testament Masculinities* (Atlanta, GA: SBL, 2003), pp. 325–7

Goldberg, D. T., *The Threat of Race: Reflections on Racial Neoliberalism* (Oxford: Wiley-Blackwell, 2009)

Goodacre, M., 'Criticizing the Criterion of Multiple Attestation: The Historical Jesus and the Question of Sources', in C. Keith and A. Le Donne (eds), *Jesus, Criteria and the Demise of Authenticity* (London: T&T Clark, 2012), pp. 152–69

Green, J. B., *Gospel of Luke* (Grand Rapids: Eerdmans, 1997)

Guelich, R. A., *Mark 1–8:26* (Dallas: Word, 1989)

Gundry, R. H., *Mark: A Commentary on His Apology for the Cross* (Grand Rapids and Cambridge: Eerdmans, 1993)
Hägerland, T., 'Jesus and the Rites of Repentance', *NTS* 52 (2006), pp. 166–87
Hanson, K. C., and D. E. Oakman, *Palestine in the Time of Jesus: Social Structures and Social Conflicts* (Minneapolis: Augsburg Fortress, 1998)
Harland, P. A., *Associations, Synagogues, and Congregations: Claiming a Place in Ancient Mediterranean Society* (Minneapolis: Fortress, 2003)
Harland, P. A., *The Dynamics of Identity in the World of the Early Christians* (London and New York: T&T Clark/Continuum, 2009)
Harrington, H. K., 'Did Pharisees Eat Ordinary Food in a State of Ritual Purity?', *JSJ* 26 (1995), pp. 42–54
Harris, S., *The End of Faith: Religion, Terror, and the Future of Reason* (London: Simon & Schuster, 2004)
Harvey, D., *The Condition of Postmodernity* (Oxford: Blackwell, 1989)
Harvey, D., *A Brief History of Neoliberalism* (Oxford: Oxford University Press, 2005)
Hayes, C. E., *Gentile Impurities and Jewish Identities: Intermarriage and Conversion from the Bible to the Talmud* (Oxford: Oxford University Press, 2002)
Head, P. M., and P. J. Williams, 'Q Review', *Tyn. Bul.* 54 (2003), pp. 119–44
Hellerman, J. H., *Jesus and the People of God: Reconfiguring Ethnic Identity* (Sheffield: Sheffield Academic Press, 2007)
Hengel, M., *The Charismatic Leader and His Followers* (Edinburgh: T&T Clark, 1981)
Hengel, M., and R. Deines, 'E. P. Sanders' "Common Judaism", Jesus, and the Pharisees', *JTS* 46 (1995), pp. 1–70
Hengel, M., and A. M. Schwemer, *Jesus und das Judentum* (Tübingen: Mohr Siebeck, 2007)
Herzog, W. R., *Prophet and Teacher: An Introduction to the Historical Jesus* (Louisville: WJK, 2005)
Hill, C., *The World Turned Upside Down: Radical Ideas during the English Revolution* (London: Temple Smith, 1972)
Hilton, R. H., 'Peasant Society, Peasant Movements and Feudalism in Medieval Europe,' in H. A. Landsberger (ed.), *Rural Protest: Peasant Movements and Social Change* (New York: Macmillan, 1973), pp. 67–94
Hobsbawm, E. J., *Nations and Nationalism Since 1780: Programme, Myth, Reality* (second edition; Cambridge: Cambridge University Press/Canto, 1992)
Hobsbawm, E. J., *The Age of Extremes: The Short Twentieth Century, 1914–1991* (London: Abacus, 1994)
Hobsbawm, E. J., *Uncommon People: Resistance, Rebellion and Jazz* (London: Abacus, 1998)
Hobsbawm, E. J., *Revolutionaries* (London: Abacus, 1999)

Hobsbawm, E. J., *Interesting Times: A Twentieth Century Life* (London: Abacus, 2002)

Hoehner, H. W., *Herod Antipas* (Cambridge: Cambridge University Press, 1972)

Hoffmann, R. J. (ed.), *Sources of the Jesus Tradition: Separating History from Myth* (Amherst: Prometheus, 2010)

Hooker, M. D., *Jesus and the Servant: The Influence of the Servant Concept of Deutero-Isaiah in the New Testament* (London: SPCK, 1959)

Hooker, M. D., 'Christology and Methodology', *NTS* 17 (1970–1), pp. 480–7

Hooker, M. D., 'On Using the Wrong Tool', *Theology* 75 (1972), pp. 570–81

Hooker, M. D., *The Gospel According to St Mark* (London: A&C Black, 1991)

Horrell, D. G., 'Models and Methods in Social-Scientific Interpretation: A Response to Philip Esler', *JSNT* 22 (2000), pp. 83–105

Horsley, R. A., *Jesus and the Spiral of Violence: Popular Jewish Resistance in Roman Palestine* (San Francisco: Harper & Row, 1987)

Horsley, R. A., *Jesus and Empire: The Kingdom of God and the New World Disorder* (Fortress: Minneapolis, 2003)

Horsley, R. A., and N. A. Silberman, *The Message and the Kingdom: How Jesus and Paul Ignited a Revolution and Transformed the Ancient World* (Minneapolis: Fortress, 2002)

Hourani, A., *A History of the Arab Peoples with an Afterword by Malise Ruthven* (London: Faber, 2002)

Hübner, H., *Das Gesetz in der synoptischen Tradition* (Witten: Luther-Verlag, 1973)

Hughes, A., *Gender and the English Revolution* (London: Routledge, 2012)

Huie-Jolly, M., 'Maori "Jews" and a Resistant Reading of John 5.10–47', in M. W. Dube and J. L. Staley (eds), *John and Postcolonialism: Travel, Space and Power* (London: T&T Clark, 2002), pp. 94–110

Hurtado, L. W., *One Lord, One God: Early Christian Devotion and Ancient Jewish Monotheism* (Philadelphia: Fortress, 1988)

Hurtado, L. W., *Lord Jesus Christ: Devotion to Jesus in Earliest Christianity* (Grand Rapids: Eerdmans, 2003)

Hurtado, L. W., 'Resurrection-Faith and the "Historical" Jesus', *JSHJ* 11 (2011), pp. 35–52

Ilan, T., *Jewish Women in Greco-Roman Palestine: An Inquiry into Image and Status* (Tübingen: Mohr Siebeck, 1995)

Ipsen, A., *Sex Working and the Bible* (London and Oakville: Equinox, 2009)

Jameson, F., *The Political Unconscious: Narrative as a Socially Symbolic Act* (Ithaca: Cornell University Press, 1981)

Jameson, F., *Postmodernism, or, The Cultural Logic of Late Capitalism* (Durham: Duke University Press, 1991)

Jensen, M. H., *Herod Antipas in Galilee* (Tubingen: Mohr Siebeck, 2006)

Jensen, M. H., 'Herod Antipas in Galilee: Friend or Foe of the Historical Jesus?', *JSHJ* 5 (2007), pp. 7–32

Jeremias, J., 'Zöllner und Sünder', *ZNW* 30 (1931), pp. 293–300

Jeremias, J., *New Testament Theology*, part 1: *The Proclamation of Jesus* (London: SCM, 1971)

Kautsky, J. H., *The Politics of Aristocratic Empires* (Chapel Hill: University of North Carolina, 1982)

Kautsky, K., *Foundations of Christianity: A Study in Christian Origins* (London: Orbach & Chambers, 1925)

Kazen, T., *Jesus and Purity Halakhah: Was Jesus Indifferent to Impurity?* (Stockholm: Almqvist & Wiksell International, 2002)

Kazen, T., *Issues of Impurity in Early Judaism* (Winona Lake: Eisenbrauns, 2010)

Kazen, T., *Scripture, Interpretation or Authority? Motives and Argument in Jesus' Halakic Conflicts* (Tübingen: Mohr Siebeck, 2013)

Keener, C. S., *The Gospel of John: A Commentary* (2 vols; Peabody, MA: Hendrickson, 2003)

Keener, C. S., *The Historical Jesus of the Gospels* (Grand Rapids: Eerdmans, 2009), pp. 144–53

Keener, C. S., '"We Beheld His Glory!" (John 1:14)', in P. N. Anderson, F. Just, and T. Thatcher (eds), *John, Jesus, and History*, vol. 2: *Aspects of Historicity in the Fourth Gospel* (Atlanta: SBL, 2009), pp. 15–25

Keith, C., 'Memory and Authenticity: Jesus Tradition and What Really Happened', *ZNW* 102 (2011), pp. 155–77

Keith, C., 'The Indebtedness of the Criteria Approach to Form Criticism and Recent Attempts to Rehabilitate the Search for an Authentic Jesus', in C. Keith and A. Le Donne (eds), *Jesus, Criteria and the Demise of Authenticity* (London: T&T Clark, 2012)

Keith, C., *Jesus against the Scribal Elite: The Origins of the Conflict* (Ada, MI: Baker, 2014)

Keith, C., and A. Le Donne (eds), *Jesus, Criteria and the Demise of Authenticity* (London: T&T Clark, 2012)

Kelley, S., *Racializing Jesus: Race, Ideology and the Formation of Modern Biblical Scholarship* (London and New York: Routledge, 2002)

Kelley, S., 'Hear Then No More Parables: The Case against "Parable"', *JSHJ* 11 (2013), pp. 153–69

Kepel, G., *The Roots of Radical Islam* (London: Saqi, 2005)

Kessler, G., 'Bodies in Motion: Preliminary Notes on Queer Theory and Rabbinic Literature', in T. Penner and C. vander Stichele (eds), *Mapping Gender in Ancient Religious Discourses* (Leiden: Brill, 2007), pp. 389–409

Kirk, A., 'Memory Theory and Jesus Research', in T. Holmén and S. E. Porter (eds), *Handbook for the Study of the Historical Jesus*, vol. 1 (Leiden: Brill, 2011), pp. 809–42

Klawans, J., 'Notions of Gentile Impurity in Ancient Judaism', *Association for Jewish Studies Review* 20 (1995), pp. 285–312

Klawans, J., 'The Impurity of Immorality in Ancient Judaism', *JJS* 48 (1997), pp. 1–16

Klawans, J., *Impurity and Sin in Ancient Judaism* (Oxford: Oxford University Press, 2000)

Kloppenborg, J. S., 'Nomos and Ethos in Q', in J. E. Goehring, J. T. Sanders, and C. W. Hedrick (eds), *Gospel Origins and Christian Beginnings: In Honor of James M. Robinson* (Sonoma: Polebridge, 1990), pp. 35–48

Kloppenborg, J. S., 'Memory, Performance, and the Sayings of Jesus', *JSHJ* 10 (2012), pp. 97–132

Koester, C. R., 'Aspects of Historicity in John 1–4: A Response', in P. N. Anderson, F. Just, and T. Thatcher (eds), *John, Jesus, and History*, vol. 2: *Aspects of Historicity in the Fourth Gospel* (Atlanta: SBL, 2009), pp. 93–103

Kowaliński, P., 'The Genesis of Christianity in the Views of Contemporary Marxist Specialists of Religion', *Antonianum* 47 (1972), pp. 541–75

Lawrence, L. J., 'Structure, Agency and Ideology: A Response to Zeba Crook', *JSNT* 29 (2007), pp. 277–86

Le Donne, A., 'Theological Memory Distortion in the Jesus Tradition', in S. C. Barton, L. T. Stuckenbruck, and B. G. Wold, *Memory and Remembrance in the Bible and Antiquity* (Tübingen: Mohr Siebeck, 2007), pp. 163–78

Le Donne, A., *The Historiographical Jesus: Memory, Typology and the Son of David* (Baylor: Baylor University Press, 2009)

Le Donne, A., *Historical Jesus: What Can We Know and How Can We Know It?* (Grand Rapids: Eerdmans, 2011)

Le Donne, A., 'The Problem of Selectivity in Memory Research: A Response to Zeba Crook', *JSHJ* 11 (2013), pp. 77–97

Le Donne, A., *The Wife of Jesus: Ancient Texts and Modern Scandals* (New York: Oneworld, 2013)

Lee, S., 'Will Cameron's Recipe for "Successful" Films Result in a Glut of Silent Comedies?', *Observer* (22 January 2012), <http://www.guardian.co.uk/commentisfree/2012/jan/22/stewart-lee-david-cameron-pinewood-film>

Lenski, G. E., *Power and Privilege: A Theory of Social Stratification* (New York: McGraw-Hill, 1966)

Lentin A., and G. Titley, *The Crises of Multiculturalism: Racism in a Neoliberal Age* (London: Zed Books, 2011)

Levine, A.-J., *The Misunderstood Jew: The Church and the Scandal of the Jewish Jesus* (San Francisco: HarperCollins, 2006)

Levine, A.-J., et al., 'Getting Judaism, and Jesus, Wrong', *Huffington Post* (17 January 2014), http://www.huffingtonpost.com/amyjill-levine/getting-judaism-and-jesus_b_4617731.html

Lieu, J., 'The "Attraction of Women" in/to Early Judaism and Christianity: Gender and the Politics of Conversion', *JSNT* 72 (1998), pp. 5–22

Liew, T-s. B., 'Tyranny, Power and Might: Colonial Mimicry in Mark's Gospel', *JSNT* 73 (1999), pp. 7–31

Liew, T-s. B., 'Re-Mark-able Masculinities: Jesus, the Son of Man, and the (Sad) Sum of Manhood?', in S. D. Moore and J. C. Anderson (eds), *New Testament Masculinities* (Atlanta, GA: Society of Biblical Literature, 2003), pp. 93–135

Liew, T-s. B., *Politics of Parousia: Reading Mark Inter(con)textually* (Leiden: Brill, 1999)

Lilla, M., 'A New, Political Saint Paul?' *New York Review of Books* 55/16 (23 October 2008), pp. 1–9

Lincoln, A. T., '"We Know That His Testimony is True": Johannine Truth Claims and Historicity', in P. N. Anderson, F. Just, and T. Thatcher (eds), *John, Jesus, and History*, vol. 1: *Critical Appraisals of Critical Views* (Atlanta: SBL, 2007), pp. 179–97

Lincoln, B., *Religion, Empire and Torture: The Case of Achaemenian Persia, with a Postscript on Abu Ghraib* (Chicago and London: University of Chicago Press, 2007)

Loader, W., *Sexuality and the Jesus Tradition* (Grand Rapids: Eerdmans, 2005)

Lopez, D. C., *Apostle to the Conquered: Reimagining Paul's Mission* (Minneapolis: Fortress, 2008)

Maccoby, H., 'The Washing of Cups', *JSNT* 14 (1982), pp. 3–15

Maccoby, H., 'The Law about Liquids: A Rejoinder', *JSNT* 67 (1997), pp. 115–22

Maccoby, H., *Ritual and Morality: The Ritual Purity System and Its Place in Judaism* (Cambridge: Cambridge University Press, 1999)

McCutcheon, R. T., *Manufacturing Religion: The Discourse on Sui Generis Religion and the Politics of Nostalgia* (Oxford: Oxford University Press, 1997)

McCutcheon, R. T., *Religion and the Domestication of Dissent, or, How to Live in a Less than Perfect Nation* (London and Oakville: Equinox, 2005)

MacDonald, N., *Deuteronomy and the Meaning of 'Monotheism'* (Tübingen: Mohr Siebeck, 2003)

McGrath, J. F., '"Destroy This Temple": Issues of Historicity in John 2.13–22', in P. N. Anderson, F. Just, and T. Thatcher (eds), *John, Jesus, and History*, vol. 2: *Aspects of Historicity in the Fourth Gospel* (Atlanta: SBL, 2009), pp. 35–43

McGrath, J. F., *The Only True God: Early Christian Monotheism in Its Jewish Context* (Champaign, IL: University of Illinois Press, 2012)

Mack, B., *The Christian Myth: Origins, Logic, and Legacy* (New York and London: Continuum, 2001)

MacKendrick, K., 'From Cognitive Theory of Religion to Religious Cognition', *Religion Bulletin* (2012), <http://www.equinoxpub.com/blog/2012/06/from-cognitive-theory-of-religion-to-religious-cognition/>

McKnight, S., *Jesus and His Death: Historiography, the Historical Jesus, and Atonement Theory* (Waco: Baylor University Press, 2005)

Malina, B. J., *The Social World of Jesus and the Gospels* (London: Routledge, 1996)

Marchal, J. A., *The Politics of Heaven: Women, Gender and Empire in the Study of Paul* (Minneapolis: Fortress, 2008)

Marcus, J., *Mark 1–8: A New Translation with Introduction and Commentary* (New York: Doubleday, 2000)

Martin, C., *Masking Hegemony: A Genealogy of Liberalism, Religion and the Private Sphere* (London and Oakville: Equinox, 2010)

Martin, D. B., *Sex and the Single Savior: Gender and Sexuality in Biblical Interpretation* (Louisville: WJK, 2006)

Marx, K., *The Eighteenth Brumaire of Louis Bonaparte* (New York: International Publishers, 1963)

Marx, K., *A Contribution to the Critique of Hegel's 'Philosophy of Right'* (Cambridge: Cambridge University Press, 1970)

Meggitt, J. J., 'The Madness of King Jesus: Why Was Jesus Put to Death, but His Followers Were Not?', *JSNT* 29 (2007), pp. 379–413

Meggitt, J. J., 'Popular Mythology in the Early Empire and the Multiplicity of Jesus Traditions', in R. J. Hoffmann (ed.), *Sources of the Jesus Tradition: Separating History from Myth* (Amherst: Prometheus, 2010), pp. 55–80

Meier, J. P., *A Marginal Jew: Rethinking the Historical Jesus*, vol. 1: *The Roots of the Problem and the Person* (New York: Doubleday, 1991)

Meier, J. P., *A Marginal Jew: Rethinking the Historical Jesus*, vol. 3: *Companions and Competitors* (New York: Doubleday, 2001)

Meier, J. P., 'The Historical Jesus and the Plucking of the Grain on the Sabbath', *CBQ* 66 (2004), pp. 561–81

Meier, J. P., 'Did the Historical Jesus Prohibit All Oaths? Part 1', *JSHJ* 5 (2007), pp. 175–204

Meier, J. P., Did the Historical Jesus Prohibit All Oaths? Part 2', *JSHJ* 6 (2008), pp. 3–24

Meier, J. P., *A Marginal Jew: Rethinking the Historical Jesus. Law and Love* (New York: Doubleday, 2009)

Miller, S., 'The Woman at the Well: John's Portrayal of the Samaritan Woman', in P. N. Anderson, F. Just, and T. Thatcher (eds), *John, Jesus, and History*, vol. 2: *Aspects of Historicity in the Fourth Gospel* (Atlanta: SBL, 2009), pp. 73–81

Mitchell S., and P. van Nufflen (eds), *Pagan Monotheism in the Roman Empire* (Cambridge: Cambridge University Press, 2010)

Moody Smith, D., 'John: A Source for Jesus Research?' in P. N. Anderson, F. Just, and T. Thatcher (eds), *John, Jesus, and History*, vol. 1: *Critical Appraisals of Critical Views* (Atlanta: SBL, 2007), pp. 165–78

Moore, S. D., *God's Beauty Parlor and Other Queer Spaces in and around the Bible* (Stanford: Stanford University Press, 2001)

Moore, S. D., '"O Man, Who Art Thou...?" Masculinity Studies and New Testament Studies', in S. D. Moore and J. C. Anderson (eds), *New Testament Masculinities* (Atlanta, GA: SBL, 2003), pp. 1–22

Moore, S. D., *Empire and Apocalypse: Postcolonialism and the New Testament* (Sheffield: Sheffield Phoenix Press, 2006)

Moore, S. D., and J. C. Anderson, 'Taking It Like a Man: Masculinity in 4 Maccabees', *JBL* 117 (1998), pp. 249–73

Moxnes, H., *The Economy of the Kingdom: Social Conflict and Economic Relations in Luke's Gospel* (Philadelphia: Fortress, 1988)

Moxnes, H., 'The Historical Jesus: From Master Narrative to Cultural Context', *BTB* 28 (1999), pp. 135–49

Moxnes, H., *Putting Jesus in His Place: A Radical Vision of Household and Kingdom* (Louisville: WJK, 2003)

Moxnes, H., 'What Is It to Write a Biography of Jesus? Schleiermacher's *Life of Jesus* and Nineteenth-Century Nationalism', in H. Moxnes, W. Blanton, and J. G. Crossley (eds), *Jesus beyond Nationalism: Constructing the Historical Jesus in a Period of Cultural Complexity* (London and Oakville: Equinox, 2009), pp. 27–42

Moxnes, H., *Jesus and the Rise of Nationalism: A New Quest for the Nineteenth Century Historical Jesus* (London and New York: I.B. Taurus, 2011)

Moxnes, H., 'Jesus in Discourses of Dichotomies: Alternative Paradigms for the Historical Jesus', *JSHJ* 11 (2013), pp. 130–52

Moyise, S., *Evoking Scripture: Seeing the Old Testament in the New* (London and New York: T&T Clark, 2008)

Muraoka, T., 'Sir. 51:13–30: An Erotic Hymn to Wisdom?', *JSJ* 10 (1979), pp. 168–78

Myles, R. J., 'Dandy Discipleship: A Queering of Mark's Male Disciples', *Journal of Men, Masculinities, and Spirituality* 4 (2010), pp. 66–81

Myles, R. J., *Jesus the Homeless in the Gospel of Matthew* (Sheffield: Sheffield Phoenix Press, 2014)

Neale, D. A., *None but the Sinners: Religious Categories in the Gospel of Luke* (Sheffield: JSOT, 1991)

Nestle, E., '"Anise" and "Rue"', *Exp.T.* 15 (1904), p. 528

Neusner, J., 'The Conversion of Adiabene to Judaism: A New Perspective', *JBL* 83 (1964), pp. 60–6

Neusner, J., '"First Cleanse the Inside": The "Halakhic" Background of a Controversy Saying', *NTS* 22 (1976), pp. 486–95

Newton, M., *The Concept of Purity at Qumran and in the Letters of Paul* (Cambridge: Cambridge University Press, 2005)

Niederwimmer, K., 'Johannes Markus und die Frage nach dem Verfasser des zweiten Evangeliums', *ZNW* 58 (1967), pp. 172–88

Nolan P., and G. Lenski, *Human Societies: An Introduction to Macrosociology* (ninth edition; Boulder and London: Paradigm, 2004)

Noll, K. L., 'Investigating Earliest Christianity without Jesus', in T. L. Thompson and T. S. Verenna (eds), *'Is This Not the Carpenter?' The Question of the Historicity of the Figure of Jesus* (Durham: Acumen, 2012), pp. 233–66

Nolland, J. L., *Luke 9:21–18:34* (Dallas: Word, 1993)

Nunn, H., *Thatcher, Politics and Fantasy: The Political Culture of Gender and Nation* (London: Lawrence and Wishart, 2002)

Økland, J., *Women in Their Place: Paul and the Corinthian Discourse of Gender and Sanctuary Space* (London and New York: T&T Clark, 2004)

Økland, J., and R. Boer, 'Towards Marxist Feminist Biblical Criticism', in R. Boer and J. Økland (eds), *Marxist Feminist Criticism of the Bible* (Sheffield: Sheffield Phoenix Press, 2008), pp. 1–25

Oppenheimer, A., *The 'Am Ha-aretz: A Study in the Social History of the Jewish People in the Hellenistic-Roman Period* (Leiden: Brill, 1977)

Osborne, G. R., 'Jesus' Empty Tomb and His Appearance in Jerusalem', in D. L. Bock and R. L. Webb (eds), *Key Events in the Life of the Historical Jesus: A Collaborative Exploration of Context and Coherence* (Grand Rapids and Cambridge: Eerdmans, 2009), pp. 775–823

Osiek, C., and M. Y. MacDonald with J. H. Tulloch, *A Woman's Place: House Churches in Earliest Christianity* (Minneapolis: Fortress, 2006)

Painter, J., 'Memory Holds the Key: The Transformation of Memory in the Interface of History and Theology in John', in P. N. Anderson, F. Just, and T. Thatcher (eds), *John, Jesus, and History*, vol. 1: *Critical Appraisals of Critical Views* (Atlanta: SBL, 2007), pp. 229–45

Patterson, S. J., 'An Unanswered Question: Apocalyptic Expectation and Jesus' *Basileia* Proclamation', *JSHJ* 8 (2010), pp. 67–79

Pimlott, B., 'Brushstrokes', in M. Bostridge (ed.), *Lives for Sale: Biographers' Tales* (London and New York: Continuum, 2004), pp. 165–170

Poirier, J. C., 'Why Did the Pharisees Wash Their Hands?', *JJS* 47 (1996), pp. 217–33

Poirier, J. C., 'Purity beyond the Temple in the Second Temple Era', *JBL* 122 (2003), pp. 247–65

Pritchard, J. B., *Ancient Near Eastern Texts Relating to the Old Testament with Supplement* (Princeton: Princeton University Press, 1969)

Prosic, T., 'Schizoid Christ: Christ and the Feminine', in R. Boer and J. Økland (eds), *Marxist Feminist Criticism of the Bible* (Sheffield: Sheffield Phoenix Press, 2008), pp. 47–69

Rawlinson, A. E. J., *St Mark* (London: Methuen, 1925)

Redford, D. B., *Egypt, Canaan, and Israel in Ancient Times* (Princeton: Princeton University Press, 1992)

Redman, J. C. S., 'How Accurate Are Eyewitnesses? Bauckham and the Eyewitnesses in Light of Psychological Research', *JBL* 129 (2010), pp. 177–97

Regev, E., 'Pure Individualism: The Idea of Non-Priestly Purity in Ancient Judaism', *JSJ* 31 (2000), pp. 176–202

Repphun, E., 'Dysenchanted Worlds: Rationalisation, Dystopia, and Therapy Culture in Ninni Holmqvist's The Unit', *Dunedin School* (25 September 2009), <http://dunedinschool.wordpress.com/2009/09/25/dysenchanted-worlds-rationalisation-dystopia-and-therapy-culture-in-ninni-holmqvist%27s-the-unit/>

Robinson, J. A. T., *The Priority of John* (London: SCM, 1985)

Robinson, J. M., P. Hoffmann, and J. S. Kloppenborg (eds), *The Critical Edition of Q: Synopsis, Including the Gospels of Matthew and Luke, Mark and Thomas, with English, German and French Translations of Q and Thomas* (Leuven: Peeters, 2000)

Rodriguez, R., 'Authenticating Criteria: The Use and Misuse of a Critical Method', *JSHJ* 7 (2009), pp. 152–67

Rodriguez, R., *Structuring Early Christian Memory: Jesus in Tradition, Performance and Text* (London: T&T Clark, 2010)

Rodriguez, R., 'The Embarrassing Truth about Jesus: The Criterion of Embarrassment and the Failure of Historical Authenticity', in C. Keith and A. Le Donne (eds), *Jesus, Criteria and the Demise of Authenticity* (London: T&T Clark, 2012), pp. 132–51

Rosenberg, P., 'A Whole World of Heroes', in H. Bloom (ed.), *Thomas Carlyle* (New York: Chelsea House, 1986), pp. 95–108

Rowland, C., *Christian Origins: The Setting and Character of the Most Important Messianic Sect of Judaism* (London: SPCK, 1986)

Rowland, C., 'Review of J. G. Crossley, *Why Christianity Happened*', *JTS* 59 (2008), pp. 765–7

Samuel, S., *A Postcolonial Reading of Mark's Story of Jesus* (London and New York: T&T Clark, 2007)

Sanders, E. P., *Paul and Palestinian Judaism: A Comparison of Patterns of Religion* (London: SCM, 1977)

Sanders, E. P., 'Jesus and the Sinners', *JSNT* 19 (1983), pp. 5–36

Sanders, E. P., *Jesus and Judaism* (London: SCM, 1985)

Sanders, E. P., *Jewish Law from the Bible to the Mishnah* (London: SCM, 1990)

Sanders, E. P., *The Historical Figure of Jesus* (London: Penguin, 1993)

Sanders, E. P., and M. Davies, *Studying the Synoptic Gospels* (London: SCM, 1989)

Sanders, J. A., *The Psalms Scroll of Qumrân Cave 11* (Oxford: Clarendon, 1965)

Sandford, M. J., *Poverty, Wealth, and Empire: Jesus and Postcolonial Criticism* (Sheffield: Sheffield Phoenix Press, 2014)

Schaeffer, F., 'Jesus Hated Women—Right?', *Huffington Post* (15 January 2014), <http://www.huffingtonpost.com/frank-schaeffer/jesus-hated-women-right_b_4598039.html>

Schiffman, L. H., 'The Conversion of the Royal House of Adiabene in Josephus and Rabbinic Sources', in L. H. Feldman and G. Hata (eds), *Josephus, Judaism, and Christianity* (Detroit: Wayne State University Press, 1987), pp. 293–312

Schneider, N., 'Why the World Needs Religious Studies', *Religion Dispatches* (20 November 2011), <http://www.religiondispatches.org/archive/culture/4636/why_the_world_needs_religious_studies/>

Schröter, J., 'Die Frage nach dem historischen Jesus und der Charakter historischer Erkenntnis', in A. Lindemann (ed.), *The Sayings Source Q and the Historical Jesus* (Leuven: Leuven University Press, 2001), pp. 228–33

Schröter, J., 'Von der Historizität der Evangelien: Ein Beitrag zur gegenwärtigen Diskussion um den historischen Jesus', in J. Schröter and R. Brucker (eds), *Der historische Jesus: Tendenzen und Perspektiven der gegenwärtigen Forschung* (Berlin: De Gruyter, 2002), pp. 163–212

Schröter, J., *Jesus von Nazaret: Jude aus Galiläa-Retter der Welt* (second edition; Leipzig: Evangelische Verlagsanstalt, 2009)

Schultz, S., *Q: Die Spruchquelle der Evangelisten* (Zürich: TVZ, 1971)

Schwartz, D., 'God, Gentiles, and Jewish Law: On Acts 15 and Josephus' Adiabene Narrative', in H. Cancik, H. Lichtenberger, and P. Schäfer (eds), *Geschichte—Tradition—Reflection: Festschrift für Martin Hengel*, vol. 1: *Judentum* (Tübingen: Mohr Siebeck, 1996), pp. 263–282

Scobie, C. H. H., *John the Baptist* (London: SCM Press, 1964)

Sellin, G., 'Lukas als Gleichniserzähler: Die Erzählung vom Barmherzingen Samariter (Lk. 10:25–37)', *ZNW* 66 (1975), pp. 19–60

Smith, R. *Julian's Gods: Religion and Philosophy in the Thought and Action of Julian the Apostate* (London: Routledge, 1995)

Stark, R., *The Rise of Christianity: A Sociologist Reconsiders History* (Princeton: Princeton University Press, 1996)

Stark, R., *One True God: Historical Consequences of Monotheism* (Princeton and Oxford: Princeton University Press, 2001)

Stegemann, E. W., and W. Stegemann, *The Jesus Movement: A Social History of Its First Century* (Edinburgh: T&T Clark, 1999)

Stuckenbruck, L. T., '"Semitic Influence on Greek": An Authenticating Criterion in Jesus Research?', in C. Keith and A. Le Donne (eds), *Jesus, Criteria and the Demise of Authenticity* (London: T&T Clark, 2012), pp. 73–94

Stuckenbruck, L. T., and W. E. S. North (eds), *Early Jewish and Christian Monotheism* (London and New York: T&T Clark, 2004)

Sugirtharajah, R. S., *Asian Biblical Hermeneutics and Postcolonialism: Contesting the Interpretations* (Sheffield: Sheffield Academic Press, 1998)

Svartvik, J., *Mark and Mission: Mark 7.1–23 in its Narrative and Historical Contexts* (Stockholm: Almqvist & Wiksell, 2000)

Taylor, J. E., *The Immerser: John the Baptist within Second Temple Judaism* (Grand Rapids and Cambridge: Eerdmans, 1997)

Taylor, N. H., 'Palestinian Christianity and the Caligula Crisis. Part II: The Markan Eschatological Discourse', *JSNT* 62 (1996), pp. 13–41

Tétreault, M. A., 'Women and Revolution: A Framework for Analysis', in M. A. Tétreault (ed.), *Women and Revolution in Africa, Asia, and the New World* (Columbia: University of South Carolina Press, 1994), pp. 3–30

Thatcher, T., *Greater than Caesar: Christology and Empire in the Fourth Gospel* (Minneapolis: Fortress, 2009)

The Archbishop of Canterbury's Commission on Urban Priority Areas, *Faith in the City: A Call for Action by Church and Nation* (London: Church House Publishing, 1985)

Theissen, G., *The Gospels in Context: Social and Political History in the Synoptic Tradition* (Edinburgh: T&T Clark, 1992)

Theissen, G., *Social Reality and the Early Christians* (Edinburgh: T&T Clark, 1993)

Theissen, G., *A Theory of Primitive Christian Religion* (London: SCM, 1999)

Theissen, G., and A. Merz, *The Historical Jesus: A Comprehensive Guide* (London: SCM, 1998)

Theissen, G., and D. Winter, *The Quest for the Plausible Jesus: The Question of Criteria* (Louisville: WJK, 2002)

Thompson, E. P., *The Making of the English Working Class* (Harmondsworth: Pelican Books, 1963)

Thompson, M. M., 'The Historical Jesus and the Johannine Christ', in R. A. Culpepper and C. Black (eds), *Exploring the Gospel of John: In Honor of D. Moody Smith* (Louisville: WJK, 1996), pp. 21–42

Thompson, M. M., 'The "Spiritual Gospel": How John the Theologian Writes History', in P. N. Anderson, F. Just, and T. Thatcher (eds), *John, Jesus, and History*, vol. 1: *Critical Appraisals of Critical Views* (Atlanta: SBL, 2007), pp. 103–7

Thompson, T. L., *The Messiah Myth: The Near Eastern Roots of Jesus and David* (New York: Basic Books, 2005)

Thompson, T. L., and T. S. Verenna (eds), *'Is This Not the Carpenter?' The Question of the Historicity of the Figure of Jesus* (Durham: Acumen, 2012)

Thurman, E., 'Looking for a Few Good Men: Mark and Masculinity', in S. D. Moore and J. C. Anderson (eds), *New Testament Masculinities* (Atlanta, GA: Society of Biblical Literature, 2003), pp. 137–61

Torrey, C. C., *Documents of the Primitive Church* (London and New York: Harper & Brothers, 1941)

Tuckett, C. M., *Q and the History of Early Christianity: Studies on Q* (Edinburgh: T&T Clark, 1996)

Vaage, L. E., *Galilean Upstarts: Jesus' First Followers According to Q* (Valley Forge: Trinity, 1994)

van der Woude, A. S., 'Wisdom at Qumran', in J. Day, R. P. Gordon, and H. G. M. Williamson (eds), *Wisdom in Ancient Israel: Essays in Honour of J. A. Emerton* (Cambridge: Cambridge University Press), pp. 244–56

van Iersel, B. W. F., 'Die wunderbare Speisung und das Abendmahl in der synoptischen Tradition (Mk VI.35–44 par VIII.1–20 par)', *NovT* 7 (1964), pp. 167–94

Vermes, G., *Jesus the Jew: A Historian's Reading of the Gospel* (London: SCM, 1973)

Vermes, G., *The Religion of Jesus the Jew* (London: SCM, 1993)

Vermes, G., *Providential Accidents: An Autobiography* (London: SCM, 1998)

Watts, M., 'Revolutionary Islam', in D. Gregory and A. Pred (eds), *Violent Geographies: Fear, Terror, and Political Violence* (New York and London: Routledge, 2007), pp. 175–203

Webb, R. L., 'The Historical Enterprise and Historical Jesus Research', in D. L. Bock and R. L. Webb (eds), *Key Events in the Life of the Historical Jesus: A Collaborative Exploration of Content and Coherence* (Tübingen: Mohr Siebeck, 2009), pp. 9–93

Wedderburn, A. J. M., *Jesus and the Historians* (Tübingen: Mohr Siebeck, 2010)

Wellhausen, J., *Einleitung in die drei ersten Evangelien* (second edition; Berlin: G. Reimer, 1911)

Wenell, K. J., *Jesus and Land: Sacred and Social Space in Second Temple Judaism* (London: T&T Clark, 2007)

White, H., *The Content of the Form: Narrative Discourse and Historical Representation* (Baltimore: Johns Hopkins University Press, 1973)

Whitelam, K. W., *The Invention of Ancient Israel: The Silencing of Palestinian History* (London: Routledge, 1996)

Wink, W., *John the Baptist in the Gospel Tradition* (Cambridge: Cambridge University Press, 1968)

Winter, D., 'Saving the Quest for Authenticity from the Criterion of Dissimilarity: History and Plausibility', in C. Keith and A. Le Donne (eds), *Jesus, Criteria and the Demise of Authenticity* (London: T&T Clark, 2012), pp. 115–31

Witherington, B., *Women in the Ministry of Jesus: A Study of Jesus' Attitude to Women and Their Roles as Reflected in His Earthly Life* (Cambridge: Cambridge University Press, 1984)

Witherington, B., 'What's in a Name? Rethinking the Historical Figure of the Beloved Disciple in the Fourth Gospel', in P. N. Anderson, F. Just, and T. Thatcher (eds), *John, Jesus, and History*, vol. 2: *Aspects of Historicity in the Fourth Gospel* (Atlanta: SBL, 2009), pp. 209–12

Wright, N. T., *The New Testament and the People of God* (London: SPCK, 1992)

Wright, N. T., *Jesus and the Victory of God* (London: SPCK, 1996)

Wright, N. T. [Tom], *The Original Jesus: The Life and Vision of a Revolutionary* (Oxford: Lion, 1996)

Wright, N. T., *The Resurrection of the Son of God* (London: SPCK, 2003)

Würthwein, E., 'μετανοέω, etc.: B. Repentance and Conversion in the Old Testament', *TDNT* 4, pp. 980–9

Žižek, S., 'Do We Still Live in a World?' (no date), <http://www.lacan.com/zizrattlesnakeshake.html>

Žižek, S., *The Sublime Object of Ideology* (London and New York: Verso, 1989)

Žižek, S., 'Multiculturalism, or, The Cultural Logic of Multinational Capitalism', *New Left Review* (1997), pp. 28–51

Žižek, S., *Welcome to the Desert of the Real! Five Essays on September 11 and Related Dates* (London and New York: Verso, 2002)

Žižek, S., *The Puppet and the Dwarf: The Perverse Core of Christianity* (Cambridge, MA: MIT Press, 2003)

Žižek, S., *First as Tragedy, Then as Farce* (London and New York: Verso, 2009)

Žižek, S., 'Liberal Multiculturalism Masks an Old Barbarism with a Human Face', *Guardian* (3 October 2010), <http://www.theguardian.com/commentisfree/2010/oct/03/immigration-policy-roma-rightwing-europe>

Žižek, S., 'Return of the Natives', *New Statesman* (4 March 2010), <http://www.newstatesman.com/film/2010/03/avatar-reality-love-couple-sex>

Žižek, S., *Did Somebody Say Totalitarianism? Five Interventions in the (Mis) Use of a Notion* (London and New York: Verso, 2011)

Žižek, S., *Living in the End Times* (revised edition; London and New York: Verso, 2011)

Zuntz, G., 'Wann wurde das Evangelium Marci geschrieben?', in H. Cancik (ed.), *Markus-Philologie* (Tübingen: Mohr Siebeck, 1984), pp. 47–71

Zur, Y., 'Parallels between Acts of Thomas 6–7 and 4Q184', *Revue de Qumrân*, 16 (1993), pp. 103–7

Index of Passages

Old Testament/Hebrew Bible

Miscellaneous Ancient Texts

General Index